'*Among Wolves* is both masterclass and manifesto for how ethnography generates insights into the operation of power as well as providing a thoughtful exploration of the politics of ethnographic methods. Pachirat is to be congratulated on creating a vivid, evocative and accessible text that will compel readers to laugh, sigh, frown and—most frequently—pause to reflect and think. The book's multidisciplinary cast of ethnographers adroitly guide the reader through debates, dilemmas and decisions, and there is a reference, comment or idea to bookmark and explore further on almost every page. This deceptively slim and readable book insistently demands that we engage actively with the praxis of ethnography and will richly reward repeated readings and discussions whether in the classroom, the field, or wherever else we find ourselves contemplating how to understand people's experiences of the socio-political world.'

**Cai Wilkinson,** *Associate Head of School of Humanities and Social Sciences, Deakin University*

'With its bold format, Timothy Pachirat's *Among Wolves* is an intellectual and pedagogical delight. Inserting readers into lively intellectual debates that defy easy answers, it challenges us all to improve our self-knowledge as we embark on ethnographic journeys. Embracing complexity, nuance, immersion, and personal engagement—all the hallmarks of top ethnographic work—Pachirat packs dozens of insights into every page. Students and practitioners of ethnography, not to mention non-ethnographers curious about the craft, will love this book.'

**Edward Schatz,** *Professor and Chair of the Political Science Department, University of Toronto (Mississauga)*

'Such a refreshing contrast to standard texts on ethnography. This book is a joy to read. The unique writing style draws one in surprisingly quickly and makes the book hard to lay aside. In re-creating a conversation between a handful of particularly accomplished contemporary ethnographers, Pachirat has provided us with a highly original, user-friendly, exploration of the (oftentimes painfully personal) challenges of "doing" fieldwork.'

**Mark de Rond,** *Professor of Organisational Ethnography, University of Cambridge*

'While methods books may be a necessary tool, especially for students, they are often boring. Timothy Pachirat's volume revolutionizes the genre, and the result is absolutely refreshing and convincing. Imagine a play where all the major methodological and theoretical issues raised by ethnography are discussed by a prosecutor arriving on a Harley Davidson to meet with a group of well-known ethnographers in the presence of a Wolfdog! This book will be on the list of required readings for my graduate seminar on ethnographic methods.'

**Martina Avanza,** *Université de Lausanne and co-director of EthnoPol*

'In *Among Wolves* Timothy Pachirat sketches some of the practical intricacies of doing ethnography and touches upon the philosophical challenges and theoretical underpinnings of thinking ethnographically. Written as a play, the book offers an unusually dramatic account of ethnography's pros and cons. While its dialogical style allows for debate by bringing together different, sometimes competing views, the creative structure of the book takes off some of the heat that such debates tend to generate. This allows the reader to approach some of ethnography's highflying and down-to-earth questions in a light and lucid style. A fantabulous book for both experienced and less-experienced ethnographers.'

**Sierk Ybema,** *Vrije Universiteit Amsterdam and Anglia Ruskin University*

# AMONG WOLVES

Summoned by an anonymous Prosecutor, ten contemporary ethnographers gather in an aging barn to hold a trial of Alice Goffman's controversial ethnography, *On the Run*. But before the trial can get underway, a one-eyed wolfdog arrives with a mysterious liquid potion capable of rendering the ethnographers invisible in their fieldsites.

Presented as a play that unfolds in seven acts, the ensuing drama provides readers with both a practical guide for how to conduct immersive participant-observation research and a sophisticated theoretical engagement with the relationship between ethnography as a research method and the operation of power. By interpolating "how-to" aspects of ethnographic research with deeper questions about ethnography's relationship to power, this book presents a compelling introduction for those new to ethnography and rich theoretical insights for more seasoned ethnographic practitioners from across the social sciences. Just as ethnography as a research method depends crucially on serendipity, surprise, and an openness to ambiguity, the book's dramatic and dialogic format encourages novices and experts alike to approach the study of power in ways that resist linear programs and dogmatic prescriptions. The result is a playful yet provocative invitation to rekindle those foundational senses of wonder and generative uncertainty that are all too often excluded from conversations about the methodologies and methods we bring to the study of the social world.

**Timothy Pachirat** is Assistant Professor of Political Science at the University of Massachusetts at Amherst and author of *Every Twelve Seconds: Industrialized Slaughter and the Politics of Sight* (Yale University Press, 2011).

# Routledge Series on Interpretive Methods

Edited by:

*Dvora Yanow, Wageningen University, The Netherlands*
*Peregrine Schwartz-Shea, University of Utah, US*

The *Routledge Series on Interpretive Methods* comprises a collection of slim volumes, each devoted to different issues in interpretive methodology and its associated methods. The topics covered establish the methodological grounding for interpretive approaches in ways that distinguish interpretive methods from quantitative and qualitative methods in the positivist tradition. The series as a whole engages three types of concerns: 1) *methodological issues*, looking at key concepts and processes; 2) *approaches and methods*, looking at how interpretive methodologies are manifested in different forms of research; and 3) *disciplinary and subfield areas*, demonstrating how interpretive methods figure in different fields across the social sciences.

# International Advisory Board

# AMONG WOLVES

## Ethnography and the Immersive Study of Power

*Timothy Pachirat*

Routledge
Taylor & Francis Group

NEW YORK AND LONDON

First published 2018
by Routledge
711 Third Avenue, New York, NY 10017

and by Routledge
2 Park Square, Milton Park, Abingdon, Oxon, OX14 4RN

*Routledge is an imprint of the Taylor & Francis Group, an informa business*

*Library of Congress Cataloging-in-Publication Data*
A catalog record for this book has been requested

ISBN: 978-0-415-52897-9 (hbk)
ISBN: 978-0-415-52898-6 (pbk)
ISBN: 978-0-203-70110-2 (ebk)

Typeset in Bembo
by Sunrise Setting Ltd, Brixham, UK

# CONTENTS

# SERIES EDITORS' FOREWORD

Wolves?! What are wolves doing in a book series on interpretive methods? And what does it mean to be "among" them? Timothy Pachirat's volume, which we welcome to the series, takes up participant-observer ethnography's purpose, its status as a science, and the relationship between the ethnographer and those being studied. Engaging the complex philosophical, practical, ethical, and political issues generated by the study of human beings *in situ* puts researchers—especially in today's atmosphere of *methodenstreit* (methods battles or disputes)—in the midst of a thicket of methodological charges and debates, possibly leaving them feeling as if they were "among wolves," subject to attack on multiple counts. Nowhere is this more evident than in the turmoil that has surrounded an ethnography of the relationships between city police and some of the residents of a Philadelphia neighborhood, the focus of this book's penultimate chapter.

In a major, creative departure from the usual methods book, Pachirat gives us entrée into this terrain through the device of a play, in which he imagines conversations among a diverse group of "characters" who are actually the living authors of ethnographic works. Coming from anthropology, journalism, political science, and sociology, they have been subpoenaed to attend a methodological "trial" of the work of one of their number, that Philadelphia-based ethnography which has received an unusual degree of public acclaim and criticism. The tension within the play is driven by a one-eyed wolfdog from the pages of yet another group member's work, the animal having traveled great distances to bring the group a highly secret invention that promises to make ethnography "truly" scientific. Should the exhausted wolfdog be helped? What should be done with the invention? Is it the holy grail of contemporary methodological inquiry, or is it fool's gold?

For those new to ethnographic research, figuring out how to do it can be rendered especially complicated by debates over its philosophical presuppositions, its representations of those who are subjected to the researcher's gaze, and the ethical and political difficulties that can arise when researchers immerse themselves in others' lives and the organizational and/or communal settings of those lives. The methodological entanglements can be perplexing and intimidating for more seasoned scholars, as well, especially when some ethnographies are pilloried in the court of public opinion, whereas others are widely praised. The imagined dialogues among the play's characters lay out ways of thinking about how one might make sense of these varied issues.

Even though it features living ethnographers, the play is a work of fiction, albeit one that footnotes those researchers' works and other methods literature. Pachirat makes his ethnographer characters articulate and assess some of the significant methodological challenges that have emerged from the method's colonial and racist origins and which are also rooted in its philosophical underpinnings. Their voices, as he imagines them, enliven what might seem to some as dry and .even, at times, arcane topics, as they discuss them in light of their own and others' actual field research practices: following a mushroom from the forests of Oregon to the dining tables of Japan; living among the reindeer people to understand their ways of knowing; working in a slaughterhouse to observe routinized violence; and so on. Reflecting their particular disciplinary affinities, varied research settings, and fieldwork and writing experiences, the ethnographers articulate areas of consensus and, as important, dissensus, giving readers a feeling for the range of issues they may confront in their own research and how and why these authors have arrived at their viewpoints.

Pachirat skillfully interweaves all of this to challenge the rationalism and managerialism of a contemporary academic culture that seeks to hide the political implications of research beneath a pretense to neutrality and a veneer of replication. Because of where it stands on the continuum of proximity-distance between the researcher and those being studied, ethnography often makes visible the ethical issues at stake in research with humans, issues that are often obscured by methods at the continuum's more distant end, even though they are present there as well. The book brings to the fore matters concerning the ontological or reality status of what social scientists study and the epistemological conundrums those studies entail, along with the ethics of a method built upon a fundamentally relational engagement between a very human ethnographer and the human participants among whom the research is conducted. At the same time, the book does not neglect the method's everyday practices and practicalities.

Reader, be not deceived by its form and underestimate the book you are holding in your hands. It is not a light read. The dialogue is tough, at times, because of the complexity of the issues raised. Follow the one-eyed wolfdog and this baker's dozen of thinkers, and you will hear tales of objective reality and intersubjective meaning put on trial and judged, their import made even more visible in light of the animal's delivered invention. The final, brief act concludes the tale with a surprise whose meanings are left open to your interpretation. That ambiguous ending is fitting for a book that seeks to provide not final answers, but a deeply reflective consideration of how this most human of methods must cope with the pain and wonder of the human beings and communities that its researchers seek to understand and, at times, with those of the researchers themselves. Social scientists undertaking ethnographic research will have to navigate this terrain, and Timothy Pachirat's exegesis provides an astute companion for this journey.

Dvora Yanow, *Wageningen University*
Peregrine Schwartz-Shea, *University of Utah*

# PREFACE

When the editors of this Series asked me to write a book about ethnography, I happily agreed, but with three conditions. First, I did not want to create yet another dry methods book that fails to evoke, and provoke, the sense of excitement and uncertainty that ought to accompany our choices about how we ask and attempt to answer questions about the social world. Second, I wanted to engage as interlocutors the ethnographers whose books I feature in my graduate seminars in political ethnography, which I have now taught to over seven cohorts of graduate students at The New School in New York City and the University of Massachusetts Amherst, and—in a more condensed version—to hundreds of students over several annual summer sessions at The Institute for Qualitative and Multi-Method Research. And third, I wanted to experiment with writing in a non-traditional genre for the social sciences: specifically, with writing the book as a play that would bring many of the ethnographers featured in those seminars out of the footnotes and into direct dialogue with one another.

The result is *Among Wolves: Ethnography and the Immersive Study of Power*, the seven-act play in your hands. Most immediately, *Among Wolves* offers a guide for those seeking to conduct highly immersive ethnographic research on power. How does one define "the field"? How does one access it? What does it mean to build relationships with those one is researching? How does one write good fieldnotes? Readers will find ample discussion of these and other practical questions in this play. Inseparably, *Among Wolves* also goes beyond a simple "how-to" in order to pose deeper questions about the relationship between ethnography as a research method and the operation of power. If participant-observer ethnography is the one method in the social sciences in which the researcher herself is the instrument of research, as many methodologists claim, in what ways might ethnography serve as an exemplary case for examining the power relationships between social science researchers and the world(s) they seek to describe, explain, and, sometimes, to change? By interpolating the more practical "how to" aspects of ethnography's conduct with deeper, reflexive questions about ethnography's relationships with power, I hope to show that each can only be fully considered with, and is indeed co-constituted by, the other.

All this, of course, might have been successfully accomplished through a more traditional, didactic academic book format. And yet, by writing *Among Wolves* as a play, I strove for a rough—and I hope generative—homology between form and content. Just as ethnography as a method crucially depends on serendipity, surprise, and an openness to ambiguity, so too is the dramatic and dialogic structure of a play particularly useful for resisting linear, step-wise programs, argumentation that closes rather than opens avenues of thought, and heavy-handed, dogmatic prescriptions. And, in a milieu in which "method" often connotes discipline (and punishment?), rigor (mortis?), and severity, a play possesses the important added intellectual and creative virtues of being more, well, play-ful.

The anthropologists (Karen Ho, Anna Tsing, and Piers Vitebsky), sociologists (Mitchell Duneier, Alice Goffman, and Loïc Wacquant), political scientists (Séverine Autesserre and James C. Scott), and journalist (Katherine Boo) featured in this play do so by conscription rather than as eager volunteers. I selected these contemporary ethnographers because they represent an interdisciplinary range, because they are well known in their fields, and because many cohorts of my political ethnography students have found their work good for thinking with.

The words and thoughts attributed to each character are *my own interpretations and representations, not theirs*. I shared the play with the ethnographers represented as characters in this play, and a few provided comments and feedback. Still, I alone am responsible for the dialogue presented here, with the exception of the rare moments when a character's speech is taken verbatim from their prior published work. Such instances are always flagged by quotation marks and citations, although I forgo customary indented block quotations in order to preserve a sense of conversational flow. You are therefore cautioned to approach the play for the overall themes and questions it develops rather than as any sort of assertion of what each character would or would not argue for in real life. Indeed, as should be abundantly clear from the inclusion of an invisibility potion and a talking wolfdog, the play is a work of fiction, albeit fiction in Geertz's second- and third-order interpretive sense of "something made, something fashioned—the original meaning of *ficti* ."[1]

Nowhere is this truer than in the play's penultimate act, entitled "The Trial," which stages the central public criticisms and defenses of Alice Goffman's widely read 2014 ethnography, *On the Run: Fugitive Life in an American City*. A remarkable debut work of academic ethnography, *On the Run* crossed over into the public discourse at a time when anti-Black police violence in the United States was beginning to capture the sustained attention of the mainstream media. For this and other reasons, *On the Run* quickly became a synecdoche both for the highly charged politics of anti-Black police practices and for the value of (or skepticism toward) ethnography as a mode of research and writing.

Other ethnographies, including my own 2011 *Every Twelve Seconds: Industrialized Slaughter and the Politics of Sight*, might be subjected to many of the criticisms (and defenses) surrounding Goffman's book. What makes *On the Run* an exemplary case to think with is the attention it has attracted from both inside and outside academia, and the way that the broader critiques of ethnography which it catalyzes create space for a productive discussion of ethnography's value as a research method and its relationship to the operation of power. Indeed, "few studies offer a better, closer, or more intense depiction and forthright confrontation of the moral dilemmas that are more or less baked into immersion ethnography."[2] Finally, the act's conceit of a trial puts the tone of many of the criticisms of Goffman's book itself on trial, and asks whether such a tone is a fair and productive way to evaluate ethnographic work.

*Among Wolves* possesses a dramatic arc and is best read (or performed!) as a whole. Nonetheless, readers short on time or wishing to assign individual acts for classroom use may still benefit from partial readings. Without spoiling the story, I might point readers to Acts One through Three as a useful introduction to the embodied quality of ethnographic research, and the question of what, if any, difference the (in)visibility of the researcher makes to the research process. Act Four provides an in-depth exploration of ethnography's relationship to power and includes a discussion of the method's troubled and troubling colonial and racist origins. Act Five offers the most sustained discussion of the practical aspects of conducting ethnography and is the most "how-to" portion of the play. Act Six stages a trial of Alice Goffman's *On the Run*, providing a specific case in which the tensions of ethnography's relationship to power and the practical conduct of ethnography are brought to the fore. And finally, Act Seven offers a brief, if intentionally ambiguous, conclusion to the play's dramatic arc.

Readers seeking even more depth than the play offers will find the ethnographies written by each of the ten "characters" an excellent interdisciplinary starting point (see the Dramatis Personae for a full listing). A semester-long class on ethnography, for example, might assign these ten books as companion texts to the play. Additional endnotes throughout the play provide further avenues for exploring particular themes or questions.

I harbor no illusions that *Among Wolves* will ever be featured on Broadway, and I leave playwriting with a deep appreciation bordering on awe for those who write and think dialogically. Living day to day with the voices of nine other ethnographers—not to mention a one-eyed wolfdog who can see the future—has proved more difficult than I imagined it would be. I am happy to bid them farewell in an eager and overdue return to the solitude and author-itarian safety and relative ease of more traditional academic projects.

I especially want to thank Dvora Yanow and Peregrine Schwartz-Shea for soliciting this project and steadfastly believing in it throughout; those among the characters featured in the play who provided feedback; Fred Schaffer, Amel Ahmed, Barbara Cruikshank, Richard Payne, Sandra Ragsdale, and Samantha Pachirat for careful readings of various drafts; Lorna Somerville for extraordinary copyediting; and Routledge Senior Political Science Editor Natalja Mortensen and Editorial Assistant María Landschoot for overseeing the production and publication process.

Above all, I am grateful to my political ethnography students at The University of Massachusetts Amherst, The New School for Social Research, and the Institute for Qualitative and Multi-Method Research for countless conversations and fieldwork projects that have shaped, reshaped, and continue to shape my thinking about and practice of the immersive study of power. This play is dedicated to all of them: past, present, and future.

And with that, let us now go forth among wolves!

Timothy Pachirat
Brooklyn, NY

## Notes

1  Geertz 1973a: 15.
2  Van Maanen and de Rond 2017: 396, Manning, Jammal, and Shimola 2016.

# DRAMATIS PERSONAE

## (in order of appearance)

A one-eyed wolfdog

Timothy Pachirat, author of this book and of *Every Twelve Seconds* (2011)

Dr. Popper Will Falsify

Anonymous graduate student

Michio Kaku, theoretical physicist and host of nationally syndicated radio show
   *Science Fantastic*

Dr. Cy N. Salthaway

Dr. Maura D. Scripshon

Séverine Autesserre, author of *Peaceland* (2014)

Katherine Boo, author of *Behind the Beautiful Forevers* (2012a)

Mitchell Duneier, author of *Sidewalk* (1999)

Alice Goffman, author of *On the Run* (2014)

Karen Ho, author of *Liquidated* (2009)

James C. Scott, author of *Weapons of the Weak* (1985)

Anna Tsing, author of *The Mushroom at the End of the World* (2015)

Piers Vitebsky, author of *The Reindeer People* (2005)

Loïc Wacquant, author of *Body & Soul* (2004a, 2016)

The Prosecutor

# ACT ONE: WOLFDOG

Lycanthropy (n.)

1. In folklore, the magical ability to assume the form and characteristics of a wolf.
2. A delusion that one has become or assumed the characteristics of a wolf or other animal.

*American Heritage Dictionary of the English Language,*
5th ed., s.v. "lycanthropy."

Wolves were demonized immediately. They became a potent symbol of the dangerous, fearful and godless wilderness that surrounded the settlers and threatened the physical safety of their fragile homes and the order of their social and religious lives.

Garry Marvin, *Wolf* (2012: 87)

## Scene

Predawn summer. In the wrinkled topography of New York State's Finger Lakes, a one-eyed wolfdog is on the move. Trotting along packed dirt shoulders of black asphalt roads, skirting vineyards tipsy with sightseers, and bisecting riotous swards of iris and milkweed, she peaks a hill and halts, nose twitching. In the fold of land below, an octogenarian barn humps against an unruly field like a beached whale, its once-upon-a-time red planks a frostbitten, sun-scorched gray, strips of desiccated skin clinging to ancient, bleached-white bones.

Human scent. Circling the barn's perimeter, the wolfdog cautiously enters an opening on its lower level. At an oak desk planted firmly in the dark dirt of the barn's ground floor, a man clickety-clacks on a laptop. To his left, several dozen books occupy a rough plank bridging weathered logs.

WOLFDOG: Hello.

[Long silence.]

WOLFDOG: Hello.
HUMAN: Who's there?
WOLFDOG: Hello.
HUMAN [seeing the wolfdog but looking for the source of the voice]: Who's there?
WOLFDOG: Me. Obviously.
HUMAN [matching speech to wolfdog for the first time]: You speak!
WOLFDOG [padding closer to the human and sitting, her massive size nearly putting her at eye-level with him]: For those with ears to hear, what doesn't speak? But, yes, I speak your English.

*be filled with a feeling of love for*

[Human sits silent, in shock.]

WOLFDOG: You so-called civilized humans are so enamored of your language magic—your emails, your texts and tweets, your handheld portals—and yet you dwell in profound deafness. Where I come from, humans have ears for the many languages of the sky and her winds, for the subtlest seasonal shifts, for the forests with their many mysteries, for the freeze and flow of the mighty rivers. And, above all else, for the reindeer.
HUMAN: The reindeer?
WOLFDOG: Yes, I am from the land of the reindeer and the people of the reindeer, a vast expanse of extreme temperatures populated by animals and spirits.

[Pauses.]

In categories comprehensible to you, I am from the Verkhoyansk Mountains of northeast Siberia where I live amongst the reindeer and their humans, the Eveny People. There, I am known to all simply as the one-eyed wolfdog who can see into the future.

*unlimited power*

HUMAN: See into the future? Wolf [pauses] dog?
WOLFDOG: I have mystical powers, but I am not omnipotent. My future-seeing powers are brought forth only in relationship with others. They are never a thing made but are always in the making. Wolf and dog are *your* categories, not ours, and the need to distinguish sharply between the two is your need, not ours.
HUMAN [recovering]: Aren't you a long way from home?
WOLFDOG: Yes, I've run hard for almost three moons across open tundra, into forest, and through labyrinthine mazes of steel, concrete, and plastic. But today the running ends.
HUMAN: Ends?
WOLFDOG: Yes, my running has led to you.
HUMAN: Me?

WOLFDOG: Yes, you are the ethnographer known as Timothy, and you told the story of a hidden house that slaughters cattle by the millions.

HUMAN [startled]: How do you know that?

WOLFDOG [raising her right lip in a smile]: Mystical powers.

HUMAN: So?

WOLFDOG: You're about to stage a trial? A trial of a certain Alice Goffman?

HUMAN [even more startled]: Yes, an ethnographic trial. But nobody knows except the handful of people involved.

WOLFDOG [smiling again]: I know it.

HUMAN: You're here for the trial?

WOLFDOG: Not exactly. Call it synchronicity. I didn't come here for the trial, but my coming may end up being important to the trial. Here, help me loosen this harness around my back and take hold of the thing I have brought you.

HUMAN [rising from chair and walking around table to the wolfdog, where he unfastens a worn rawhide harness holding a package wrapped in reindeer skin]: You brought this all the way from Siberia?

WOLFDOG [suddenly tired]: Open it, and I shall tell you its story.

HUMAN [untying the rawhide and gently unrolling the reindeer skin on the oak table, revealing a small, rubber-stopped glass vial containing an incandescent green liquid and a sheaf of papers covered in writing and complex mathematical equations]: *What?*

WOLFDOG [rising to full height and voice becoming fainter and eyes growing distant]: Revealer of cattle killing

> Still now your heart and mind
>
> Open your ears
>
> To receive the tale of this gift....

[Voice growing trance-like. Timothy sits back down at his desk.]

Four moons ago, Terrapin and Nikolay were traveling with their reindeer herd through a pass in the Verkhoyansk Mountains when the lead reindeer began to snort and summon the herd into a tight circle, youngest and weakest in the middle. Seeing no obvious predator, Nikolay urged his own reindeer to the head of the herd. There, at the zenith of the pass, he noticed an irregular shape underneath the snow and ice. Scraping away the fallen snow, he let out a shout of surprise and alarm, for there, frozen solid, was the perfectly preserved corpse of a dark-eyed, bearded man dressed in Western clothing. After extricating the man from his icy tomb, Nikolay and his companions fashioned a makeshift sled, harnessed it to their reindeer, and pulled him back to their camp.

There, the local shaman was summoned, and when he arrived he immediately asked that two wooden bowls of reindeer milk and a bottle of vodka be brought to him. Sprinkling the milk over the body of the man and throwing a cupful of vodka into the fire, he began to chant as the residents of the camp gathered in a circle around him and beat on drums of stretched reindeer skin.

After a time of this drumming, the shaman's eyes rolled upward in his head as he entered into a trance and was transformed into a flying reindeer on a soul flight to the sun. There, he met with the spirit of the dead man, who told him that he possessed a terrible and mighty secret such as the world had never known and that it would have been better if his body had never been discovered. But, now that the secret had been untombed, it was of the utmost importance to select the people's most trusted messenger to carry the secret east, across the tundra and the sea, to a man who would be waiting in a blood-red house overlooking a lake. And with this, the spirit of the dead man vanished into the burning center of the sun.

Thus informed, the camp dwellers searched the body of the dead man and found, sewn into a secret compartment on the inside of his vest, the vial and the sheaf of papers that now sit before you. Some of the camp dwellers, led by a strong young man many expected to become the next leader of the village, argued that the vial and papers should immediately be cast into the fire and destroyed, that nothing good would come of the discovery of the body of this man or of his great and terrible secret. Others, led by a second young man known for his savvy in dealing with the outside world, argued that the vial and papers should be taken to the place of trading and sold to the many merchants who passed by that place. The soft voice of Granny, indisputable matriarch of the camp, interrupted their dispute.

Having lived through the time of Stalin and the near-eradication of the Eveny shamans, Granny spoke with the authority of one-who-has-suffered. "We've been entrusted," she said, "with the secret and charged by the spirit of the dead man with taking it east. For such an important and dangerous journey, there is only one messenger." Then she turned to face me, the one-eyed wolfdog.

The people prepared the vial and papers for their long journey, wrapping them in the reindeer hide that now lies on your desk. Harnessing the package to my chest, they sent me away with much sorrow. Night after night, I ran east against the passage of the moon across the sky, my only company the winds of forests and mountain passes. By day, I burrowed under deep roots or between rocks and slept. In the early days of my journey, my sleep was a dead sleep. But as I continued east, my dreams began to take on a substance more vivid than the shadowy world of my nightly runs.

In the beginning, I dreamed nightmares of a vast and blood-soaked house in which thousands of innocent creatures were led each day to be killed and butchered by men and women who were themselves strangers to the land. In these dreams, I saw you, Timothy, working in such a blood-soaked house by day and returning to your own house to write about your work by night. These nightmares haunted me during my nightly runs, for although I have seen many reindeer killed for their meat and hides, in my land it is always done with thanksgiving, gratitude, and sorrow, never with the casual and callous disregard for the spirits of the animals that I saw in these dreams. From this first dream, I knew that my task was to bring the secret gift to you.

HUMAN: But why?

WOLFDOG: Please do not interrupt me any further, for my tale is long and its speaking wearies me.

HUMAN: I'm sorry.

WOLFDOG: In the second week, my dreams transported me from the house of killing to a vertigo-inducing jungle of concrete and steel on an island called Manhattan where humans clothed in all manner of finery scurried to and fro like rodents escaping a rising flood. In this jungle, I was led to a tall building emblazoned in gold like the sun. Inside, humans stared hypnotized at blinking screens while bloodthirsty screams of, "Buy! Sell! Trade!" rushed from their throats.

Far, far away from the screaming automatons, yet bound to them by invisible chains, were entire realms of creation: men, women, children, factories, towns, forests, rivers, vast fields, and animals of all kinds. As the humans in the tall building shouted "Sell!", some chains would be tightened and others loosened, and like puppets, some men, women, and children would topple over, and entire forests and fields would be demolished. Then, when the tall building people shouted "Buy!", other chains would be tightened and entire herds of animals would be brought into existence from nothingness, only to be sold, slaughtered, then sold again. From dawn until long after darkness, the people in the tall buildings pulled and pushed on these chains, unleashing destructive convulsions through every corner of the earth.

In the third week, my dreams carried me, spore-like, along the trail of the matsutake mushroom, from their human discovery by Hmong, Cambodian, Lao, and Vietnam War veteran pickers in the mountains of Oregon to their sale to buyers in roadside tents along the highway before their bulking and transformation into homogenous export commodities in Vancouver. From there, I flew across the Pacific Ocean with them as they traveled to Japanese wholesalers. Then, once in Japan, I continued to follow their re-individuation as high-status gifts signifying serious commitments between gift giver and receiver. My dream of the matsutake mushroom expanded, and I found myself roaming the peasant landscapes of Yunnan, China, and Honshu, Japan, and the industrial pine forests of Oregon and northern Finland, trying to understand the interspecies encounters between humans and pines that create the conditions where matsutake mushrooms are most likely to flourish.

HUMAN: That sounds amazing!

WOLFDOG [letting the interruption pass]: In week four of my long run to the east, I returned in my dreams to the streets of Manhattan and entered the lives of Alice, Marvin, Ron, Keith, and others as they struggled to get by, some by selling books on sidewalk tables, some by panhandling. I listened in as the Grand Central Partnership and their lawyers discussed strategies for reducing the number of sidewalk vendors in New York City, arguing that their presence was disruptive and dirty.

In week five, I dreamed of a small, rice-farming peasant village in Malaysia and of pilfering, gossip, slander, and shirking deployed as weapons wielded by the weak against the strong in the village. I saw how one poor farmer slowly moved the earth, dividing his meager plot of land from his wealthy neighbor's huge paddies, centimeter by centimeter, year after year, gradually and imperceptibly increasing his growing area. I laughed when I saw how other poor farmers slipped grain into their pockets as they threshed the rice of the rich farmers in the village. And I listened as the poor farmers spread stories about the stinginess and small-heartedness of the rich farmers.

In the sixth week, my dreams led me to a slum in India. It was hidden behind billboards advertising flooring tiles that would stay beautiful forever, and in this slum little boys picked through garbage for objects to sell and recycle, adolescent girls swallowed poison to kill themselves in their despair, and grown women set themselves on fire to spite their neighbors.

In week seven, my dreams transported me to a boxing gym on the South Side of Chicago where I was placed in the ring itself, feeling the blows and sweat of my opponents upon my body and returning them in equal measure. I trained under a man named DeeDee who sat at his desk with a stopwatch, supervising the sparring, as well as my floorwork, tablework, and ringwork.

In the eighth week of my running, I became engrossed in the international world of self-described "peacekeepers," joining employees of international agencies, non-governmental organizations, and diplomatic missions in Congo, South Sudan, Burundi, Cyprus, Israel and the Palestinian Territories, and Timor-Leste as they tried in various ways to "help" their host countries achieve peace. I spent time behind the fortified walls of the compounds where these expatriates lived, following the rules of their security protocols (No going out at night! Report your location to base at all times!), immersing myself in their daily routines, attending their frequent going-away parties, and sitting with them as they created their endless reports and PowerPoint presentations recounting universalized "lessons learned."

In the ninth week, I dreamed of an inner-city neighborhood in Philadelphia where I joined Mike, Chuck, Alex, and other members of the 6th Street Boys in dodging and running from the police. I accompanied some of them after they were caught and beaten, making their way through the labyrinth of arraignment, bail hearing, trial, sentencing hearing, lengthy prison time, and then their return home. I watched as the police broke down the doors of their mothers' and girlfriends' houses and threatened them with jail if they didn't reveal the whereabouts of their sons and boyfriends.

HUMAN: Wait, that's exactly the topic of the ethnographic trial!

[Wolfdog glares at the interruption and the human sinks back in his chair, subdued.]

WOLFDOG: And last of all, just as I was farthest from home, the tenth week of my dreams returned me to the vast landscape of mountains and tundra that I had started from. Only it was not the home of my memories and my perceptions, but rather my home as seen through another's eyes, a stranger's eyes, the eyes of a tall ethnographer who calls himself Piers Vitebsky. In my dream, I saw the reindeer herders of my camp, Terrapin, Nikolay, and Bison, and I saw Ivan, the head herder, as well as Yura, his younger brother. I also saw Granny, the camp's matriarch.

And I saw myself, the one-eyed wolfdog, but I saw myself through the eyes of this white outsider, this man Piers Vitebsky. And I saw that this stranger, Piers, believed neither in my mystical powers nor in the others' understanding of my powers. He was kind, courteous, and friendly. He ate as we ate and learned to ride behind a dog sled as we rode behind a dog sled. He brought with him an open and inquiring mind and a big heart. But it was an openness and a curiosity that at once sought to understand our land as it is and as we ourselves see it—and simultaneously to translate our land and ourselves into a language and a way of seeing not our own; a language and way of seeing meant for other eyes, other ways of being, other ways of making the world.

And when this stranger took out his notebook and his lead pencil and his tape recorder and began to inscribe us in a strange language, through strange eyes, through trained eyes that sorted everything they perceived into strange boxes he called theories...

[Voice trails off into a hoarse whisper.]

composed of material

/...well, then, at that moment in my dream I felt myself for the first time as pure materiality, as mere wolfdog, nothing more than my bone, flesh, fur, and teeth. My birthright powers, the powers that came into being in the spaces of possibility between myself and all the worlds around me, vanished under his gaze.

[As she speaks, the wolfdog's body sinks lower and lower to the ground until she is curled up tightly into a ball, nose to tail. Her body stiffens before going completely limp.]

HUMAN [rising from his seat, alarmed]: Are you all right? Are you all right? Wolfdog!

[No response.]

HUMAN [walks around his desk to the one-eyed wolfdog and, failing to rouse her with gentle shakes, sits on the dirt floor next to her with a hand resting gently

on her head, silent for some time before speaking]: Do you know, wise wolfdog, you dream the books of the ethnographers about to gather here?

[Looks at books on the wooden plank next to the desk, while photographs
of the covers of each book are projected onto a screen at back of the stage.]

The secret house of cattle killing you dreamed is my own *Every Twelve Seconds: Industrialized Slaughter and the Politics of Sight*. It sits next to Karen Ho's
*Liquidated: An Ethnography of Wall Street*, which tells the tale of the men and
women shouting "Buy! Sell! Trade!" Then there's Anna Tsing's *The Mushroom
at the End of the World*, an ethnography of the matsutake mushroom, the worlds
that make it possible, and the further worlds that it in turn calls into being.
And *Sidewalk*, Mitchell Duneier's account of Sixth Avenue's booksellers and
panhandlers in Greenwich Village. Also, James C. Scott's *Weapons of the Weak*,
an analysis of everyday forms of resistance in a Malaysian peasant village.
Next is Katherine Boo's *Behind the Beautiful Forevers*, a story about the people
living in the Mumbai slum of Annawadi. Your seventh dream, of a boxing
gym on the South Side of Chicago, corresponds to Loïc Wacquant's *Body &
Soul: Notebooks of an Apprentice Boxer*. And then there's Séverine Autesserre's
*Peaceland*, which unpacks the culture of international interveners around the
world. Also, Alice Goffman's *On the Run*, the book about fugitive lives in
Philadelphia, and the reason for the ethnographic trial we are about to hold
here. And the last, the one in which you dreamed your own diminished self
through the eyes of another, is Piers Vitebsky's *The Reindeer People: Living with
Animals and Spirits in Siberia*.

What can be the meaning of your arrival, wolfdog, and your dreaming of
these authors' books?

[Falls silent, then rises and walks to the table, where he holds up the vial of
incandescent green liquid which glows eerily in the early morning light.
Then, sets down vial, unrolls sheaf of papers, and begins to read aloud.]

Undated Memo
To: Unidentified Principal Investigators
From: Special Operations Branch, The National Science Foundation Social
Science Directorate
Subject: Field Invisibility Potion
Classification: Top Secret
Pursuant to prior classified communication between ourselves and the rele-
vant Congressional committees, we write to authorize….

[Voice fades. Lights dim to darkness.]

## End of Act One

# ACT TWO: FIELDWORK
# INVISIBILITY POTION

It seemed that the ring he had was a magic ring: it made you invisible! He had
heard of such things, of course, in old tales; but it was hard to believe that he had
really found one, by accident.

J.R.R.Tolkien, *The Hobbit* ([1937] 1966: 79)

Then charm me, that I
May be invisible, to do what I please
Unseen of any...

Christopher Marlowe, *Dr. Faustus* (1994: 32)

## Scene

Windowless room in the basement of unidentified Camelot University building. Beakers, burners, and test tubes cover several long lab tables. Assisted by an
anonymous, bearded graduate student, Dr. Popper Will Falsify moves about the
room, adjusting burners, measuring liquids and powders into the test tubes, and
scribbling elaborate mathematical formulas onto yellow legal pads. Both Popper
and the graduate student wear white lab coats and safety goggles.

As the two work, the lights dim slightly and an offstage voice reads the following memo in a bureaucratic tone:

To: Unidentified Principal Investigators
From: Special Operations Branch, The National Science Foundation Social
Science Directorate
Subject: Field Invisibility Potion
Classification: Top Secret

Pursuant to prior classified communication between ourselves and the relevant Congressional committees, we write to authorize unrestricted funding for National Science Foundation secret project 00-000-001-2539, also to be known as the "Field Invisibility Potion," or FIP.

The express purpose of this project is to internationally advance United States military, political, economic, and social interests by laying the foundation for a more rigorous, objective, and replicable science of understanding of non-American countries and cultures. The project has two rationales.

The first is that the advancement of United States' interests cannot depend on brute military strength alone. Development and deployment of nuclear weaponry and other advanced military capacities should be seen as a strategy of last resort, bolstered and supplemented by softer strategies of persuasion and control that are rooted in a deeper understanding of the cultural, linguistic, and ideological obstacles currently preventing large segments of the world's population and their governments from adopting what might be known as "the American Way." Although less likely to yield immediate results in the short run, such strategies will prove immeasurably more cost-effective in the long run in achieving American dominance throughout the globe.

The project's second rationale lies in the underdeveloped, nascent state of academic ethnography. Developed largely in anthropology and sociology, and increasingly common in political science, organization studies, education studies, nursing studies, and a range of other disciplines, ethnography has in the past led to occasional actionable insight, as when, for example, instructors at the John F. Kennedy Special Warfare School taught Raphael Patai's 1973 ethnography, *The Arab Mind*, in order to give US soldiers better insight into behavior they encountered on the battlefield.[1] Notwithstanding these sporadic contributions, however, the studies overall have been marred by the subjectivity introduced by the presence of the researcher in the site of research, leading to contamination and bias of the results. Ethnography's actual contributions to actionable knowledge in the service of United States' interests have relied primarily on flashes of insight derived from non-replicable interactions that are highly specific to the qualities of the individual researcher.

The re-authorization of this secret program, particularly pressing in the context of the current Global War on Terror, seeks the development of the technical means for realizing a rigorous scientific approach to ethnography that retains the benefits of a close-range, emic encounter with national and cultural others while nonetheless overcoming the bias introduced by the messy, embodied presence of the ethnographer.

To this end, building on the foundation laid by scientific breakthroughs in molecular physics during the past decades of the Manhattan Project, we authorize the commencement of FIP. The primary goal of the project is the design, invention, and implementation of an injectable or ingestible liquid ("the potion") that will render ethnographers impervious to physical detection in the field ("invisible"). Audacious, perhaps even unimaginable on its face, we believe the basic science is now in place to make this possible.

Principal Investigators for FIP shall comprise, in equal numbers, leading physicists and social scientists. There is no end date for the completion of the project. Its funding is unrestricted, subject to ten-year renewals. Because of the military and political sensitivity of the project, it is designated top secret.

Signed,

[name redacted]

Director, National Science Foundation

[Stage lights grow brighter.]

DR. POPPER WILL FALSIFY: We are almost there, I can feel it, we are almost there.

GRADUATE STUDENT: Unbelievable, after over five decades of effort!

POPPER: This must be how Moses felt after forty years in the desert. On the cusp of the Promised Land, yet unable to enter himself. I would give my right arm for a chance to go back into the field with this potion.

GRADUATE STUDENT [fiddling with the flame under a beaker]: Approaching the specified temperature now.

POPPER: That's it! We did it!

[Lights fade to darkness. After thirty seconds of silence, an illuminated multimedia screen begins to display a collage of newspaper headlines and play clips of prime-time news announcements heralding the invention of the Field Invisibility Potion in various languages. A loud voice babble of partial headlines and news reports fades out as Michio Kaku's voice announces: "From Talk Radio Network, this is *Science Fantastic*, and I'm Dr. Michio Kaku."]

## End of Act Two

## Note

1   Patai 1973, De Atkine 2004; see also McCoy 2006.

# ACT THREE: SCIENCE FANTASTIC

To render oneself invisible is a very easy matter, [but] it is not altogether permissi-
ble, because that by such a means we can annoy our neighbour in his [daily] life…
and we can also work an infinitude of evils.

S. Liddell Macgregor Mathers, *The Book of the Sacred Magic
of Abramelin the Mage* (1932: 147)

And perhaps in this is the whole difference; perhaps all the wisdom, and all truth,
and all sincerity, are just compressed into that inappreciable moment of time in
which we step over the threshold of the invisible.

Joseph Conrad, *Heart of Darkness* (1973: 101)

## Scene

Complete darkness. Voices of Dr. Michio Kaku, Dr. Cy N. Salthaway, and
Dr. Maura D. Scripshon are heard.[1]

Michio Kaku: Broadcasting live on Talk Radio Network on over 100 com-
mercial radio stations around the country and live streaming on Talk Radio
Network.com, this is *Science Fantastic* with Dr. Michio Kaku. As you know,
listeners, on this show we talk about "black holes, time travel, higher dimensions, string theory, wormholes, search for extra-terrestrial life, dark matter
and dark energy, the future of space travel, genetic engineering, the aging
process, the future of medicine, the human body shop, artificial intelligence,
the future of computers and robots, as well as topics from science fiction."[2]
"When I was a kid, I used to love reading science fiction. I read about telep-
athy, that is reading minds. I read about telekinesis, moving objects with the

mind. I read about recording memories. I read about photographing dreams. Well, today we can do all of the above."[3]

And, today, listeners, our topic is invisibility. Yes, invisibility! As many of you are probably already aware, social scientists spilled from their offices and gathered on campus quads this week to celebrate the invention of the Fieldwork Invisibility Potion, or FIP. The culmination of decades of top-secret research funded by the Special Operations Branch of the Social Science Directorate of the National Science Foundation, the breakthrough invention of FIP allows for the first time the possibility of ethnographic field research uncontaminated by observer-observed interactions. Variously termed "bias" and "subjectivity" by leading social science practitioners, these forms of contamination have long plagued the quest for a replicable, objective, and systematic ethnographic method.

The project's current principal investigator, Dr. Popper Will Falsify, released a statement that reads, in part: "With FIP's invention, such sources of uncontrolled error in ethnographic method may very well join flat-earth theories, witch burning, and medical bloodletting in the dustbin of prescientific history. The observer effect has been a known feature of theoretical physics and quantum mechanics since Heisenberg first articulated it in the early part of the 20th century, so it's no small irony that it should be the social sciences that have now discovered the key to overcoming the Heisenberg effect in the quest for a truly scientific study of the social world. We believe FIP may very well usher in a new era of comity between the so-called social and natural sciences, one that finally secures social science's place as an equal partner, rather than an envious younger sibling, to the so-called hard sciences."

On our show today, I welcome two leading social scientists, Dr. Cy N. Salthaway and Dr. Maura D. Scripshon, to share their perspectives on the invention of FIP. Professor Salthaway is founder and director of the prestigious Institute for Cumulative Knowledge (ICK) and is widely known across the social sciences as a leading proponent of a more scientific approach to social knowledge. He joins us from ICK's headquarters at Harper University. Professor Scripshon is convener of the Political Ethnography Collective (PEC), an upstart group of social scientists seeking to challenge what they call an unproductive emphasis on scientism in the social sciences. She joins us on the phone from the high plains of Mongolia, where she is currently conducting research on equine–human relationships.

Welcome to *Science Fantastic Live*, Professors.

Dr. Cy N. Salthaway: Thank you, Michio, it's a pleasure to be here.

Dr. Maura D. Scripshon [static on the line]: Yes, thanks for having me on, Michio!

Michio: Before we get started with questions for each of the professors, I want to read for my listeners an excerpt from a recent book by Frederic Schaffer, entitled *Elucidating Social Science Concepts*. As a theoretical physicist, I must things cannot be objective evidence; they include subjective values... not directly observed 3 (counter

admit to ignorance when it comes to the many differences inside of the social sciences. So, I did a little digging to try to understand one difference that I kept hearing over and over as I talked to my social science friends about the invention of FIP. And that is the difference between positivism on the one hand and interpretivism on the other.

human knowledge is produced by the scientific interpretation of observational data

[Dr. Salthaway and Dr. Scripshon chuckle in unison.]

DR. SCRIPSHON: Yes, that's a big one, all right!

MICHIO: Well, here is what Professor Frederic Schaffer has to say on the topic:

> A widely shared methodological commitment of positivism, as I understand it, is a belief that social scientists can directly and neutrally observe a social world that is made up of entities (like families and classes and revolutions) that enjoy, or are treated as if they enjoy, a real existence independent of how people think about them. An interpretivist approach to social science, in contrast, usually starts from the dual premises that there are no "real" social entities, only culturally mediated social facts, and that social science is always perspectival and entwined with the pursuit of moral or material goods. The aim of much interpretivist inquiry, consequently, is to shed light on how shared meanings and their relation to power inform or structure the social world and the study of the social world.[4]

Professors, how does the quote I just read resonate with your own views?

DR. SALTHAWAY: As a rough generalization, I think it does a nice job of summing up one of the key differences in how social scientists approach their work. My work, of course, tends to fall within what Schaffer calls a positivist logic of inquiry.

MICHIO: Professor Scripshon?

DR. SCRIPSHON: Yes, I agree with Dr. Salthaway that Schaffer's distinction provides a nice working definition. And, as you know, unlike Dr. Salthaway, my own work tends to be identified with an interpretivist approach.

MICHIO: Wonderful, so I got things right by inviting the two of you to comment on FIP. Dr. Salthaway, let's start with you. Those working within a logic of inquiry informed broadly by positivist commitments seem extremely optimistic about the invention of FIP. What's your take on it?

DR. SALTHAWAY: Unfortunately, politicians and governments often have a vested interest in portraying certain images of their societies. Ethnography, in-depth immersion, and participant observation are sometimes the only ways of getting a better handle on realities as they actually exist on the ground. But the obvious advantages of immersive fieldwork that gets closer to ground-level facts are diluted if not actually reversed by their "just anecdotal" quality, namely, that because the fieldworker is necessarily only observing interactions highly contingent upon her location in time and space, there is really no way to systematize and generalize the data she collects. Of course, another important worry when it comes to researchers who rely extensively or exclusively on ethnographic research is that the data they collect are more an artifact of their presence than a reflection of what is actually there. Combined, these concerns make it exceedingly difficult for ethnography to justify itself as sufficiently systematic or replicable to qualify as science.

MICHIO: Could you give any examples?

DR. SALTHAWAY: We recently had a job candidate for a prestigious senior position with ICK. He had invested years to learn Malay and live in a remote Southeast Asian village of approximately seventy families. His job talk offered some remarkably vivid descriptions of pilfering, gossip, and foot-dragging that came out of this fieldwork, but when a respected senior member of our department interrupted the candidate halfway through his talk to ask whether the research amounted to anything more than an anthropological monograph about a specific researcher living in a specific village at a specific historical moment, it really put a damper on things. That, I think, is generally the problem that ethnography suffers from as a method.

MICHIO: So, prior to the invention of FIP, was ethnography really doomed to produce only anecdotal stories that, while interesting and occasionally entertaining, didn't amount to anything resembling science?

DR. SALTHAWAY: Well, Michio, I'm loath to throw the baby out with the bathwater, and it's why I advocate what you might call a three-legged stool approach to the scientific study of politics. Under this approach, ethnography is immensely useful for generating hypotheses, exploring peculiar residuals that appear in statistical analyses, or helping the researcher uncover potential causal mechanisms linking dependent and independent variables.

But, ultimately, to produce what I would consider truly valid scientific knowledge, ethnography must be subsumed within a broader research program in which the other two legs of the stool—statistical and formal analysis—serve to test, and ultimately verify or falsify, the hypotheses and hunches developed by fieldwork.

MICHIO: So has the invention of FIP changed your thinking on the role that ethnography might potentially play in the social sciences?

DR. SALTHAWAY: Well, it's an interesting question. On the one hand, by containing the potential to eliminate entirely the participant in participant observation and produce a pure observer *qua* observer, it does strengthen the capacity of ethnography to be more objective. On the other hand, FIP does not do much for the "just anecdotal" problem insofar as an observer, no matter how invisible, is still only observing highly specific interactions and settings. So, ultimately, I think that even fieldwork conducted using FIP would still need to be combined with statistical and formal analyses.

I suppose you could say that one anxiety I have is that by making ethnography somewhat more rigorous without overcoming all of its limitations, FIP may give the dangerous illusion of strengthening arguments for the stand-alone value of ethnography in the social sciences. If you'll indulge the extended metaphor, proponents of ethnography's stand-alone value have always seemed to me a bit like creators of one-legged stools. Now, I grant you that one-legged stools might be very aesthetically pleasing, they might make for wonderful conceptual or installation art, and it might even be possible to create an entire tradition or discipline of one-legged stools in which earlier styles are compared with later styles, different types of wood are employed for the stool, different varnishes are put on it, passionate debates erupt over whether this or that wood is more ethical and environmentally sustainable, over whether this or that kind of varnish better respects the underlying grain or "voice" of the wood, and so on and so forth. This kind of thing might continue to the point where these debates replace the actual making of stools as the primary concern of the one-legged stool school or tradition or discipline. But, ultimately, for those concerned with the advancement of *science*, all of this hyper-reflexivity and navel-gazing boils down to the rather straightforward question of whether you would ever want to sit on a one-legged stool. And just as no one would ever want to sit on a one-legged stool, no matter how beautifully crafted, so too would we be better off the sooner we abandon the fantastical notion that stand-alone ethnography, absent a kind of disciplining or stabilization by statistical and formal analysis, can serve to move the project of a scientific study of social relations forward? FIP undoubtedly makes the ethnography leg of the three-legged stool of science stronger, but it does nothing to eliminate the need for the other two legs of the stool.

MICHIO: It sounds like you're rather less sanguine than Dr. Popper Will Falsify about the implications of FIP for ethnography's capacity to become a true science.

DR. SALTHAWAY: I have the highest respect for Dr. Popper Will Falsify and what he has accomplished with the invention of FIP, but I just don't think we're quite there yet in terms of a truly scientific, truly replicable, truly systematic ethnographic capacity in the social sciences.

MICHIO: So, what, in your opinion, would we need in order to get there?

DR. SALTHAWAY [laughing]: Oh, a time machine, for starters. And a do-over button. And a hermetically sealed social world in which our publications had no chance of being read by those they analyze, since that too might alter their behavior.

MICHIO: Ah, you laugh, Dr. Salthaway, but "my *New York Times* bestselling book, *Physics Of the Impossible: A Scientific Exploration into the World of Phasers, Force Fields, Teleportation, and Time*, goes not just fifty years into the future, it goes 500 years into the future, when we might have starships, we might have teleportation, we might even have time machines.[5] And in this book I answer the question, according to Einstein's theory: is it possible to go back in time and meet your teenage mother, before you were born, and she falls in love with you? Well, [laughing] if your teenage mother falls in love with you before you were born, you're in deep doo-doo."[6]

DR. SALTHAWAY [laughing]: Yes, I suppose if we do one day invent time machines and teleportation, people falling in love with their teenage mothers before they were born will be the least of our problems. Time machines would render our current notion of social sciences completely irrelevant!

DR. SCRIPSHON: Oh, I wouldn't be so sure about that, Dr. Salthaway! I'm not sure that the realization of any of those current impossibilities would fundamentally alter the core task of social sciences, which is understanding.

DR. SALTHAWAY: Understanding and not prediction?

DR. SCRIPSHON: Yes, Dr. Salthaway, understanding and not prediction.

MICHIO: Ah, thank you for that interjection, Dr. Scripshon! You know, although I am a physicist who writes about the future, and even though I believe "we can predict the evolution of the universe billions of years from now," I can certainly appreciate your reticence when it comes to prediction. "Let me quote from that great philosopher of the Western world, Yogi Berra. Yogi Berra once said, Prediction is awfully hard to do, especially if it's about the future!"[7]

[Laughter from both Dr. Salthaway and Dr. Scripshon.]

Well, Dr. Scripshon, let's now turn to your thoughts on the invention of FIP. You're widely recognized in the social sciences for employing what Frederic Schaffer calls an interpretive approach to social research. What's your take on FIP?

DR. SCRIPSHON: Like all revolutions in technologies of observation and analysis from the microscope to the telescope to the explication of the bell curve to the development of ordinary least squares analysis to the delineation of fuzzy set analysis, this so-called FIP will no doubt be heralded by many as a breakthrough of magnificent proportions and magical possibilities. Fundamentally, however, I do not think the invention of FIP or any other technology, including, I would add, time travel, obviates some of the basic, unavoidable questions facing the ethnographer and, by extension, all who take the social world as their focus of analysis.

Indeed, a central motivation for organizing the Political Ethnography Collective is the contention that the power of ethnography lies not only or even primarily in its capacity to get closer to the ground, to better "collect data" as if data were like so many rocks lying about in a field, but rather precisely in the way ethnography forces us to confront the question of how we as researchers are implicated in the social worlds we study, to confront the ways we actually co-generate rather than simply collect data, and to confront the ways the knowledge we produce with these data travels back and alters the very social worlds it purports to explain.

MICHIO: So, if I understand you correctly, you are saying that FIP actually eviscerates ethnography of one of its core strengths?

DR. SCRIPSHON: Not eviscerates so much as pushes underground. For researchers utilizing an interpretive methodology, the idea of neutrality or objectivity in fieldwork is an illusion because the researcher is always intervening in specific relations and networks of power. Being invisible does not change this. Take, as one example, a researcher who studies social relations of production on a factory floor. Not only *what* but *how* that researcher sees is going to be intimately tied to whether or not she enters the factory as a guest of management or whether she enters as an entry-level line worker, just to contrast two starkly different positional locations the researcher might take. Further, the ethnographer is always situated at the intersection of multiple identities—racial, gender, sexual, class, and so forth—and these impact both how people in the field interpret and therefore respond to her and how she herself filters her observations. So, arguably, the more fraught the power relations in the field, the more accounting for these sorts of positionality matters to the quality of the research.

MICHIO: Well, but wouldn't being invisible obviate the need for attention to what you call positionality?

DR. SCRIPSHON: Not at all! The researcher-specific positionality I was just talking about is only the most obvious and least avoidable center of a successive series of positions that every research project adopts. Ethnography's attention to researcher-specific positionality is nested inside other positions, such as the ways in which the underlying logic of inquiry used in the research channels a whole series of decisions of great import, beginning with the framing of the research question to the way the researcher counts certain things as facts or observations relevant to the research and others as coincidental or unimportant. And this position is itself nested within yet another that locates any given project within larger disciplinary histories connected to broader political projects, funding programs, and specific ideologies and interests. At this level, researchers reflect on the uses of research, on the kinds of discourses one's research legitimizes and is in turn legitimized by, and on the likely effects—intended and unintended—of those discourses on the subjects of research and the broader social and political worlds they inhabit.

MICHIO: I see. So, Dr. Scripshon, are you saying that all research must give an account of its position in these three dimensions?

DR. SCRIPSHON: I would say, Michio, that all research already does so, if not through explicit reflection, then through implicit silences. One unique feature of an interpretive approach to ethnography is that it surfaces these conversations for explicit commentary, rather than allowing them to be taken for granted, and that it does so because of the analytical and ethical gains that result.

MICHIO: So, from this perspective, the idea of invisibility is a bit ironic?

DR. SCRIPSHON: Ironic, yes, because part of the impetus of an interpretive approach is to make the position of the researcher at these different levels more visible.

MICHIO: I think I already know your answer, but would you ever consider using FIP in your own research in Mongolia?

DR. SCRIPSHON: Michio, let me just ask if after three years of slowly building rapport with this community and countless bruises and not a few broken bones from trying to master the impossible art of riding smelly horses across the tundra, you really think I would squander all that hard work by swallowing some potion that makes me disappear with a puff and a poof?

MICHIO: And there you have it, listeners. Radically different takes from Professors Salthaway and Scripshon on the invention of FIP. Clearly, the place and value of ethnographic research in the social sciences is rooted in longstanding disciplinary debates defying easy resolution. It seems that FIP will intensify rather than resolve these debates.

Meanwhile, social science departments and the research ethics committees called Institutional Review Boards, or IRBs, are scrambling to deal with the practical implications of FIP's imminent release. In an effort to attract the most competitive Ph.D. applicants, some top departments are already promising funding and specialized methods courses to support FIP-enabled fieldwork, while other departments are embroiled in debates over whether FIP ought to be reserved for tenured faculty, at least in its initial years of use. And in keeping with the patchwork system of university-specific IRB procedures, some IRB committees are all but requiring ethnographers to use FIP in the field, arguing that the risk of harm to subjects is radically reduced by the invisibility of the researcher. Researchers who can't be seen are less likely to harm subjects, they say. Other IRB committees have taken an opposite approach, equating invisibility with a kind of deception, which requires difficult-to-obtain exemption from standard informed-consent requirements.

For Principal Investigator Dr. Popper Will Falsify, the intellectual and pragmatic debates ignited by the invention of FIP only serve to underscore its revolutionary importance for the social sciences. We'll end this program with this confident quote from Dr. Popper Will Falsify: "We may very well be standing at an historic junction. In one hundred years, the history of the social sciences may be divided simply into pre-FIP and post-FIP. Real progress has been made. There will be no turning back."

Listeners! More on invisibility and time travel, as well as a special live question-and-answer session on air with our guests Dr. Maura D. Scripshon and Dr. Cy N. Salthaway after these short messages from our sponsors.

[Lights fade to darkness as futuristic music plays to end radio segment.]

## End of Act Three

# Notes

1  My thanks to Lee Ann Fujii for helping name Drs. Salthaway and Scripshon.
2  Kaku 2016a
3  Kaku 2016b
4  Schaffer 2016: 2
5  Kaku 2008
6  Kaku 2016b
7  Kaku 2016b

# ACT FOUR: ETHNOGRAPHY AND POWER

The political organization of a native tribe is obviously one of the first things to be known clearly. Now the political organization of an African people may be of an advanced kind, implying a sort of monarchy, with extensive traditions and genealogies, with great ceremonial and ritual, a developed system of finance, military organization and various judiciary functions. Such native states can be allowed to run on their own lines but they have to be first expurgated and then controlled. Now it is essential to touch as little as possible of the established order, and yet to eliminate all elements which might offend European susceptibilities or be a menace to good relations. Such knowledge obviously ought to be obtained.

Bronislaw Malinowski, "Practical Anthropology" (1929: 24–25)

Cultural knowledge of adversaries should be considered a national security priority.

Montgomery McFate, "The Military Utility of Understanding Adversary Culture" (2005a: 43)

There are armies, and armies of scholars at work politically, militarily, ideologically.

Edward Said, "Representing the Colonized: Anthropology's Interlocutors" (2006: 373)

[F]ieldwork itself reproduces modes of knowing straight out of plantation slavery, plantation management, and plantation geographies that were laboratories for black subjection and black resistance.

Christina Sharpe, "Black Life, Annotated" (2014)

I have never approved of the very public manner in which some of our western friends have conducted what they call the underground railroad, but which I think, by their open declarations, has been made most emphatically the upperground railroad. ...I see and feel assured that those open declarations are a positive evil to the slaves remaining, who are seeking to escape. They do nothing towards enlightening the slave, whilst they do much towards enlightening the master. They stimulate him to greater watchfulness, and enhance his power to capture his slave.

Frederick Douglass, *Narrative of the Life of Frederick Douglass, an American Slave* (2017 [1845]: 86)

## Scene

Back in the Finger Lakes Barn. Séverine Autesserre, Katherine Boo, Mitchell Duneier, Alice Goffman, Karen Ho, Timothy Pachirat, James C. Scott, Anna Tsing, Piers Vitebsky, and Loïc Wacquant mingle, the curled-up wolfdog nearly lifeless at their feet.

LOÏC WACQUANT [impatient]: The complication of this dog aside, I would like to state from the outset my opposition to this ridiculous idea.

MITCHELL (MITCH) DUNEIER: I agree with you, Loïc. This is just not a good idea.

ALICE GOFFMAN [sighing]: So I assume all of you received the same letter I did?

ANNA TSING: The one from someone calling themself The Prosecutor that summoned us here to hold an ethnographic trial of your book?

ALICE: Yes, the one that opens with, "In the name of the public interest and the integrity of science, I demand that you present yourselves for an ethnographic trial to be held on the eleventh of May in the old barn off Lake Keuka." Did everyone else receive it as well?

[Nods all around.]

LOÏC [looking around]: So where is this so-called prosecutor?

ALICE: Doesn't look like he or she is here yet.

[Pauses and looks around the room.]

Unless it's one of you?

[Everyone shakes their heads no.]

KATHERINE BOO: Well, The Prosecutor's letter of summons did mention that they would be wearing "A flowing black cloak woven with the strands of truth and carrying an oak staff fashioned from justice." Doesn't look like anyone here is dressed like that!

SÉVERINE AUTESSERRE [smiling]: I laughed pretty hard when I read that. I mean, it is a joke, right?

[Silence and serious faces.]

Right?

[Her smile fades.]

ALICE: Well, this person who calls her- or himself The Prosecutor *has* been racking up some very public victories against a whole series of junior scholars lately, most of them ethnographers. It's resulted in the early end of many promising intellectual futures and intimidated many other young scholars from pursuing the kind of work we all do.

ANNA: Yes, I've seen that happen, too, Alice, and I thought it was serious enough that I should come.

[All nod glumly.]

JAMES C. (JIM) SCOTT [smiling, trying to break the tension]: Hey, speaking of jokes, I assume you all know the one that goes, "three anthropologists, three sociologists, three political scientists, and a journalist meet a hooded prosecutor in an old barn to hold a trial?"

[General laughter breaks the tension.]

ANNA: Don't forget the sleeping dog.
TIMOTHY PACHIRAT: Wolfdog.
JIM: Oh, right. "Three anthropologists, three sociologists, three political scientists, one journalist, *and* a wolfdog meet in an old barn to hold a trial…."
KAREN HO: The dog doesn't actually look so hot.
ANNA: Wolfdog.
TIMOTHY: Do you recognize her, Piers?
PIERS VITEBSKY: Why? Should I?
TIMOTHY: Look more closely.
PIERS [stepping closer and peering down, brow furrowed]: What? The one-eyed wolfdog who can see the future?
TIMOTHY: Yes, it's the one-eyed wolfdog from your fieldwork among the Eveny reindeer herders.
PIERS: She's lost a lot of weight.
TIMOTHY: She's been running.
PIERS: No!
TIMOTHY: Yes! All the way here.
KATHERINE: For the trial?
TIMOTHY: I'm not sure.
ANNA: The wolfdog from *The Reindeer People*?
PIERS: Exactly.
SÉVERINE: Great book!
PIERS: Thanks!
KAREN: Twenty years is a long time for fieldwork.
LOÏC: Yeah, I'm not really sure how you have so much direct quotation in there or how you remembered it all.
PIERS: Conditions were a bit more inclement than a boxing gym a few miles from my university dorm room, but I still managed. Lead pencils work better than pens when it's −80 Fahrenheit.
LOÏC: I would never measure distance traversed in miles alone, Piers. As far as the University of Chicago was concerned, The Woodlawn Boy's Club where I did my fieldwork might as well have been in Siberia.
TIMOTHY: The wolfdog ran here from Siberia.

[Scattered exclamations of surprise and disbelief. Everyone interjecting questions at once.]

ALICE [nervously]: Everyone!

[General silence.]

Since it's my work that we're ostensibly gathered here to put on trial, and since I'm understandably quite nervous about this, may I get an explanation for what's going on with this wolfdog?

[Voices quiet down.]

TIMOTHY: Last week, I was sitting in this very barn, writing, or at least trying to write, when the creature you see before you appeared at my feet and began speaking to me.

LOÏC: Whoa, what are you smoking, Timothy? How long have you been out here alone?

ALICE: Let him tell his story.

TIMOTHY: She was very weak and tired, on the verge of collapsing into the coma you now see her in.

KATHERINE: Why haven't you taken her to the vet?

PIERS: A vet would kill this animal. She needs to see a shaman.

ANNA: Or a Diamond Queen.

ALICE: Can we all please stop interrupting and hear the story?

TIMOTHY: So she staggered into the barn and began speaking to me. She told me that she had run all the way from Siberia, by night, and that each day she slept and dreamed a series of different dreams.

LOÏC: Quite a tale, but what's it to do with us?

TIMOTHY: Everything! She arrived here, exhausted, and asked if we were about to stage an ethnographic trial. I said yes.

ALICE: She knew about the trial?

TIMOTHY: Yes. Then she began recounting the dreams she had each day as she slept. The first was of a slaughterhouse. The second was of Wall Street investment banks. Then it was matsutake mushrooms, peasants in a Malaysian village, a Mumbai slum, a Chicago boxing gym…you get the picture.

JIM: Sorry to be the dense one here, but I don't get it at all.

KATHERINE: I don't either.

ALICE: She was dreaming the books written by each person gathered here.

MITCH: Unreal.

LOÏC: That's one word for it.

TIMOTHY: I tried to write down as much of what she said about each of your books as I could remember. It wasn't your first-year college student kind of summary. It was more pointed. The description itself carried a viewpoint.

ANNA [aside]: Don't all descriptions carry a viewpoint?

TIMOTHY [looking at Karen]: She has this strangely poetic description of your book, for example. Instead of it being about stakeholders and shareholders and the Princeton to Wall Street pipeline, she dreamed about people screaming "Buy! Sell! Trade!" into telephones and about the chains connect-ing these screams to forests, oceans, animals, and other people all around the world. Every time they screamed, the chains would get yanked, taking down anyone or anything on the other end of them.

KAREN: Wow. That's depressing.

TIMOTHY [looking at Piers]: And her recounting of your book, Piers, was the strangest of all.

[Piers raises eyebrows.]

She said she dreamed of herself, not as she was, but as you saw her and wrote about her. She said that as her dreams went on across several days, she began to feel herself not as the venerated one-eyed wolfdog who could see the future, but simply as the product of superstitious beliefs of a primitive people.

ANNA [under her breath]: I have lots to say about the use of the word "primitive."

TIMOTHY: As she was recounting this, her voice grew fainter and fainter, until, finally, she said something like, "I feel like I have been killed."

JIM: Maudlin.

KATHERINE: Is she breathing? I still think we should take her to the vet.

KAREN [kneeling to get closer to the wolfdog]: Yes, she's still breathing. Just very faintly.

PIERS: So it wasn't the running that wore her down, then.

TIMOTHY: It doesn't seem so.

PIERS: It was experiencing herself through my eyes. How horrid. How absolutely horrid. Although I do write that by the end of my twenty years among the Eveny, I was beginning to question my own application of a Western world-view to their ways of thinking.

ALICE [softly]: Is that all?

TIMOTHY: No, there is more.

PIERS: I was afraid of that.

TIMOTHY: She also delivered these to me.

[Holds up sheaf of equations and vial of serum.]

KATHERINE: What *are* those?

JIM: This story gets stranger and stranger.

TIMOTHY: As the one-eyed dog told it to me, it is this.

[Recounts story of the discovery of the frozen body, the shaman's consulta-tion, and the secret memo.]

MITCH: This is the Fieldwork Invisibility Potion that we have been hearing about in the news?

TIMOTHY: Yes, according to the wolfdog, this is it.

LOÏC: One of the dumbest things I've ever heard of.

SÉVERINE: What is?

LOÏC: This idea of an invisibility potion.

SÉVERINE: Well, it's not an idea anymore, it's a reality.

LOÏC: An asinine reality that completely negates the purpose of ethnography, which is embodiment.

ANNA: Is this the only vial of the serum?

KAREN: I think I remember them saying on the news that they had only been able to produce a single vial.

MITCH: What should we do with it?

ANNA [joking]: How about we pass it around right now and take some shots!

LOÏC [scowling]: I refuse.

JIM [smiling]: I think Anna was playing around, Loïc.

ANNA [smiling]: Oh, was I now?

[General nervous silence as everyone stares at the incandescent serum.]

But seriously, what should we do with it?

KAREN: Since the wolfdog dreamed of our books, knew about the mock trial we were going to stage, and brought the serum to us, it seems incumbent on us to figure out together what to do with the serum.

MITCH [looking at Loïc]: Seems unlikely we'll all agree.

KAREN: True, but at least we'll have a chance to air the issues, and who knows, maybe talking about the serum will also help us with the trial as well.

ALICE: How would it do that?

JIM: Since it's Alice's trial that we're all gathered here for, maybe we ought to ask her.

ANNA: Spoken like a true anarchist.

JIM: Hey, it's two cheers for anarchism, not three. And anyway, I don't think a true anarchist would support anything like a trial in the first place.

ALICE [looking down at the wolfdog]: This is not really a theoretical discussion, folks. This dog is doing extremely poorly, and I think we ought to figure out quickly what to do with the potion and with her.

SÉVERINE: There's far too many of us here for this to be a productive discussion in a single big group. While we're waiting for The Prosecutor, assuming they are even coming, why don't we split into smaller groups to talk about the serum? Maybe we'll be able to reach a consensus on what to do with that by the time The Prosecutor arrives.

PIERS: That seems reasonable given what's at stake here.

ALICE: I'm okay with that plan too. But how should we split up?

TIMOTHY: Why don't we divide up based on the location of our ethnographies? Mitch, Loïc, Alice, Karen, and I have written ethnographies based here in the United States. Anna, Jim, and Katherine's work is based in Asia. And Piers's work is in Russia, while Séverine's is in Democratic Republic of Congo.

ANNA: Well, I'm not sure I agree with that characterization of my work. My book actually travels quite a bit, following the path of the matsutake mushroom from Oregon to Japan and even further afield than that, including forestry efforts in Lapland, Finland, and Yunnan, China. Like the matsutake mushroom itself, my book works with both patches—localities spread out in time and space but interconnected along a common commodity chain—and spores, which can take flight and spread in very open-ended ways. So I wouldn't be so quick to say, Timothy, that my book is based in Asia.

SÉVERINE: Yes, I agree with you, Anna. This location-based way of thinking about ethnography leaves me out as well. *Peaceland* is hardly location-based. While my research for the book did involve extensive time in specific locations, particularly North Kivu, Congo, I also draw on extensive experience in many other places: Kosovo, Cyprus, Nicaragua, Israel and the Palestinian Territories, Afghanistan, Timor-Leste, South Sudan, and Burundi. In fact, the ultimate "field" that I'm studying is non-locatable in geographic terms and is one that I create a metaphorical name for—*Peaceland*—which signifies the common practices and narratives of international interveners wherever they find themselves geographically.[1]

JIM: My first book was definitely based in one location, in a very out-of-the-way peasant village in Malaysia! Even in that book, however, I look at things that travel: rumors, speculation, gossip, and character assassination. I increasingly feel that location is a bit of an old-fashioned way to think about our work. It's an artifact, I think, of ethnography's academic history.

PIERS: But if we look at the classics of anthropological ethnography—Malinowski, Radcliffe-Brown, Evans-Pritchard—they are all based on the idea of going into a single, bounded society, a single "place," and trying to capture the totality of that place—its customs, kinship structures, rituals, beliefs, food avoidances, sexual mores, and so on—and then to present the totality of that place to the reader.

ANNA [aside]: Usually, the Western white male reader.

JIM: Thus, the term "fieldwork" for what we do when we do research.

KAREN: What a misnomer! My so-called "fieldwork" took place in lower Manhattan's concrete and steel jungle, not in any sort of faraway "field"! Much better to call it steelwork than fieldwork.

PIERS: Well, I hear what you are all saying about multi-sited ethnography. But whatever we choose to call it—"fieldwork" or "steelwork"—I don't want to completely let go of locality. People, ideas, and things travel, as do the ethnographers who research them, but I would still want to insist on the primacy of the local specificity of ethnography, of its commitment to long-term immersion in a place.[2]

KAREN: Long-term immersion and place are two elements of ethnography that I am interested in unsettling a little bit. Certainly, many ethnographies still rightly rely on long-term, immersive, single-site "fieldwork." But we must also create space for studies of things that move quickly or that present in multiple places, sometimes ephemerally.

SÉVERINE: Like mushroom spores!

ANNA: Yes, like mushroom spores! Even if it isn't based on long-term immersion in a single place, like the twenty years Piers spent amongst the Eveny reindeer herders, I still think it's possible to apply an ethnographic approach and sensibility to the study of non-localizable things like mushroom spores and international peacekeepers.

SÉVERINE [laughing]: I never thought I'd hear international peacekeepers and mushroom spores in the same sentence.

[General laughter.]

ALICE [laughing then turning serious]: OK, OK, everyone! This is all very merry, but let me remind you that we have an invisibility potion to deal with, an ailing wolfdog to save, and a trial to stage. So, if we can't reach consensus on splitting into location-based groups, would it perhaps be more productive for us to organize ourselves by the kinds of themes and ideas our works engage?

MITCH: Great question, Alice. It perfectly parallels the distinction Clifford Geertz makes between the locus of study and the object of study. He puts it something like, Ethnographers don't study villages, they study in villages.[3]

KATHERINE: Meaning?

MITCH: Meaning that where we study and what we study are two different things. Two people can have radically different fieldsites but still study the same thing. Alternatively, two people can share the exact same fieldsite but study radically different things.

KATHERINE: Makes sense.

KAREN: Geertz famously goes on to talk about making sheep raids speak to revolutions and winks to epistemology. The primary task of ethnography, for Geertz, lies in making what he calls its "microscopic nature" speak to made-in-the-academy mega-concepts, or as he inimitably puts it, how to make the complex specificity of ethnography "present the sociological mind with bodied stuff on which to feed."[4]

PIERS: You have that memorized?

KAREN: It's a memorable line.

JIM: Yes, it seems that Piers and others who defend the importance of place to ethnography are speaking, perhaps, to the sheep raid and wink side of that relationship, while Karen, Anna, Séverine, and others who reference the promise of multi-sited ethnography are perhaps identifying more with the revolutions and epistemology side of the relationship.

SÉVERINE: So some of us identify ourselves more with the locus of study and others with object of study?

JIM: Something like that, yes.

SÉVERINE: I hear what you're saying, Jim, but, at least in my case, I don't think that's quite right. I'm just as interested in the sheep raid as the revolution, and I don't think that good ethnography privileges one over the other. But, in my own work, I couldn't even get to the revolution or the epistemology if I didn't attend to sheep raids and winks in not one, but multiple locations, because the kind of revolution and epistemology that I'm after is constituted by and legible only because of its circulation through multiple locations. Or in the language of my own work, there is no way for me to get to the object of my study—the practices, habits, and narratives of international interveners—without attending to multiple localities.

MITCH: My own work is very location-based, but I am open to the possibility of grouping ourselves by theme. Although I must say that I hardly know at the outset of my work what the specific themes and analysis are going to be. I put a lot of value on place, on location, and, most importantly, on what emerges from the people with whom I interact.

LOÏC [sarcastically]: Well, Mitch, there you go again, singing the epistemological fairy tale of diagnostic ethnography and grounded theory.[5] That nonsense is exactly what produces an unsophisticated raw empiricism and theoretical absentmindedness that in turn leads to the mistaking of folk sayings for actual categories of analysis, among other errors.

MITCH: First of all, Loïc, I don't even think of myself as a theorist, much less a grounded theorist. Unlike you, I don't think the apex of every ethnography needs to culminate in the reconstruction of theory in order for that ethnography to have value. Theory has never been the pivotal agenda of my own work, and I would even go so far as to say that the best ethnographies are not remembered for their theories but rather for their ability to show the lives and social situations of those they study.

LOÏC: If the point of ethnography is not to develop or illuminate theory then what is it there for?

MITCH: "Part of my criticism of ethnography as a frame for doing theory for theory's sake is not simply that the people in the studies can't recognize themselves in the work, but they don't even have a sense of how they mattered. I mean how did it matter, why did it matter that this ethnographer spent all this time with me? So he could enter into a dialogue with theory that is utterly trivial, even by academic standards? What is the ethics of that? I want the books I write to contribute to a greater understanding of the world. I want to be able to say to them, the people in my books, that students are going to be able to read this book and they're going to understand homeless people in a better way. To me that's a perfectly legitimate minimal warrant for this work, and in fact the best that I've been able to come up with."[6]

LOÏC: That's the best warrant you can come up with for why to do ethnography?

MITCH: I said minimal warrant. And I was referring to my own work. I would never legislate a universal goal for every ethnography. But even your own book *Body & Soul* is a great example of what I mean here, Loïc. Although you are an outstanding theorist, I don't think the enduring value of your book lies in its reconstruction or elaboration of a theory of habitus, but rather in the compelling ways it evokes the lives and social situations of the men in the boxing gym.

LOÏC: I appreciate the attempted compliment, but I disagree. I do think that the theoretical reconstruction of habitus and development of a carnal sociology in *Body & Soul* are its most important and enduring contributions. And the development of theory certainly is the goal of my own ethnographic work!

But, Mitch, even accepting that theory isn't your aim, there must be *some* way that you think about ideas and themes, even at the very outset of your work. You surely don't just walk into a place and say, out of nowhere, I think I'm going to do an ethnography here, without having any idea whatsoever of what might be conceptually or theoretically interesting about the place! To begin with, you can't even separate a studied "here" from a non-studied "there" without exercising some sort of theoretical and conceptual control.

MITCH [evenly]: Well, yes, if reduced to a caricature, of course it is absurd to say that an ethnographer starts doing fieldwork without any notion whatsoever of what interests them. And while I don't utilize a grounded theory approach, even Glaser and Straus, the two people most associated with grounded theory, state clearly and early in their book that no researcher approaches reality as a tabula rasa and always has a point of view that they bring to the field.[7]

What I actually find more worrying is the inverse of your concern: ethnographers so completely controlled by an *a priori* theoretical interest that they are incapable of actually noticing anything in their fieldsites, much less being surprised by it. In this inverted caricature, "the field" exists purely as an inert illustrative putty, shaped at will by ethnographers according to the dictates and needs of their theoretical and scholarly proclivities.

Look, if there's any epistemological fairy tale that needs debunking, it's the notion that there is one single or best way to do ethnography. "As... ethnographers, we walk a line, many lines: romanticizing versus condemning; bringing theoretical questions to the field versus discovering them while working at the site; protecting anonymity versus replication and/or accountability; political agendas versus naive tabula rasa; fully theorized versus open to issues and empirical events; redistributing ethnographic authority versus maintaining the authority of the social scientist; seeing agency/resistance versus all determining structures; accumulating many thinner observations versus a few thick ones; using an in-depth description to enter into a dialogue with a theory versus telling readers only as much about people and places as they need to know to reconstruct a theory. These are real dilemmas that become embodied as practical trade-offs and enduring tensions in the descriptions and arguments of ethnographies."[8]

SÉVERINE: That's well said. But how do you navigate these dilemmas in your own work, Mitch, especially the one between bringing theoretical questions to the field versus discovering them while working at the site?

MITCH: Some of my earlier work was guided by a personal and theoretical interest in how moral behavior is or is not constructed. That interest provided the broad parameters for what I was alert to, both in initially recognizing certain social fields as potential fieldsites and then again once I conducted research in those defined social fields. Beyond that, however, I was very deliberate in not setting out with particular theories I knew I wanted to reconstruct. And when I did move from data collection to theory reconstruction, it was almost in spite of myself. In fact, "when I went back to Sixth Avenue to work as a magazine vendor, I hadn't yet formulated a precise research question. I had no theories that I wanted to test or reconstruct, and I didn't have any particular scholarly literature to which I knew I wanted to contribute."[9]

SÉVERINE: I have to say, Mitch, as refreshing as I find what you're saying, it seems radically counter to the way we political scientists are trained to represent the research process. I can't imagine anyone in our discipline getting a grant or even passing a dissertation proposal defense if they wrote, "I plan to go to X fieldsite without a specific research question or scholarly literature that I know I want to contribute to."

LOÏC [muttering]: I don't think it should be any different in sociology either.

MITCH: Look, I admit that "the fact that I did not know my specific research question at the start may seem counter to the way that sociologists are supposed to operate."[10] But, actually, think about it this way: "In much of social science, especially much of quantitative research using large data sets, a research design often emerges *after* the data has been collected.... Like quantitative researchers who get an idea of what to look for by mulling over existing data, I began to get ideas from the things I was seeing and hearing on the street."[11]

TIMOTHY: Well, that may be the reality of how much positivist research is conducted, but it is certainly not held up as an acceptable approach. One widely influential ideal for both quantitative and qualitative researchers is for the research question to shape data collection, not vice versa. And, in particular, the ideal is that any data that inform the hypotheses in the research design should not be the same data against which those hypotheses are later tested.[12]

JIM: Yes, but now we are dealing with the difference between the fiction of how "rigorous" research is supposed to be carried out as opposed to the reality of how it is actually carried out. Think about the whole notion of "kitchen sink" regressions, in which every variable in a data set is run against every other possible variable, and whatever emerges as "statistically significant" gets conscripted for post-hoc theorizing and a backdated research design. This backdated design, by the way, is often later presented in an article or book's "theory" section as having informed the theoretical interest in those variables to begin with.

TIMOTHY: So true. But these fictions matter, especially when they are enforced by grants and other professional awards that lead to the perpetuation of a recurring narrative that everyone parrots and strives to conform to regardless of whether it reflects actual practice or not.

SÉVERINE: So would you say, Mitch, that your approach is more inductive while Loïc's is more deductive?

MITCH: Look, "my approach is not strictly inductive or deductive: I engage a variety of theoretical/sociological questions, some of which I brought to the site from the beginning, some of which I discovered through various routes as I worked in the site." What Loïc's comment misses is that "in one sense, every sociologist, when they bring questions to a site, 'projects' the question onto the site. The real question is whether or not they project their answer: Did the research allow for any learning from the site?"[13] That, to me, is the key question, and I approach my fieldsites in order to maximize the possibilities of actually learning something from them, even at the expense of the kinds of *ex ante* theoretical control that Loïc seems to advocate.

LOÏC: That's a complete misrepresentation of my approach.

[Uncomfortable silence.]

ALICE: Returning to the question of how we should split up into smaller groups, don't you think it would be quite hard to divide our work thematically anyway? I mean, I work on power, broadly speaking, but then again it seems there's hardly a person in the room whose work doesn't centrally engage with power in one way or another.

PIERS: But isn't that just another way of saying that power is everywhere, so a good ethnography, by virtue of being a good ethnography, will not be able to help but pick up on power?

KATHERINE: I come at this question from the perspective of a journalist, not an academic ethnographer.

TIMOTHY: Well, I think your work represents some of the very best contemporary work in the ethnographic tradition, whether classified as academic or not.

KATHERINE: Thanks, Timothy! Anyway, what I wanted to say is that from my perspective as a journalist, what makes an immersive sensibility compelling is its capacity to depict the particular and the specific. As I emphasize to any and all who will listen, I am keenly interested in power, but not in some abstract, theoretical, or more academic sense. My work is animated by a conviction that "small stories in so-called hidden places matter. And one of the reasons they matter, I think, is because they implicate and complicate what we generally consider to be the larger story in this country and throughout the world, which is the story of people who do have political and economic power."[14]

KAREN: That's so true, Katherine. In an abstract sense, your work is about class power in a Mumbai slum, but to leave it at that would be a disservice. What makes your writing so compelling is that it never feels didactic. *Behind the Beautiful Forevers* draws us into the intimate details of individual lives, and it's out of that rich and complex storytelling that dominant stories about those in power become complicated and implicated.

KATHERINE: I think that's right, Karen. Although I'm interested in power, I didn't say to myself that I was going to write about this slum in order to teach people this or that abstract lesson about power. I am more interested in understanding who people are and how they live and experience life under those very specific conditions, and then in letting those specifics speak back to the larger stories we tend to hear by and about people who wield more political and economic power.

PIERS [smiling]: And you just happened to win a National Book Award in the process?

KATHERINE: What do you mean by that?

PIERS: It seems a bit of an oversimplification to say that you just wanted to understand who people were and how people lived. The characters you feature in *Behind the Beautiful Forevers*—Sunil, Manju, Abdul, and others—they were chosen by you out of a much wider range of people whom you could have written about, but you chose not to.

KATHERINE: Well, in some ways I didn't choose them, they chose me.

KAREN: What do you mean by that?

KATHERINE: They were the people I happened to get to know best, the ones who allowed me into their lives and who had the most compelling life experiences to share.

PIERS: OK, but still, there was a very deliberate crafting of a narrative, of a story.

KATHERINE: Well, of course! But that story did not come about because I decided from the outset to write about some abstract theory of power.

ANNA: I'm very sympathetic to this. Some of us come to our work serendipitously, by complete accident. Others of us are much more intentional, animated by what some might call conceptual or theoretical questions or by generalized "puzzles" about something we observe in the world.

TIMOTHY: I think the way we write our ethnographies, especially in academia, has something to do with this. There is a bias to the way we present our work—which we often call our arguments, rather than our stories—that causes us to write deductive intentionality backwards into the research process.

MITCH: Because we wish to represent ourselves as in control and knowing at all times?

TIMOTHY [laughing]: Maybe, a bit. But I think it has as much to do with our writing conventions as with anything else. Most books in the social sciences usually lead with what we call a theory chapter, followed by a methods chapter, followed by several chapters of so-called data, and close with a conclusion that reiterates how the data chapters have demonstrated the arguments put forward in the theory chapter.

JIM: A handy little structure.

TIMOTHY: But you can see how the standardization of this structure, through peer reviews for university presses, through dissertation committees, and through sheer repetition can lead to a construction of social science as dominated by theoretical concerns that we then go out into the empirical world to try to address.

JIM: As opposed to a social science dominated by accidents?

TIMOTHY: As opposed to a social science that recognizes its debts to serendipity.

MITCH: Right. Regardless of how ethnographers *actually* came to their subject matter, it typically gets represented as being theoretically driven.

TIMOTHY: I just think there is so much value in laying bare the serendipitous, even accidental, nature of a lot of ethnographic research projects.

KAREN: What is the value you see in doing that?

TIMOTHY: For one, I think it keeps our ethnographies truer to their origins. Rather than constructing some cosmic Origin Myth rooted in abstract theoretical concerns, rooted in logic and rationality, it preserves a space for the sensual actuality of lived experience.

KAREN: But why should we do that?

TIMOTHY: Because it keeps our feet on the ground.

LOÏC: But in the end, don't we all want to reach for something larger and more constant than the serendipitous and the accidental? We are not just short-story writers or novelists, moving through the world weaving threads of our own fancy. We do social science because we care about ideas that are larger than the particular, about arguments and theories that reach beyond a specific locale. I think I am unique in this gathering in that I don't practice ethnography as an exclusive craft; I argue it should be always combined with comparative institutional analysis. *Body & Soul* is complemented by *Urban Outcasts*.[15]

JIM: I wouldn't say you are completely unique in that regard, Loïc. *Weapons of the Weak* is the only work I've done that is strongly ethnographic, if by that we mean based on firsthand participant observation. My book *Seeing Like a State*, for example, utilizes what you might call comparative institutional analysis. And *The Art of Not Being Governed* relies heavily on historical analysis and interpretation.[16]

MITCH: And my book on the ghetto from the early modern Jews to the present is based on historical research.[17] I would go so far as to say that many ethnographers must, of necessity, do other kinds of work because it can become more difficult to do deeply immersive fieldwork once you get entangled in university or family life. Many of these other kinds of studies are quite complementary to the earlier work, completing some aspect of that work which could not have been fulfilled "on the ground."

ANNA: Here we are again, right back in the tension between the sheep raid and the revolution, between winks and epistemology.

TIMOTHY: Exactly! That entire passage is worth reading.

[Walks to bookshelf and thumbs through Geertz's *The Interpretation of Cultures*. Finds the right page and reads aloud.]

> *The methodological problem which the microscopic nature of ethnography presents is both real and critical. But it is not to be resolved by regarding a remote locality as the world in a teacup or as the sociological equivalent of a cloud chamber. It is to be resolved—or, anyway, decently kept at bay—by realizing that social actions are comments on more than themselves; that where an interpretation comes from does not determine where it can be impelled to go. Small facts speak to large issues, winks to epistemology, or sheep raids to revolution, because they are made to.*[18]

I love this passage because it brings to the forefront the creative tension inhabited by the ethnographer, a creative tension generated by this space between the locus and the object. How to make small facts speak to large issues, winks to epistemology, sheep raids to revolution? To live only among the small facts, the winks, and the sheep raids leads to irrelevance. We learn about small facts, winks, and sheep raids, but we have no ability to signal why they matter. Yet to talk only about large issues like epistemology and revolution is to resign ourselves to an irrelevance of a different kind, an irrelevance of made-in-the-academy concepts.

KAREN: Nice, but how to relate the two?

MITCH: Always imperfectly, I think. This is what it means for them to be in creative tension. They are not antagonists, but neither do they fit neatly into some sort of formulaic ratio: take two-parts locus, three-parts object, stir vigorously, and presto: out comes ethnography!

JIM: Exactly. It's interesting to look more closely at Geertz's language in this passage. First, he intimates that there may not be *resolution* to this methodological problem of how to relate small facts to large issues, but only better and worse ways of keeping the problem at bay.

KATHERINE: At bay! Inspired by present company [nodding gently at the sleeping wolfdog], it brings to mind the starving wolf pack chasing the two dog-sledders across the frozen Alaskan Tundra in the opening chapters of Jack London's *White Fang*.

[The wolfdog stirs in her sleep, makes a low growl, and the hairs on her neck rise. Nervous laughter among the ethnographers.]

The wolves and the men are locked in a precarious shadow dance. All day long, the wolves follow at a close enough distance for the men to hear them, and sometimes to see them, but far enough away that the men can't shoot them.

ALICE [remembering]: And in any case, I think they only have like three or four bullets left.

KATHERINE: Right! And then at night, when the men stop to make camp, the wolves circle around the very edges of the firelight. And soon, the entire existence of these two men is defined by how to keep these wolves at bay for enough time that they can make it to the next fort.

ALICE: But then the men begin losing their sled dogs one by one. And soon it proves too much for one of the men, who goes charging after the wolves with his handful of bullets and is taken down.

JIM: A pretty grim metaphor for ethnography!

KATHERINE: Yes, but look at the language Geertz uses to evoke how to keep this methodological problem at bay. It's the language of realization and willpower. The ethnographer must *realize* that social actions are commentaries on more than themselves. That is, she must realize that the space of her work is in the tension between the locus (the social actions) and this larger thing (the objects) that extends beyond the social actions. Then, Geertz goes on to use two highly interesting phrases: the first is that interpretation must be *impelled* to go somewhere. And the second is that small facts speak to large issues because they are *made* to. In other words, there is no formula or method or step-wise process for getting from small facts to large issues. It is the task of the ethnographer to impel this connection, to, quite literally, make it happen.

ALICE: Yes, and even then the end result is that the methodological problem of ethnography's microscopic nature is merely kept at bay, rather than being resolved in any final way.

JIM: Michael Burawoy's essay on the extended case method is another example of how ethnographers have tried to navigate this tension.[19]

TIMOTHY: Yes, as its title suggests, one of the central questions Burawoy deals with is how the specificity of ethnographic research can be made to speak to larger questions and issues. How a case can be extended to theory.

MITCH: I'd just point out, again, that it need not be the goal of every ethnography to reconstruct or extend to theory. Sometimes we're in danger of fetishizing theory to the point that it becomes the tail that wags the dog, to the point that the holy grail of theory makes the people and their social situations secondary. This, I think, is a danger to avoid. What ethnography excels at—and I would even say that this is one of the moral functions of ethnography in the social sciences—is showing the people and the social situations behind the theories and the statistics that we construct.

JIM: Right. We simply should not do social science behind the backs of the people we claim to study.

ANNA: We've been talking about this tension between the microscopic and the macroscopic in the context of ethnography, but I think all research, all knowledge creation, regardless of its specific method, wrestles with these tensions in one way or another. We are, so to speak, always among wolves.

[The wolfdog growls even more loudly in her sleep.]

PIERS: Including, quite literally, the wolfdog on this floor.

MITCH: And so, at least on this dimension, you could imagine methods and methodologies as specific ways that have been devised in different research traditions to deal with the wolf pack.

KAREN: I like it. Playing with this a bit, you could imagine that programmatic extermination is one methodological option. These wolves, these enduring tensions between small facts and large issues, are pesky, dangerous, and evil, so let's put a bounty on the wolves and exterminate them, try to make them extinct. Let's play it completely safe and try to deal with the wolf problem by getting rid of the wolves altogether. The method itself acts as a kind of poisoned bait that you can, by virtue of employing it, just scatter throughout the forest and along the trail with relative certainty that it will get rid of the wolves altogether.

JIM: Well, which method or methodologies would that be?

TIMOTHY: Anything that creates a step-wise, formulaic series of actions for the researcher to take in order to programmatically eliminate, or at least domesticate, the ravenous wolves.

MITCH [getting in on the metaphor]: And other researchers run out into the pack of wolves like the dogsledder did, with just a few bullets in his rifle, hoping for the best. Once in a while, someone comes out alive, having vanquished the wolves, but for the most part, those approaches tend to swallow up the researcher completely, leaving them ravaged either by the fangs of too-much-about-the-small-facts or the death grip of too-much-about-the-large-issues.

JIM: And which method or methodology would that be?

MITCH: I don't know—something completely idiosyncratic?

ANNA: But must it always be about the extermination and killing of the wolves? What about a heightened understanding of and sensitivity to their movements and to who they are, understandings and sensitivities that make something amazing more likely without eliminating all danger?

TIMOTHY: Great questions, Anna. Many readings of *The Call of the Wild* and *White Fang* emphasize the Darwinian "survival of the fittest" themes in London's work. In that sense, there are clear affinities between the notion of willpower in London's work and Geertz's emphasis on small facts being *made* to speak to large issues. But more recently, other, more subversive readings of London have emerged, readings that create space for genuine interspecies relationships between humans and wolves.[20]

ANNA: Yes, *The Call of the Wild* and *White Fang* are mirrored tales about the movement from civilized to barbarian and back. In *The Call of the Wild*, Buck is a dog who eventually becomes a wolf. In the other, White Fang is a half-dog, half-wolf who gradually becomes more and more domesticated and doglike.

[Wolfdog growls even more loudly, her hair bristling.]

PIERS [stepping back with some alarm and speaking under his breath]: Well, I wonder which direction this wolfdog is moving in.

ANNA [continuing]: But in both cases, London opens up spaces of possibility for new kinds of interspecies relationships to be formed with these wolfdogs. It's not always, or necessarily, reduced to humans shooting wolves or wolves killing humans.

KATHERINE: Oh, I see, Anna. So instead of thinking about an antagonistic relationship, pitting humans against wolves, we might think of the ethnographic sensibility as offering the possibility of living among wolves.

ANNA: Living among wolves! Yes, I think that's more promising.

TIMOTHY: This is where the magic of ethnography happens, in this uncomfortable but generative tension between locus and object. Unlike other methods, which bypass this discomfort with step-wise formulas—"just follow these steps in linear order and all will be well"—ethnography asks its practitioners to live in the creative tension between locus and object, to—as Katherine said—live among wolves.

ANNA: Yes, and to do so with keen attention to one's own reflexivity and positionality.

[Wolfdog growls again. Again, Piers steps back.]

PIERS [still under his breath]: I'm not so sure this wolfdog is very interested in living with me.

ANNA [continuing]: All this wolf talk closely parallels the way I think about ethnography's capacity to tell multiple stories. "To listen to and to tell a rush of stories is a *method*. And why not make a strong claim and call it a science, an addition to knowledge? Its research object is contaminated diversity; its unit of analysis is the indeterminate encounter. To learn anything we must revitalize the arts of noticing and include ethnography and natural history."[21]

SÉVERINE: I'm sympathetic! But, again, hearing this through the lens of my disciplinary training in political science, I can't help but hear the refrain that stories are only anecdotes and that the task of the social scientist is to somehow extract data from those stories, data that is reliable and valid and reproducible. As some of my political science colleagues claim, all social science involves extracting information from the social world and analyzing it as data.[22]

TIMOTHY: All this talk of extraction makes us sound like mountaintop coal miners, deep-water oil drillers, Great Plains frackers, or, for that matter, dentists!

[General laughter in the group.]

ANNA: I advocate for an approach wholly contrary to what's suggested by an extraction metaphor. In insisting on the importance of stories, "we [run into] a problem with scale. A rush of stories cannot be neatly summed up. Its scales do not nest neatly; they draw attention to interrupting geographies and tempos. These interruptions elicit more stories. This is the rush of stories' power as a science. Yet it is just these interruptions that step out of the bounds of most modern science, which demands the possibility for infinite expansion without changing the research framework."[23]

SÉVERINE: Yes, exactly.

ANNA: "Arts of noticing are considered archaic because they are unable to 'scale up' in this way."[24]

SÉVERINE: By 'scale up' you mean generalize? That it's hard to generalize from ethnography because ethnography is so specific?

ANNA: Yes, "the ability to make one's research framework apply to greater scales, without changing the research questions, has become a hallmark of modern knowledge."[25]

LOÏC: Are you saying that ethnography cuts against the grain of modern knowledge?

ANNA: Ethnography that privileges the arts of noticing and that views a rush of stories as a method does, yes. I myself have always tried to privilege curiosity over coherence in my work.[26]

JIM: Maybe it's not so much against the grain of modern knowledge, per se, as it is against certain conceptions of what science is or should be. When people in political science say ethnography is not scientific, "the snotty reply is, Too bad for political science if it ends up excluding a lot of insight about politics that does not come in a certain package or format. But the real question is, does the book say something about power and the state? If it does and it's presented in an easy-to-swallow way, then so much the better."[27]

LOÏC: It seems like it's a very slick slope from there to producing mere journalism.

KATHERINE: Hey now, don't be so quick to denigrate journalism!

JIM: I agree with Katherine. And I'm reminded "of something my colleague Charles Lindblom once said about a student's thesis, 'It's a failure, but it addresses big questions that are formulated in a brilliant way. Even though the student failed to answer these questions, the thesis still advances political insight further than lots of things that are rigorous but address trivial and banal questions.'"[28]

SÉVERINE: Listen, as sympathetic as I am, we still run into this question of how to convince our colleagues, particularly in political science, that ethnographic work meets their standards of what constitutes science.

JIM: You know, "I read David Laitin's review of *Seeing Like a State*, and it's a rather interesting review. He says, 'The book is good, it will last forever, and it will become a classic.' But he also says, 'It ain't social science, because methodologically it's a mess; Scott selected cases on the dependent variable and so on.' A colleague of mine actually ran into Robert Bates and David Laitin at a political science meeting shortly after *Seeing Like a State* came out, and he asked them what they thought of the book. I think it was Laitin who said, 'What an artist, he's a real artist.' At one level it was a compliment, but at another level it was meant as a put down, because he was saying my work was not scientific. Well, I am happy to be called an artist because I don't believe political science is a natural science in the first place. I like Laitin's work, and I think he's an interesting intellectual. But I also think he is less of a social scientist than he believes himself to be, and I think the interesting ideas that Laitin has had don't really add up to anything particularly 'scientific.'"[29]

ANNA: From the perspective of dominant knowledge systems which prize scalability, criticisms like the one leveled by David Laitin make sense. But from another perspective, a perspective more skeptical or even critical of scalability, returning to a rush of stories as method may be a way forward. And, as Jim points out, it's worth asking whether our most provocative and generative insights about power come from highly technical work that addresses relatively small and banal questions, or whether they come from more risk-taking work, from a sense of artistry.

MITCH: What you're saying resonates with me, Anna, but can you say more about what you mean by scalability and why it is problematic?

ANNA: By scalability, I don't just mean certain conceptions of science or of research methods, although the idea certainly applies there as well. We should understand that "progress itself has often been defined by its ability to make projects expand without changing their framing assumptions. This quality is 'scalability.'.... A scalable business, for example, does not change its organization as it expands. This is possible only if business relations are not transformative, changing the business as new relations are added. Similarly, a scalable research project admits only data that already fit the research frame. Scalability requires that project elements be oblivious to the indeterminacies of encounter; that's how they allow smooth expansion. Thus, too, scalability banishes meaningful diversity, that is, diversity that might change things."[30]

LOÏC: Could you give a concrete example of what you mean by progress being defined by scalability?

ANNA: Think about "the European colonial plantation. In the sixteenth- and seventeenth-century sugarcane plantations in Brazil, for example, Portuguese planters stumbled on a formula for smooth expansion. They crafted self-contained, interchangeable project elements as follows: exterminate local people and plants; prepare now-empty, unclaimed land; and bring in exotic and isolated labor and crops for production. This landscape model of scalability became an inspiration for later industrialization and modernization.... It was a success: Great profits were made in Europe, and most Europeans were too far away to see the effects. The project was, for the first time, scalable—or, more accurately, seemingly scalable. Sugarcane plantations expanded and spread across the warm regions of the world. Their contingent components—cloned planting stock, coerced labor, conquered and thus open land—showed how alienation, interchangeability, and expansion could lead to unprecedented profits. This formula shaped the dreams we have come to call progress and modernity...sugarcane plantations were the model for factories during industrialization; factories built plantation-style alienation into their plans.... By envisioning more and more of the world through the lens of the plantation, investors devised all kinds of new commodities. Eventually, they posited that everything on earth—and beyond—might be scalable, and thus exchangeable at market values. This was utilitarianism, which eventually congealed as modern economics and contributed to forging more scalability—at least in appearance."[31]

LOÏC: Strong claims.

ALICE: So research methods that prize scalability are like European colonial plantations? They are in league with colonialism and capitalist modernization?

ANNA [laughing]: Perhaps it is not just that they are "like" European colonial plantations. Perhaps the relationship is closer than that. Perhaps modern research methods and the expansion of global capitalism have co-constituted each other, each drawing strength from the other and seeing in the other its outward sign of success.

KAREN: There's a lot of talk about scalability here, but what about the non-scalable?

ANNA: Yes, exactly, Karen. "It is time to turn our attention to the non-scalable, not only as objects for description but also as incitements to theory."[32] That's why I am so interested in matsutake mushrooms! Their existence relies on a highly non-scalable and relational ecology and political economy that, so far anyway, have resisted all efforts at imposing a plantation model. Matsutake mushrooms are my own incitement to theory.

JIM: So, then, Anna, if the dominant methods of modern science are plantation-like in their emphasis on scalability, do you think that ethnography as a method is "anti-plantation" in the same way that matsutake mushrooms are anti-plantation?

ANNA: Matsutake mushrooms are anti-plantation in the sense that they cannot be farmed. But, fascinatingly, they often thrive in the ruins of abandoned scalable projects, in the ruins of capitalism. So, for example, in the US Pacific Northwest, matsutake mushrooms often thrive amongst the firs and lodgepole pines that replaced the great ponderosas once a plantation model was applied to forestry. So it is not that matsutake mushrooms are absolutely "anti-plantation," but rather that they exist in spite of, or perhaps because of, scalable projects. So, I would say that ethnography, while not inherently anti-plantation, exists in spite of, or perhaps because of, scalable approaches to research. It is this quality that makes it more likely to be anti-plantation.

KAREN: I like the idea of using these mushrooms as an "incitement to theory," a way to think about the anti-plantation qualities of ethnography in relation to other methods that prize scalability. Might we say that ethnography is anti-scalable insofar as it privileges a rush of stories that sit uneasily with one another and that cannot be formulaically generalized across time and space? And that this ethnographic method can thrive within—indeed, is in some ways dependent on—the very ruins of scalability, both in terms of our notions of progress and modernity and in terms of our dominant notions of what constitutes good research?

SÉVERINE: Ethnography as a way of thinking about the possibility of life amongst the ruins of dominant research approaches: that's a provocative metaphor.

ANNA: Yes, and more specifically, an ethnography attuned to a rush of stories as a method. An ethnography that valorizes the arts of noticing.

TIMOTHY: We are now talking about ethnography as a kind of counter-discourse, a kind of counter-conduct within the dominant array of research methods. We are talking about ethnography as anti-plantation, and, by extension, as anti-colonial. But positing ethnography as anti-plantation, and, by extension, anti-colonial, curiously inverts the history of anthropology, the academic discipline most closely associated with ethnography as a method.

KAREN: Yes, and it's not a history we anthropologists are particularly proud of.

KATHERINE: What do you mean?

KAREN: Well, the history of ethnography within anthropology is bound up with projects of colonialism and empire. The European and American "discovery" of "new" lands and peoples developed in conjunction with the establishment of the study of those lands and peoples as a field of academic expertise. And that field in turn informed—some would even say served as a handmaiden to—colonial projects of power.

JIM: Ethnography became a way of making the unknown legible so that it could be conquered and ruled.

KAREN: Exactly. If you look at the history of ethnic highland "tribes" in Southeast Asia, for example, you can see very clearly how Western ethnographers and their colonially trained counterparts calcified identities that were previously incredibly fluid.

JIM: I would even argue that those identities were fluid by design, as escape hatches from oppressive structures.

KAREN: Right. But the work of ethnographers who entered those areas under the auspices of colonial and state power created fixed identities. So "authoritative" field guides were created, stating that those who wear these kinds of garments and practice these kinds of rituals shall be known as the Lahu, and those who wear those kinds of garments and practice those kinds of rituals shall be known as the Akha, and so on and so forth.

JIM: Like the creation of a *Peterson's Field Guide for Birds*, except for highland peoples instead.[33]

KAREN: And the effect of this was twofold. First, it offered colonial and state powers a ready-made grid onto which to map people. And because of the power behind that mapping, the mapping—which ethnographers thought corresponded to reality, but which was in fact only an artifact of the specific moment of entry and interaction of the ethnographer—actually inscribed and created new realities for the peoples being mapped.

JIM: In some ways, the combination of ethnographers and state power called those people into being and fixed them in relation to one another and in relation to colonial and state power.

PIERS: It's a story you see replayed again and again in the history of anthropology and ethnography. Such that you could actually rewrite the history of ethnography as a history of spying, intelligence gathering, and incursion on behalf of empire.

KATHERINE: Wow, that's a strong statement!

PIERS: Not just intelligence gathering, but the creation of new facts on the ground that those ostensibly being studied would then have to conform to in order to navigate the colonial or state realities that were being imposed on them through the gridlines of the "knowledge" that the ethnographers were producing.

JIM: The irony, of course, is that the only way we know this is with the help of other ethnographies. So, it's Edmund Leach's *Political Systems of Highland Burma* that gives us a sense for the fluidity of political structure and ethnic identity in highland Burma.[34] We wouldn't know about the artificiality of the fixing of identities independent of other ethnographic work.

KAREN: True! And so we're caught in a kind of conundrum. The fallacies and follies of ethnography in the service of colonialism could only be undone by other ethnographic work.

ANNA: A rush of stories.

KAREN: But in both cases, it is still the production of knowledge by outsiders.

JIM: Yes, and the story is even more complicated still. In many cases, the ethnographic work done by Western anthropologists was explicitly meant to be protective of, rather than destructive of, the peoples it was studying.

KATHERINE: Protective from whose perspective?

JIM: An astute question! Take, for example, in the early 1950s, the Tribal Research Institute that was created in Chiangmai, Thailand. The whole stated purpose of this institute was to protect highland peoples from the pressures of state power. At the time, Thailand viewed highland peoples living in the mountainous border region between Thailand, Burma, and Laos as threats to national security. These highland people were seen as poppy growers and opium producers and as potential communist sympathizers. The approach at that point was conversion or killing; they either were to become homogenized as Thai or else eliminated or driven across the border entirely.

Seeing this, several Western anthropologists and the sympathetic Thai anthropologists they worked with embarked on a project to catalogue and document the "tribes" of northern Thailand. They created a museum of tribal peoples that showed them in their "native" costumes and persuaded the Thai government to officially recognize nine tribal groups and hill minority peoples in Thailand.[35]

KATHERINE: So was that a good thing or a bad thing?

JIM: It was a complicated thing. On the one hand, it slowed or blunted some of the most oppressive policies of the Thai state towards these peoples. But on the other hand, much like all colonial ethnography preceding it, it froze, both in time and as established knowledge, a particular moment in a broader and more fluid series of power relations and identity constructions.

KATHERINE: It's almost as if you're saying that the anthropologists invented these ethnicities?

JIM: Yes, I think that's correct. They invented them in order to save them. But, in doing so, they harnessed the power of the Thai state and the legitimacy of Western academia to their cause, and these inventions in fact became the new realities on the ground. They set the parameters for identity within which these peoples either had to work with or push against.[36]

KATHERINE: So the moral of the story is?

KAREN: Well, I think one moral of the story is that even at its best-intentioned, ethnographic work is always implicated in larger projects of power.

KATHERINE: Well, OK, but isn't that true of everything: that it's implicated in larger projects of power?

KAREN: Sure, so as a general claim, maybe that's not so interesting or important. What matters is to always look at the what and the how of the implication and the nature of the projects of power themselves. And when we begin to look specifically at the ways ethnography has aided and abetted colonial regimes or state projects of control and domination, or when we look specifically at how anthropologists with progressive aims end up constructing dynamics that further control and domination, then I think we can begin to talk about the ways in which ethnography is always already a deeply problematic enterprise.

MITCH: Differently problematic from any other enterprise of knowledge creation?

JIM: Well, yes, I think so. Or at least more visibly so. Because ethnography takes as its stated aim the understanding of the other from the perspective of the other, it creates a much more tangible and palpable tension than other kinds of projects of knowledge creation that do not make those kinds of claims. Other projects of knowledge creation, you might say, are already much more explicit about their aims and ends being separate from the aims and ends of those they purport to study.

SÉVERINE: I'm not so sure that ethnography is the only method that claims to understand and represent the worldview or lived experience of those being studied. Think, for example, about survey research, which is also trying to get at how those being studied understand the world.

MITCH: You might even say that large-N regression analysis and formal modeling, in their own registers, are trying to represent some aspect of the lived experiences of those they study. Of course, ethnography is typically the method that does this in its most concentrated form, but I think we are talking about differences of degree, not of kind. After all, if there's no point of connection at all, no place where the method meets up with lived experience, then what is the point of the method?

JIM: Good points. But with ethnography, I think there is a singularly unique emphasis on the accessing of participant meanings. And this emphasis often leads ethnographers to question whether surveys, and even some types of interviews, are really able to capture those meanings.[37] And certainly to question whether large-N regression analysis and formal modeling are capable of accessing the lived experiences of the researched from their own internal perspectives.

PIERS: Yes, and the intensity of ethnography's interest in the lived experience of its research subjects is true, I would argue, even for ethnographers who ultimately and self-consciously impose interpretations that their subjects would disagree with.

KAREN: What do you mean?

PIERS: Well, some ethnography—we might call this ethnography that employs a hermeneutic of trust—explicitly takes as its criterion an attempt by the ethnographer to enter into and represent the understandings that the ethnographic subjects have of themselves and their worlds. The ethnography, in this hermeneutic, is a success or a failure based on the degree to which it accurately conveys how the subjects themselves construct and understand their worlds. Other ethnography—and, following Paul Ricoeur, we might call this an ethnography that employs a hermeneutic of suspicion—does not make itself exclusively beholden to its accuracy in representing the subjects' self-understandings for its legitimacy. In this kind of ethnography, the researcher is free to, and indeed often expected to, impose interpretations that might run quite counter to the subjects' self-understandings.[38]

MITCH: Can you give an example?

PIERS: Well, in my own work, I think there are examples of both kinds of hermeneutics being applied. When I studied the Eveny reindeer herders in Siberia, I quickly became alert to the power of omens and dreams in their social lives. Initially, as a Western ethnographer, I approached the omens and dreams rationally and with skepticism. Rather than being expressions of what the future held, I interpreted these dreams and omens psychoanalytically in accord with my own training as a Western academic. I saw the dreams and omens as expressions of repressed anxieties, desires, and tensions.

MITCH: OK. And what about the hermeneutics of trust?

PIERS: Well, as I spent more and more time in the field, I found myself becoming inducted into an entirely different way of understanding. Inducted not just as a researcher or an ethnographer, but as a person. It was as if my years of graduate training were slowly being eroded and replaced by the ways of seeing presented by the Eveny. So, one of the final chapters of my book is entitled "How to Summon a Helicopter," and it reflects my own adoption of the Eveny ways of seeing the world, in quite clear opposition to the Western modes of thinking that I had started out with. And because the book reflects over twenty years of fieldwork amongst the Eveny, there are parts of it that are written with a hermeneutic of trust and parts of it that are written with a hermeneutic of suspicion.

MITCH: You know, "sometimes whether or not a story is true or false is really not important. What matters a lot more is that the story somebody tells can be an index to the kind of person that they are or the kind of life that they live."[39]

ANNA: I really agree with that point, Mitch. I think sometimes we fixate on the facticity of the things we hear in the field to the neglect of broader and ultimately more generative questions about what kinds of work the stories we hear are doing. Political work, social work, identity-building work, and even performative work in the context of a relationship between the teller and the ethnographer. I'm reminded of stories I heard in the fieldwork I did for *In the Realm of the Diamond Queen* about government head hunters in Kalimantan, Indonesia. I spent a bit of time trying to figure out if the stories were factually "true"—where were the graves for the bodies of the people killed for their heads?—before realizing that what was most central was that the stories said something extremely important about how the storytellers saw their relationships with government officials.[40]

KAREN: That's a nice invocation of the hermeneutics of trust and of suspicion, Piers. And I take your points, Mitch and Anna, about the facticity of what ethnographers hear in the field sometimes being less important than the work those stories do. But I would also make the point that regardless of which hermeneutic the ethnographer is employing, sussing out the facticity of stories or taking them as an index to the social situation of the storyteller, ultimately the legitimacy and authority of the ethnographic claims still rely on a bedrock assertion that the ethnographer is able to—has been able to—enter into a shared lived experience with those she studies. And this, I think, is what makes ethnography so visibly troublesome as a method, given its historical and contemporary entanglement with projects of dominating and oppressing power.

JIM: Right, and therefore, when ethnography is so blatantly used to oppress or dominate or even to create out of thin air the groups it studies, there is a more apparent tension than with other methods of knowledge creation.

ALICE: OK. So, is the answer to stop making claims about representation, to be more naked and truthful about ethnography's imperialist ambitions, or is the problem with all knowledge creation regardless of what its claims are?

KAREN: Deep, important questions. One thing that's interesting is how anthropology has taken a serious turn in recent decades towards critically examining its own history and its own complicities with projects of colonial and state power. A lot of the substance of anthropology in relation to ethnography is no longer about the actual conduct of ethnographic fieldwork but rather about the examination of the power relations between researcher and researched.

TIMOTHY: Some have even said that the whole enterprise of anthropology has become so consumed by these questions that it has become an exercise in navel-gazing.

KAREN: I think that's an easy enough criticism for anyone to make. But even recent history shows us that these debates are far from settled and that critical self-reflection is anything but navel-gazing.

TIMOTHY: How so?

KAREN: Take, as the latest example, the brouhaha over the United States military's so-called Human Terrain System (HTS), operative from 2006 to 2014.

JIM [sighing]: Ah, yes.

KAREN: The $725 million-dollar program recruited anthropologists and other social scientists to aid the United States military in places like Iraq and Afghanistan. In small units that included armed soldiers, these anthropologists entered villages and towns and "mapped" the local "human terrain" in service of US aims. Montgomery McFate, a Yale Ph.D. in anthropology and one of the early champions of the program, published several essays arguing that cultural knowledge is an integral part of warfare and celebrating anthropology's return to its roots as a "warfighting discipline."[41]

TIMOTHY: Yes, and many of these anthropologists also used the information gleaned while working for the US military in warzones as the basis for academic articles and dissertations.[42] I don't think you could find a more blatant example of how ethnography is, even today, tied up with projects of imperial power.

KAREN: The debates that HTS has ignited within the American Anthropological Association (AAA) have been fascinating. In 2010, several hundred anthropologists sent a signed statement to the Speaker of the US House of Representatives expressing strong opposition to the HTS. They noted that the executive board of the AAA had determined in 2007 that the use of anthropologists and ethnographers in the direct service of war was unacceptable.[43]

JIM: To be provocative, isn't HTS simply a formalization of a longstanding power dynamic that has characterized ethnography's relationships to its subjects from its very founding as a method? That is, one in which the knowledges produced by the ethnographer are enlisted, whether explicitly or not, whether with the express consent of the researcher or not, in the service of projects of control and domination?

KAREN [upset]: Are you saying we should not oppose projects like the Human Terrain System?

JIM: No, of course we should. But we should also stop to ask ourselves about how other kinds of ethnography, even seemingly innocent ethnography, might contain undercurrents similar to those made painfully explicit by HTS. There is a way in which the overt and highly vocal opposition to this one program might serve to deflect attention from the ways other kinds of ethnographic work also serve the agendas of those in power, agendas that the researchers who produce that ethnographic work might themselves be opposed to.

KAREN: Like what?

JIM: The feminist anthropologist Kathleen Gough wrote a terrific piece in the late 1960s in which she argued that anthropology is basically a child of Western imperialism.[44]

LOÏC: That seems like a rather sweeping claim. I've also heard of anthropology referred to as the handmaiden of colonialism and the tool of colonialism.

JIM: Yes, but I like the way Gough puts it. She lays out the position of the anthropologist very nicely, likening her to the white liberal reformer. Anthropologists, especially the first ones, were located higher in terms of social status than the people they studied, and were usually white. This put them in the curious position of benefiting from imperialist and racist orders while at the same time often trying to soften or protect their research subjects from the worst effects of those same structures.[45] It's an inherent contradiction: the anthropologist is there because, and only because, of the very colonial power whose worst effects she is often trying to blunt.

KAREN: Yes, as Talal Asad writes, from the beginning the very enterprise of anthropology, and of anthropological ethnography in particular, has been tied up with the context of power in which it was born.[46]

PIERS: All these terms—handmaiden, child, tool—make it sound like anthropological ethnography was somehow central to projects of power. And they risk making it sound like projects of domination and exploitation somehow continue to rely centrally on ethnographic work to advance their aims. Yet I think it's in that same essay of Asad's, Karen, where he makes a point of cautioning against attributing too much centrality to anthropology's contributions to colonial power.[47] After all, colonial power also relied heavily on the knowledges being constructed by missionaries, traders, travelers, and bureaucrats.

ANNA: All of whom were traveling on the tailwinds of colonial power and dependent, in one way or another, on the success of the colonial project.

KAREN: According to Oscar Salemink's history of ethnographies in the Central Highlands of Vietnam, the earliest anthropologists were preoccupied with establishing their legitimacy as scientists and professionals, unlike "mere" missionaries, administrators, and travelers.[48]

PIERS: That's so true! Bronislaw Malinowski, considered by many to be one of the most influential founders of modern fieldwork methods, goes to great lengths to establish the scientific credibility of professional anthropology. You could read the entire first section of his famous *Argonauts of the Western Pacific* as an attempt to show how academic anthropology is scientific and rigorous where the accounts of missionaries and travelers are not.[49]

ANNA: That is accurate but incomplete. Malinowski argues against an additional antagonist in that classic essay: those who would advance academic knowledge from afar, without grasping the lived experiences of those they claim to study. In contrast, Malinowski argued for what he called the "imponderabilia of actual life," and he insisted that the ultimate goal of the ethnographer is "to grasp the native's point of view, his relation to life, to realise *his* vision of *his* world."[50]

[Laughing.]

And that's a direct quote that I still have memorized from my days in graduate school!

JIM: Yes. So there's this double-sided charge against early ethnographers: on the one hand, they were like spies or agents of the state, agents of imperialism. Then, on the other hand, they were not different from travel writers, traders, and missionaries. Against those two charges they had to create a space of their own that insisted on their autonomy, their immersion, and their scientific credentials.

KAREN: I don't know how much autonomy from the colonial state they were seeking. Malinowski may have championed the importance of the "imponderabilia of actual life," but his essay on "Practical Anthropology" argues for the importance of pressing such anthropological knowledge into the service of colonial administrators.[51]

PIERS: That's not the whole story, though. Across the Atlantic, Franz Boas, the other founder of modern anthropology, was waging his own battle against military and colonial applications of anthropology. In 1916, Boas published an essay in *The Nation* decrying four unnamed anthropologists for using their status as academics as a cover for intelligence gathering and spying activities in South America.[52] Boas was furious about the use of academic cover as a pretext for espionage, and wrote a fiery missive exposing, but not directly naming, the four anthropologists. He even said that the academics had "prostituted science!"[53]

KAREN: Quite telling to see the nearly opposite stances taken on the right relationship between anthropology and state power by two of the most important
founders of the discipline. While Malinowski was penning essays encouraging the use of anthropological knowledge in the service of the colonial project, Boas was exposing espionage activities that used academic credentials as
a cover. This tension suggests a schism at the earliest moments of the method
about the ethical relationship between ethnography and power and continues
to play out in the recent debates over HTS.

LOÏC: Quite telling also to see how furiously Anglo-centric this whole discussion is, with no mention whatsoever of Francophone contributions to early
anthropology, and in particular the signal importance of Marcel Mauss to the
development of both anthropology and sociology![54]

JIM: That's a great point, Loïc, but again I'd just caution us to return to the insight
that the entire discipline—whether we are talking about in the UK, the US,
or France—had as a condition of its existence the colonial project.

KAREN: Indeed. The involvement of star anthropologists with war projects
exploded during the Second World War. Anthropologist Gregory Bateson,
known for his ethnographic research in New Guinea that was published as
*Naven* in 1936, served with the Office of Strategic Services (OSS) in the
Arakan Mountains of Burma and aided with the development of propaganda.
Margaret Mead also worked with OSS to establish a Far East psychological
warfare unit. And a Harvard professor of anthropology named Carleton Coon
trained and smuggled weapons to resistance groups in German-occupied
Morocco and wrote about it in *A North Africa Story: The Anthropologist as
OSS Agent, 1941–1943*.[55]

PIERS: To this list we can add Ruth Benedict, who in 1943 headed the Basic
Analysis Section of the Bureau of Overseas Intelligence of the US Office
of War Information. While there, she authored a book that combatted the
racial superiority theories of the Nazi regime. Titled *Races of Mankind*, it sold
more than 750,000 copies and was even turned into a Broadway musical.[56]
Later, from 1947 to 1952, Mead and Benedict would form the "culture-at-
a-distance" program at Columbia University with direct sponsorship and
oversight from the US Office of Naval Research. The goal of the program
was to reconstruct whole cultures from afar using artifacts and textual sources
when wartime conditions would not permit close, immersive ethnographic
encounters.

KAREN: All throughout the 1950s, anthropologists continued to contribute actively
to military efforts. Major General Edward Landsale used anthropological
knowledge about folklore amongst the Huk in the Philippines to devise
psychological warfare operations that included, for example, snatching the
last person in a Huk guerrilla patrol, killing him, puncturing his neck with
two holes, then placing his body back on the path in order to exploit Huk
fears of *asaung*, or vampires. Also in the 1950s, Charles Bohannan, who had

advanced anthropology degrees, co-authored *Counter-Guerrilla Operations: The Philippine Experience*, which is still widely respected in the military as a classic in counterinsurgency literature. In 1959, Bohannan led a secret team in Colombia for the US military, traveling more than 14,000 miles and using anthropological and ethnographic techniques to interview more than 2,000 officials, civilians, and guerilla leaders. He published the results of this work in a three-volume report.[57]

SÉVERINE: Probably worth keeping in mind here that not all military endeavors are necessarily colonial or imperialist. It sounds like at least some of these anthropologists were involved in aiding resistance efforts. And certainly many contemporary peacekeepers, including military peacekeepers whom I did research among, were not there for colonial or imperialist purposes.

ANNA: True, but one person's resistance is another person's occupation. And the larger point is that anthropologists were explicitly using their craft to help state projects, whatever your normative judgment of those state projects might be.

PIERS: Continuing with this history, the mid-1960s and early 1970s is when things really reached a boiling point. In 1964, the Special Operations Research Office (SORO), founded by the US Department of Defense in response to the particular challenges of counterinsurgency wars, partnered with American University in Washington, D.C. to start Project Camelot, a research program whose aim was to identify what made societies vulnerable to internal warfare and conflict, and to manipulate those factors so as to either encourage or discourage internal wars. The first target of Project Camelot was Chile; its lead researcher was Hugo Nuttini, a professor of anthropology at the University of Pittsburgh. Although Nuttini tried to be covert about the project's military origins, the Chilean government found him out and filed a formal diplomatic protest with the US Ambassador. After the Congressional hearings that followed, Project Camelot was cancelled in 1965.

KAREN: Yes, the blowup over Project Camelot and the politics of what is known in the United States as the Vietnam War in the subsequent decade led many in anthropology to renounce any direct service to the military and the interests of empire. And this renunciation set the stage for increased and ongoing scrutiny of the historical, ethical, and epistemological origins of anthropology as a discipline, as well as to the sources of ethnographic authority.

JIM: It's interesting, though, that even though she writes from that same spirit of scrutiny, Kathleen Gough calls for nearly the same kinds of research as Project Camelot was after, but does so with an anti-imperialist sensibility.[58]

ANNA: Like I just said, one person's resistance is another person's occupation.

JIM: Exactly. The problem, in my view, is not primarily one of motivations. McFate wants ethnographers to create knowledge for the US military. Gough wants ethnographers to create knowledge that resists imperialism. But both are creating knowledge all the same. Gough's argument—that progressive, critical anthropologists go after the same kinds of questions as the ones that are of keen interest to the Department of Defense and the economic interests it represents, but that they do so in their own way—seems to ignore the possible uses of that information regardless of our motives in creating it. Let's say we are pro-insurgent researchers operating in Guatemala. We would like to see an overthrow of the current US-supported regime and its replacement by a socialist government with a redistributive agenda. So we begin to conduct research on the questions that Gough lays out: who the guerrilla leaders are, who the labor organizers are, what the likely conditions are for their successes, and what they have learned from other resistance movements elsewhere. We conduct all of this research as truly independent scholars, taking not a penny of money from the US military or even from the US government. What then? Will our findings be of any less interest to—or, more to the point—of any less usefulness to the US military and the US government?

ALICE: This question could certainly be raised about my work.

TIMOTHY: Mine too. And yours too, Jim, for that matter.

JIM: Agreed. But it gets us back to an issue I have been trying to raise all along. What, in the end, distinguishes any ethnographer from a spy? Or a merchant? Or an administrator? Or a missionary? Or a journalist? Or from anyone else in the business of gathering information and disseminating it? Information on people who are below them in social status, information on people who, despite their best intentions of providing aid, are only being made more legible, and therefore more controllable and more vulnerable to the designs of those who wish to oppress them? If the history of ethnography's relationship to colonial power has anything to teach us, it surely must be that it is not primarily a question of motivation or intention, but rather one of consequences, of effects, that most matters.

KAREN: So, I wonder where all this leaves us in terms of understanding ethnography as anti-plantation? From this history, it seems ethnography is quite capable of serving the needs of capitalist and colonial power.

ANNA: Yes, of course I agree. It's not so much that ethnography is necessarily anti-plantation, but that of all methods in the social sciences, it contains the greatest potential to be anti-plantation.

JIM: Why's that?

ANNA: Because of its insistence on the increasingly archaic arts of noticing, and because of the space it creates to tell a rush of stories, stories that interrupt scalability and linear notions of temporality and progress.

KAREN: So it's possible to think an anti-plantation ethnographic method, one that's needed for our times? Isn't this just a new version of Gough's call for an anti-imperialist anthropology? And what keeps the information generated by these ethnographies—these rushes of stories—from being co-opted by projects of domination?

ANNA: Nothing. There is no guarantee. But I do think it's possible to think and write and listen in ways that contest rather than contribute to domination, and that—its troubled history notwithstanding—ethnography provides us with some of the best tools for doing so.

MITCH: As I listen to this genealogy of ethnography in anthropology, I can't help but think about the equally troubled and troubling history of ethnography within the discipline of sociology.

LOÏC: Me too, Mitch. It's lamentable how often ethnography is automatically associated with anthropology when, in fact, it has roots in sociology that are just as deep. Some of the very first ethnographies were produced not by anthropologists studying faraway places and cultures, but rather by sociologists and activists conducting empirical studies of their own cities and countries. Ethnography was first honed to study the "savages of the interior" of the Western world, workers, immigrants, and peasants. Read Friedrich Engels's *The Condition of the Working Class in England*, first published in 1845![59]

MITCH: Yes, exactly. We already talked about anthropologist Bronislaw Malinowski's *Argonauts of the Western Pacific*, which is seen by many as one of the founding examples of ethnography. But Malinowski didn't publish his book until 1922, well after some of the first ethnographic studies of urban communities had been published.

PIERS: Which studies?

MITCH: As Aldon D. Morris points out in *The Scholar Denied: W.E.B. Du Bois and the Birth of Modern Sociology*,[60] one of the first recognizable ethnographies produced by a self-identified sociologist is Du Bois's *The Philadelphia Negro*, published in 1899.[61]

JIM: I've always associated Du Bois with *The Souls of Black Folk*![62]

MITCH: I think a lot of people don't realize that in addition to being a theorist of race in the United States, Du Bois was also a pioneering ethnographer.

TIMOTHY: I've always heard that ethnography in sociology began with *The Polish Peasant in Europe and America* by William I. Thomas and Florian Znaniecki published in five volumes from 1918 to 1920.[63] In the story I usually hear from my sociology colleagues, *The Polish Peasant* was a founding text of their discipline and a landmark transition away from armchair theorizing to deep empirical engagement with the world.[64] And that Thomas was deeply shaped by—and in turn shaped—the Chicago School of Sociology of the early 20th century and the symbolic interactionists who are mostly closely associated with ethnography in sociology.[65]

LOÏC: I would dispute that conventional history. I think the real movement from armchair theorizing to deep empirical engagement actually occurred in the work of the Durkheimians around the same time. But no matter whether we attribute the rise of ethnography in sociology to Du Bois or Thomas and Znaniecki or the Durkheimians, the larger point still stands: sociology has as much or more of a claim as anthropology to the creation of academic ethnography as a mode of research and writing.

KAREN: Wait, am I hearing this right? W.E.B. Du Bois published his ethnographic work decades before *The Polish Peasant?*

ALICE: That's exactly right, Karen! Long before *The Polish Peasant*, Du Bois was conducting studies of race and race relations in the United States, drawing in particular on the earlier work of social reformers Jane Addams and Charles Booth. They argued that a close-to-ground empirical understanding of poverty in urban areas—one that used maps, census data, descriptive statistics, in-depth interviews, and ethnography—was essential to creating positive change.[66]

ANNA: So why don't we typically hear much about Du Bois in relation to the origins of ethnography?

ALICE: Aldon Morris's *The Scholar Denied*, which Mitch just referenced, demonstrates how anti-Black racism prevented Du Bois from being hired in a top US department after his return from Germany, where he had studied alongside and deeply influenced the intellectual development of one of his contemporaries, Max Weber. And Morris shows how Du Bois, despite a lack of resources, pioneered a new school of empirical sociology at Atlanta University, long before the Chicago School became prominent.

MITCH: That's right. Du Bois strongly believed in the power of empirical sociology to combat the anti-Black racism prevalent in society and the academy. His research for *The Philadelphia Negro*, for example, was funded by Susan P. Wharton and facilitated through the University of Pennsylvania Sociology Department, which wanted a black scholar to carry out research on blacks in Philadelphia because they thought it would therefore be more credible.[67] As Du Bois would later reflect in his book *Dusk of Dawn: An Essay toward an Autobiography of a Race Concept*, he saw the research as an opportunity to use ethnography and other close-to-the-ground empirical methods to fight back against the racist theories of his time, including those held by his funders.[68]

TIMOTHY: Wow, sounds like a pretty anti-plantation way to deploy ethnography!

MITCH: If we take seriously Morris's claim that Du Bois was a pioneer of the ethnographic method, it's not just that Du Bois deployed ethnography in an anti-plantation way, but that he actually *developed it* for its anti-plantation capacities.

ALICE: And as is often the case in academia, the story gets even more personal! Robert E. Park, the man most often credited as being the genius behind the Chicago School of sociology, worked as an assistant to Booker T. Washington before he ended up at the University of Chicago. Washington, of course, was one of Du Bois's main rivals, primarily because he espoused a conservative and racist vision of blacks in America, arguing that blacks were primitive and that their best hope lay in vocational training for manual and service labor. Because Washington's views were safe for the system of white supremacy, white funders were content to let Washington serve as a gatekeeper to funding and support.

Park worked as Washington's ghostwriter and assistant for seven years, and he agreed with Washington's views of race relations in the US and held similar ideas about the status of blacks. According to Aldon Morris, Park and others at the Chicago School wanted to create an academic approach to understanding white supremacy as a positive good. They argued that both African colonization and African slavery were important steps in lifting blacks into the superior civilization of whites.[69] What's more, while working for Washington, Park perpetrated a smear against Du Bois and then, once at Chicago, proceeded to appropriate Du Bois's work without acknowledgment.

MITCH: And here's perhaps the greatest irony of all: the racist perspectives of Robert E. Park and other members of the Chicago School were presented under the guise of neutral, universal science, while Du Bois was portrayed as a partisan and denied funding because of his lack of "objectivity." Park took for granted white biological and political supremacy, all the while simultaneously telling his students at Chicago that their role was to be calm and detached scientists who investigated race relations with objectivity.[70]

LOÏC: So, the supporter of the racist status quo represents himself and his method of study as objective and detached while portraying competing scholars who use close-to-the-ground methods to challenge that status quo as crusading partisans! And so it is that the contributions of Du Bois, and the seminal role he played in pioneering ethnography and other close-to-the-ground research methods as a way of combatting scientific and societal racism, remain repressed to this day.[71]

MITCH: That's a damning counter-history. Damning not only on account of the racism that Du Bois faced personally, but also on account of the founding racisms of sociological theory itself.

ANNA: Yes, but it's also a hopeful history.

MITCH: How so?

ANNA: It suggests, as Du Bois himself believed, that ethnographic work, work that is close-to-the-ground, work that interrogates made-in-the-academy racist theories with the complexity and specificity of lived experience, contains the power to counteract these theories, to locate them and place them as the handmaidens of power that they are.

LOÏC: Yes, or more pessimistically, and perhaps more realistically, it also shows how ethnography, on its own, is not capable of countering anything. After all, if Aldon Morris's counter-history is correct, then Park and the other founders of the Chicago School were more than able to advance theories about natural racial hierarchies and biological determinism using ethnographic methods.

ALICE: True, but that itself is an ethnographic insight, insofar as it shows that power shapes what counts as legitimate knowledge, that there is no sphere of knowledge independent of power.[72] Du Bois himself practiced a science that engaged with, rather than detached from, the power relations shaping both its practitioners and the "subjects" of its study. For Du Bois, "One could not be a calm, cool, detached scientist while Negroes were lynched, murdered, and starved";[73] he saw the purpose of his life's work as "leading to the emancipation of the American Negro." In his words, "history and the other social sciences were to be my weapons, to be sharpened and applied by research and writing."[74]

ANNA [admiringly]: Sounds like you have that memorized, Alice.

ALICE [laughing]: I do.

TIMOTHY: I'm also interested in the ways power operates internally, within the conduct of ethnography itself. I'm familiar with the passage that Alice referenced earlier from Du Bois's *Dusk of Dawn*. One of the things I find most intriguing about it is that Du Bois writes about not only the racism of his white financial backers, but also the resistance to his research from blacks in Philadelphia. "Are we animals to be dissected and by an unknown Negro at that?" he imagines the blacks of Philadelphia asking in response to encountering him as a researcher.[75] It's a provocative line, because it highlights the way in which this sociological and ethnographic movement inward to the inaccessible urban center was—even for Du Bois—still marked by a crossing of boundaries and an establishment of power relations which mimic the move by anthropology's later ethnographers to cross the boundaries of nation-state and language. Du Bois was alert to this tension and to the resistance on the part of his "subjects" to being treated like animals to be dissected.

[Wolfdog growls and shows her fangs. Silence for a long moment as the ethnographers look at her with concern before Timothy continues.]

So despite its focus on the "local" and the "urban," there is still an exoticization of the other that is possible even within sociological work that is ethnographic.

PIERS: There's that fascinating fragment, "and by an unknown Negro at that?" So, Du Bois, chosen by his white racist funders because of supposed "insider" status as a fellow black person, recognizes his own outsider status in relation to the communities he is studying.

ALICE: Du Bois was known, actually, for being quite reserved and aloof, for dressing conservatively, carrying a walking stick, and for speaking in a New England accent.[76] So it's intriguing to think of him in the seventh ward of Philadelphia, administering surveys and conducting interviews. The animosity that he anticipated towards his research and even himself as a researcher shows that there can be gaps to bridge even when others perceive the researcher to be "native" to a situation.

MITCH: Yes, absolutely. And when the researcher is clearly an outsider, the tensions are even more obvious. It's a charge that's sometimes been leveled against my work in both *Slim's Table* and *Sidewalk*.[77] I'm a white Jewish male, so what gives me the right to study poor, black men? And in particular, what makes me think I am able to understand them and make claims about them that they themselves might not agree with?

PIERS: Right. So are you a kind of modern-day colonialist ethnographer?

MITCH: That's the implication.

PIERS: Well, what's your response to those charges?

MITCH: This is a complicated question that I've done a lot of thinking about.[78] The first thing to note is that I always understood there to be a metaphorical chain-linked fence that existed between me and those I was studying.

KATHERINE: A chain-linked fence?

MITCH: Yes, the metaphor comes from Elliot Leibow's *Tally's Corner*, which, alongside Carol Stack's *All Our Kin*, still offers, to my thinking, one of the best exemplars of how to think about the privilege of white ethnographers in the United States who study nonwhite others.[79]

TIMOTHY: These themes seem to recur over and over throughout the history of ethnography.

KATHERINE: So what about the chain-linked fence?

MITCH: Well, the metaphor suggests that there is a very real racial separation, one that is informed by "the historical relations between the kinds of people being studied and the kind of person doing the study, in this case a privileged white man and a group of poor US black descendants of slaves."[80] But it also suggests that this separation does not need to be absolute, that there is an opening for, as Leibow demonstrates in his own work, "the possibility of a white man entering into a serious dialogue with the lives of poor blacks and producing a book that was not nothing, that gave you something significant, even if was not a full understanding, which we can never get."[81]

PIERS: I like the metaphor. But it still leaves the question of how you negotiate the specific relationships in the field.

MITCH: One way I deal with them is by making sure I include as much of the voices of my participants as possible. In *Sidewalk*, I even invited one of my participants, Hakim Hasan, to write an afterward to the book and co-teach a seminar with me at the University of California, Santa Barbara.[82] I see this not as an attempt at resolution but as a way of recognizing the tensions and of trying to move through them by redistributing ethnographic authority.

ANNA: I wonder if that really gets around the problem? Selecting one or two model subjects and granting them symbolic co-authorship or inviting them to teach with you might only serve to obscure the larger power dynamics at play.

MITCH: My aim is not to obscure the larger power dynamics but rather to surface them so that we can acknowledge them and think about them. As I said, inviting Hakim to write an afterword to the book or co-teach a seminar does not resolve the tensions. If anything, it makes them more available to the reader. This is what I mean by redistributing ethnographic authority.

Loïc: What qualifies a member of a given universe to co-teach a seminar on his own universe? Since when is the average person a sociological expert on their life as opposed to just another informant? That's the real question that's avoided here in the name of seeming "inclusive" and "respectful" of the subject of research, and it is epistemological nonsense and political farce. Would you do it if you were studying 'up'? Would you invite the prison warden and the prosecutor to co-teach a course on the ethnography of incarceration? You wouldn't, for fear of being seen as a shill.[83] But perhaps I can also speak a bit to this from a different perspective, as several of my critics charged me with a kind of imperialist ethnography of the boxing gym.

Piers: How is that?

Loïc: Well, I am a white Frenchman who claims in my book to have somewhat sidestepped or superseded the problem of white–black racial relations in the US more broadly and on the South Side of Chicago more specifically by virtue of my nationality. I further make the claim that in the boxing gym, and especially in the squared circle of the ring, race is conditionally suspended as it gets pushed to the background and overtaken by properties more relevant in the urgency of practice: do you have a good left hook, can you exchange sparring sessions, do you live by the ethic of "sacrifice"?[84]

Mitch: And isn't it also the case that in your book you go to some lengths to persuade readers that you've been accepted by the black men in the gym as one of their own?

Loïc: Well, in fact, I think I was accepted that way. My whiteness was interpreted by the members of the boxing gym through the lens of my Frenchness, which I came to view as a kind of propitious prop. As a non-US citizen, and as a cultural outsider, my racial naïveté, in US racial terms, really played to my advantage. As my ringmate Ashante once put it, "'French people ain't crackers, they always had good rapport with blacks, goin' all d'way back,' by which he meant that a Frenchman is not directly implicated in the bitter black–white dualism that organizes American society and may even have cultural affinities with his community."[85]

Mitch: I'm not sure that's entirely persuasive, though. I think it's a bit naïve to accept at face value comments like these, believing that we have become one of them. "I am reminded of my own experience of being told by poor blacks that they and I have a special rapport, owing to the relationship between Jews and blacks during the civil rights movement. I would later learn that the very same people were saying anti-Jewish things behind my back. I am skeptical that any white researcher could ever really know what his poor black subjects think of him on the basis of the things they say to him."[86] This is why I keep returning to the metaphor of the chain-linked fence first articulated by Leibow.

In ethnography, as in life, the possibility certainly exists for extraordinary moments of solidarity and even friendship across race and class lines, but we should not be overly romantic in ways that lead us to imagine a complete dissolution of the chain-linked fence erected by long and still ongoing histories of racial domination.

ALICE: I think this raises an important question about the role that ethnography has historically played in the discipline of sociology. This tradition of relatively privileged, outside academics studying various aspects of the social lives of classes ranked lower on society's hierarchy continues largely to this day. We can think, for example, of Sudhir Venkatesh's *Gang Leader for a Day*, an ethnography of his research on gang life, also on the South Side of Chicago.[87] Both Loïc's research for *Body & Soul* and Mitch's work in *Sidewalk* could be similarly understood. And as I'm sure we'll hear if The Prosecutor ever shows up, my book, *On the Run*, has also been explicitly criticized along these lines.

ANNA: Well, not to bring it back to anthropology, but I think Karen's book is also unique in this way.

TIMOTHY: How so?

ANNA: *Liquidated* is very much a book that "studies up," to invoke anthropologist Laura Nader's felicitous phrasing. Nader was writing in the 1970s, but her argument that anthropology, and by extension, ethnography, needs to do much more to study those in positions of power in society, to study the colonizer rather than the colonized, the affluent rather than the culture of poverty, continues to be relevant today.

KAREN: I agree, Anna. And Nader's point isn't just about what knowledges are produced by whether ethnographers study up or down, but also about how the power relations we have with our so-called "subjects" exert an influence over how we ask questions and define problems in the first place. Studying up, Nader argues, might lead us to turn a lot of our conventional questions on their heads. Instead of asking why people are poor, we might explore why some are rich. Instead of studying the ghetto, we might study the institutions—banks, real estate agencies, and school districting—that create those areas.[88]

PIERS: But think of all the problems with access when it comes to studying up.

JIM: Yes.

KAREN: I think that's exactly Nader's point, though. She's raising a critically important question: does ethnography inherently favor objects of study that place the researcher in a dominant–subordinate relationship with her "subjects"? And could part of the reason for that be that access is typically easier when one is studying down than when one is studying up?

TIMOTHY: You could take it a step further, if you wanted, and critically ask whether urban sociology specifically, and ethnography more generally, tends towards a voyeurism of the poor, or the perverted, or the deviant. There is a long and distinguished list of reputations and careers that have been built on ethnographies based on the infiltration and elucidation of subcultures otherwise closed off to a middle-class readership base. This critique could be made of my book too, based on undercover work in the slaughterhouse.

JIM: It's not just academically driven work, either. Think of *Nickled and Dimed* by Barbara Ehrenreich.[89] Work of that kind deserves a mention inasmuch as it involves full immersion in another life-world, trying to "live that life." It's interesting that our own society's poorest people are so remote from our experience that we have to send anthropologists to them as if they were a tribe in the New Guinea Highlands.

LOÏC: I object to being lumped into this critique. The object of my study was carnal sociology, not a voyeuristic look at what it was like to be a member of a black boxing gym.

ANNA [laughing]: Well, Loïc, surely you can't deny that entering a hidden world was also part of the attraction for your readers? After all, you even wrote part of *Body & Soul* as a sociological novella!

LOÏC: Well, the narrative I offer in *Body & Soul* is just a "prelude and stepping-stone to a second, more explicitly theoretical work."[90] It's meant to elaborate the notion of habitus and aims to contribute to a sociology of flesh and blood capable of capturing the carnality of social action.[91]

ANNA: Yes, but the theoretical work in *Body & Soul* is inseparable from the visceral, voyeuristic thrill of entering a boxing gym, a space hidden and unknown to the vast majority of us.

TIMOTHY: You can't have the object of study without the locus of study. That's what we were arguing before. In ethnography, no theoretical diamonds can be washed clean of the mud in which they were found.

PIERS: Nor would we ever want to wash them clean. That's the beauty and power of ethnography.

TIMOTHY: I completely agree, Piers. In my ethnography of an industrialized slaughterhouse, I even warn my readers against the "impulse to thumb through the pages so as to locate, separate, and segregate the sterile, abstract arguments from the flat, ugly, day-in, day-out minutiae of the work of killing."[92]

KATHERINE: But wait, can't the thrill also be in the other direction? There is a reason why celebrity-focused magazines and tabloids sell so well.

ANNA: Oh, I see. So we could have *Wall Street Investment Banker for a Day* and *Elite Prep School Student for a Day*.

ALICE: Yes, or in the case of Ashley Mear's book on the New York City fashion industry, *Top Fashion Model for a Day*.[93]

JIM: You know, whether studying up or down, it's not always outsiders who offer the most compelling accounts. Sometimes it's insiders who have decided to write ethnographically about their own social situations. Think here of Ben

Hamper's *Rivethead: Tales from the Assembly Line* on one end and John Perkins's *Confessions of an Economic Hit Man* on the other.[94]

KAREN: Whether or not all ethnography indulges a voyeuristic impulse is one question, but Nader's point is different. She would say, I think, that the political, normative, and theoretical consequences of directing the ethnographic gaze predominantly downward are serious and important.

TIMOTHY: I'm fascinated by this discussion of the history of ethnography within anthropology and sociology, but I think it's important to remember that ethnography has also been taken up in a wide range of other disciplines, including political science, education, organizational studies, nursing, and even journalism, and that the word ethnography takes on different valences within each of those disciplines.

KATHERINE: Yes, that's a good point. And I think there are particular debates and tensions and "schools" of thought about ethnography within each of those disciplinary histories.

PIERS: And yet—returning to the situation at hand [looks at wolfdog on the ground]—I would say that it is not our disciplinary or even academic identities that matter most here, but rather our common practice of deep, immersive research and writing of some kind.

KAREN: A kind of research and writing that might loosely be identified as ethnographic.

[General silence.]

TIMOTHY [holding up potion]: At the risk of speaking too broadly, I do think there is a common theme that holds all of our discussion together so far, and that relates directly back to the question of what we should do with this Fieldwork Invisibility Potion.

[The wolfdog growls.]

ALICE: And what's that?

TIMOTHY: I would call it attention to positionality, to our locations within structures of power.

MITCH: That is pretty broad.

TIMOTHY: Let me try to be more specific then. Most importantly, I think our conversations so far illustrate how ethnographers need to attend to their positionality within networks of power in the fieldsite itself. As we've already suggested with our discussion of ethnography's tortured relationship to power, there is no such thing as a neutral position from which to conduct ethnography.

KATHERINE: Can you illustrate?

TIMOTHY: In my own research, for example, I made a conscious decision to enter the fieldsite as an entry-level worker rather than as a guest of management. This had a significant impact, not only on the kinds of information I was able to access in the field, but also on how I interpreted and understood that information.

KAREN: I imagine it also had a huge impact on how others in the field perceived you.

TIMOTHY: Exactly. Imagine, for example, if in your ethnography of Wall Street you had conducted your research from the vantage point of one of the janitors or cafeteria workers rather than as an investment banker.

KAREN [laughing]: Well, I doubt I would have had very much sustained interaction with the traders at all!

TIMOTHY: True, but if you'd had them, those interactions would have been profoundly shaped by your vantage point.

KAREN: This is such an important point. People criticize my work for not being sufficiently immersive, but what they don't understand is how difficult it is to study Wall Street investment bankers as a participant-observer. Those positions are highly competitive. It is not simply a matter of walking in and getting a position there in order to study them.

ANNA: Right. It's the point about studying up versus studying down.

TIMOTHY: Definitely. My fieldwork is nicely illustrative just because the hierarchies were so explicitly encoded in the site itself. As a workplace, the slaughterhouse had very clear and very consequential divisions of authority.

JIM: Well, and even within those divisions, there were further divisions of labor that really mattered, right?

TIMOTHY: Yes. So, it mattered a great deal that I worked first as a liver hanger, then as a chute worker, then finally as a quality control worker.

JIM: So this level of positionality you are talking about—it's not just a matter of power, is it?

TIMOTHY: No, I guess you're right. It's not just overt or implicit power hierarchies in the fieldsite—manager vs. line worker, guard vs. prisoner, etc.—but also other distinctions that are not as immediately obvious as power distinctions.

ANNA: I think one of the exciting things about ethnography is that you can't always know what those distinctions are until you get into the fieldwork. It's the fieldwork itself, in a way, that illuminates what those distinctions are and why they matter.

JIM: Yes, exactly. Thinking back to Timothy's research again, research that I supervised, I doubt he would have even known the difference between a liver hanger and a liver packer, before starting his fieldwork, much less that it would prove so important to his research.

KAREN [eyebrows raised]: Liver hanger and liver packer? Do tell!

TIMOTHY: Well, I don't know if it's completely relevant here.

PIERS: Oh, come on, do tell us.

TIMOTHY: Well, OK. My first job in the slaughterhouse was working in the cooler as a liver hanger. Basically, I stood in a damp, near-freezing cooler for nine hours a day taking freshly gutted livers off a line of overhead hooks and hanging them on carts to be chilled.

KAREN: Gross.

TIMOTHY: Yes, at first. But then it became overwhelmingly monotonous.

ANNA: So where do the liver packers come in?

TIMOTHY: Well, after hanging and then sitting on the carts for a period of time, the livers are taken off the carts by the liver packers and put in boxes.

KAREN: Still gross, but why does this matter?

TIMOTHY: See, there was a fierce and recurring conflict between the liver hangers and the liver packers over who was supposed to wash the liver carts after they had been used. The liver packers had a much easier job overall than the liver hangers because they weren't tied to the line in the same way. The liver hangers had to attend to the overhead line of moving hooks, so they couldn't step away from their stations for even a second because if they missed a liver and it went back upstairs to the kill floor without being taken off the hook, they would be fired.

KAREN: And the liver packers?

TIMOTHY: They weren't tied to the line. All they had to do was to take the livers off the carts, which could be manually pushed around in the cooler. So, they could really work at their own pace and often took long breaks between bouts of work.

ANNA: Long breaks?

TIMOTHY: They seemed long to us liver hangers, because we were tied to the line and couldn't step away for even one second.

KAREN: So what happened with this conflict?

TIMOTHY: Again, the liver packers had the flow of work on their side. Because it was the liver hangers who needed to use clean carts, the liver packers could just let the dirty carts pile up without any consequences to themselves. But the liver hangers would ultimately be forced to wash the carts themselves, which caused a lot of problems given that they also had to attend to the overhead line of moving hooks.

JIM: What's interesting about this conflict, reading your book, is how completely it came to dominate your consciousness.

TIMOTHY: Exactly. Entire weeks went by where all my fellow liver hanger Ramón and I could think or talk about was how we were going to get back at the liver packers. Here we are, working in a freezing cooler for just a few bucks an hour, contributing to the mass slaughter of thousands of creatures a day, and all we could think about was this fight we were having with three guys who were also working in a freezing cooler for just a few bucks an hour.

JIM: The point here being that it was a critically important insight for your larger question about how violence is structured and normalized, a moment where you make Geertz's sheep raid speak to Geertz's revolution.

TIMOTHY: Yes.

KAREN: So what happened? Did you ever get the liver packers to wash the carts?

TIMOTHY: We did! Ramón and I appealed to our red-hat supervisor. At first, he wasn't sympathetic to our point of view at all, but he relented after we told him the slaughterhouse risked being written up by the USDA for a food safety infraction if we got our gloves dirty cleaning the carts and then touched a liver. He told the liver packers they had to wash the carts. It made Ramón and me ecstatically happy!

JIM: I imagine there are all kinds of small conflicts like that all over the slaughterhouse.

TIMOTHY: Right, and it was pure coincidence that this is where I was positioned when I was hired.

JIM: So it matters both that you were an entry-level worker and that you were positioned as a liver hanger in the cooler.

TIMOTHY: Exactly. Attending to my positionality in the fieldsite really mattered in ways that were both under and not under my control. It was my decision to access the site by seeking employment as an entry-level worker rather than as a guest of management. But once inside the slaughterhouse, I had minimal or no say about my initial placement as a liver hanger in the cooler, my movement to the chutes, where I herded the live animals into the kill box, and my promotion to quality control, which gave me access to nearly the entire slaughterhouse, including its paperwork documentation and radio communication.

SÉVERINE: It just seems so risky, because you couldn't have anticipated in advance where you would be.

TIMOTHY: I guess it's a bit like learning to live with those wolves: risky, for sure, but also exhilarating and potentially enormously generative and creative.

KATHERINE: So if I understand you right, what you mean by positionality at this level is careful attention to how you will be located in the fieldsite, both in relation to the power relationships that are already in existence there, and also in relation to particular locations that might not seem overtly connected to power but that might exert an enormous influence over what and how you perceive things in the field.

TIMOTHY: I couldn't have said it better myself. It's interesting, for example, to think about each of our research projects in this regard.

LOÏC: Yes, how would we categorize ourselves? I suppose, first of all, that each of us strove for and accomplished different degrees of immersion as participants in the sites that we studied. So, Timothy, you and I are very similar in that our research involved a high degree of immersive participation. You were a full-time, paid worker in the slaughterhouse you were studying, and I was a bona fide member of the boxing gym, participating in actual boxing matches. In terms of the ethnographers gathered here, I think we are definitely on the more immersive side of the continuum.

KAREN: My fieldwork was located somewhere in the middle of the immersion continuum. I spent part of it immersively participating as a worker at an investment bank, and part of it as a researcher interviewing people who worked in investment banks.

MITCH: Me too. In *Sidewalk*, I conducted both deeply immersive research in which I set up my own book table on Sixth Avenue while also stepping out of that bookselling role and inhabiting an obvious identity as a researcher. I also examined other locations in order to get a grasp on the forms of power at work in the site where I was more immersed. I interviewed officials working with the Business Improvement District, for example, to understand how political and class power shaped the lives of the booksellers. And, I did research with a white family from Vermont who set up a seasonal Christmas tree stand on Jane Street in order to understand how racial power played into the differential treatment received by the white family and the black booksellers. By definition, I could not have thickly immersed myself in all of these sites.

TIMOTHY: Don't you call that method the extended place method, in a play on Burawoy's extended case method?

MITCH: That's right! Our fetishization of theory so often leads us to want to extend our analyses from our immersive sites to theory when much more can sometimes be gained by extending to the other places that shape our own, sometimes at a distance.

JIM: Karen, I imagine your location in networks of power was not very high when you inhabited your role as a researcher?

KAREN [laughing]: No, not very high at all! These were all high-powered investment bankers, and me telling them I was a researcher did little to impress them or to entice them to give up their time for my project.

JIM: Right. On the other hand, as an American researcher living in a small Malay village and staying with one of the wealthier people there, I commanded a great deal of power in my fieldsite as a "researcher."

SÉVERINE: So all of this can really vary considerably. I suppose the main point here is to be acutely aware, as ethnographers, of the power positions that we do inhabit in the field. These power positions sit orthogonally to the question of how immersively participative our research is.[95]

TIMOTHY: Yes, exactly. And, there's a second level of positionality that has to do with our roles as creators of knowledge. When we think about this level of positionality, we are being attentive to how our position as knowledge creators is already located in particular historical and power contexts. Our knowledge creation is made possible only because of those contexts, and it can also come back and interact with those contexts, sometimes in surprising and unexpected ways. So, for example, earlier we had a rich conversation about the role that ethnography played in the early history of anthropology, and in particular about the role that ethnography played in assisting colonial projects of power. And we've discussed how ethnography might be playing a continued, similar role in the US military today.

KAREN: Or how it might be playing a similar role in "urban ethnographies" of communities of color in the United States, as is the case with a lot of contemporary sociology, for example.

ANNA: Right.

KATHERINE: What about the positionality of people who do ethnographic writing that isn't located in academic disciplines, work like my own?

TIMOTHY: Your book in particular is interesting, Katherine, because it has had such an influential reach. It won a National Book Award and has been widely read, at least in the United States. So the relevant question there would be about the conditions of possibility that made your research feasible and about what impact it is having on the Mumbai slum you studied, or on other similar slums.

KATHERINE: I write a little bit about this in my afterword, about the hopes I had for what impact the book might have.

TIMOTHY: Yes, you do.

ANNA: And yet what's interesting about your book, Katherine, is that even though you think explicitly about its intended impact, you very self-consciously adopt a non-presence in the narrative itself. So, at the first level of positionality that Timothy was talking about—the level that asks us to think reflectively about how we are located in our particular research sites—it seems that you are almost entirely silent.

KATHERINE: I did think long and hard about that. It's just that I chose not to communicate this with my readers, because I thought it would distract them from the story that I really wanted to get across. I didn't want to become an unwitting protagonist in the story I was telling.

ANNA: I understand your reasoning, but one might argue that in your complete absence, you actually become much more of a distracting presence than if you'd made yourself present in the text so that the reader could understand how you were located in your fieldsite and how you came to know what you know.

KATHERINE: I do write about this in a short afterword. I tell my readers about the interviews I conducted.

TIMOTHY: This particular discussion shows, I think, how these different levels of positionality are related in various ways; how there can be no simple compartmentalization of each level. Ethnography locates the researcher in the creative tension between locus and object of study, and it asks the ethnographer to think about how her disciplinary location in knowledge creation matters. It also, importantly, asks the ethnographer to be explicit about her location in networks of power in the fieldsite itself. In at least these ways, positionality becomes a central theme running through ethnographic work.

[A contemplative silence fills the room. Soon, attention begins to turn back to the sheaf of papers, the vial of liquid, and the wolfdog lying on the floor.]

PIERS: Well! This has all been very interesting, but it doesn't seem like we're any closer to solving the conundrum of what to do with the vial of liquid.

ANNA: Yes, or of what to do with the one-eyed wolfdog.

ALICE: Or of what to do about my ethnographic trial.

LoÏc: Where is The Prosecutor? I am tiring of this, and I have important field-work to do.

MITCH: Yes, where is that prosecutor?

KAREN: At least the wolfdog seems to be sleeping more peacefully now.

KATHERINE: Do you think we should call a vet?

PIERS: A vet would probably kill her!

KATHERINE: What do you mean?

PIERS: The last thing she needs is treatment at the hands of Western veterinary medicine. What she's facing now is something of an existential and spiritual crisis. I've seen it many times before when shamans reach the end of their trance journeys.

KATHERINE: OK, then, what should we do about the vial and the dog? And what about Alice's trial?

[Wolfdog starts to stir on the floor, gets up weakly, and looks at the group. She opens her mouth, but only a muffled bark comes out.]

ALICE: It looks like the wolfdog has lost her powers of speech!

KAREN: It does. But at least she's moving again.

PIERS: Look, I have an idea. Why don't a few of us take the wolfdog for a walk by the lake? Maybe the fresh air will help her feel better. I know I could use some air myself after this conversation.

ALICE: Well, but what about the trial?

LoÏc: Maybe The Prosecutor will never show up and the trial will never happen.

ALICE: That would be a bit anticlimactic, wouldn't it? The summons from The Prosecutor is the whole reason we came up here in the first place.

KAREN: OK, look, how about this? Why don't I go with Piers to walk with the wolfdog, and the rest of you hold the trial while we're gone?

TIMOTHY: I like that idea, and I'll come on the walk with you two. I've been in this barn for far too long already. And while we walk, why don't the three of us discuss what to do with the potion?

ANNA: That sounds fine. So, Karen, Piers, Timothy, and the wolfdog will go for a walk and continue discussing what to do with the potion, and the rest of us will stay here and wait for The Prosecutor. But please give us a call if anything changes with the wolfdog or if you need help.

TIMOTHY: Cell reception isn't the best up here, but we'll try!

[Lights fade out to darkness as Piers, Karen, Timothy, and the wolfdog exit stage right. A's they leave, the sound of a motorcycle engine gradually grows louder and soon a cloaked, hooded figure can be seen in the background approaching the barn on a Harley Davidson, the folds of his cloak flowing dramatically in the air. A long wooden staff is strapped to the back of the motorcycle.]

## End of Act Four

## Notes

1 For more on multi-sited ethnography, see Marcus 1995, 1998.
2 "Places…are the objects of anthropological study as well as the critical links between description and analysis in anthropological theory. [Arjun] Appadurai's crucial point is that description and analysis are systematically linked (and distinguished) by specific historical *spatializations*" (Clifford 1990: 65–66, original emphasis).
3 "Anthropologists don't study villages, they study in villages" (Geertz 1973a: 22).
4 Geertz 1973a: 23
5 For Wacquant's labeling of diagnostic ethnography and grounded theory as an "epistemological fairy tale" and for his critiques of raw empiricism and theoretical absent-mindedness, see "Scrutinizing the Street: Poverty, Morality, and the Pitfalls of Urban Ethnography" (2002: 1481). Wacquant's language in this section of Act Four draws heavily on, and at times quotes verbatim from, "Scrutinizing the Street." Verbatim language that goes beyond a few key words or phrases is indicated by quotation marks.
6 Duneier and Back 2006: 564–565
7 "Of course, the researcher does not approach reality as a tabula rasa. He must have a perspective that will help him see relevant data and abstract significant categories from his scrutiny of the data" (Glaser and Strauss 1967: 3).
8 Duneier 2002: 1574
9 Duneier 1999: 340–341
10 Duneier 1999: 341
11 Duneier 1999: 341
12 King, Keohane, and Verba 1994: 19–31
13 Duneier 2002: 1566
14 Boo 2012b
15 Wacquant 2010
16 Scott 1985, 1998, 2009
17 Duneier 2017
18 Geertz 1973a: 22
19 Burawoy 1998
20 Lundblad 2015, Jackson 2013
21 Tsing 2015: 37
22 "The methodologies political scientists use to reach evidence-based conclusions *all* involve extracting information from the social world, analyzing the resulting data, and reaching a conclusion based on that combination of the evidence and its analysis" (Elman and Kapiszewski 2014: 44, original emphasis).
23 Tsing 2015: 37
24 Tsing 2015: 37–38
25 Tsing 2015: 38
26 Tsing 1993
27 Quoted in Munck and Snyder 2008: 365.
28 Quoted in Munck and Snyder 2008: 365.
29 Munck and Snyder 2008: 366, Laitin 1999
30 Tsing 2015: 38
31 Tsing 2015: 38–40
32 Tsing 2015: 38
33 Peterson 2001
34 Leach 1954
35 Jonsson 2005
36 For the "romance of the primitive" in anthropology, see Fox 1972, Tsing 1993. For a revalorization of "the primitive," see Graeber 2006.
37 Schaffer 2014, Jerolmack and Khan 2014

38  Ricoeur 1970
39  Duneier et al. 2010
40  Tsing 1993
41  "Cultural knowledge and warfare are inextricably bound" (McFate 2005a: 42; see also McFate 2005b). For more on the Human Terrain System, see McFate and Laurence 2015, Petraeus 2015, González 2007, 2009, 2015, Gezari 2013. For broader relationships between anthropology and intelligence agencies, see Price 2000, 2005.
42  "Recently, a few social scientists have capitalized on their work with HTS, using it as the baseline for publishing academic journal articles….A few HTS personnel used the research they had conducted in the field as the basis of their dissertations" (McFate and Laurence 2015: "Introduction").
43  American Anthropological Association 2007
44  "Anthropology came into its own in the period in which the Western nations were making their final push to bring practically the whole pre-industrial, non-Western world under their political and economic control. Anthropology is a child of Western Imperialism" (Gough 1968: 12–13, Gough 1967). Decades later, Gough 1993 revisited the themes of her earlier essay.
45  "Anthropologists were of higher social status than their informants; they were usually of the dominant race; and they were protected by imperial law; yet, living closely with native peoples, they tended to take their part and to try to protect them against the worst forms of imperialist exploitation" (Gough 1968: 13).
46  "European power, as discourse and practice, was always part of the reality anthropologists sought to understand, and of the way they sought to understand it" (Asad 1991: 315).
47  "The role of anthropologists in maintaining structures of imperial domination has, despite slogans to the contrary, usually been trivial. The knowledge they produced was often too esoteric to government use, and even where it was usable it was marginal in comparison to the vast body of information routinely accumulated by merchants, missionaries, and administrators. Of course, there were professional anthropologists who were nominated (or who offered their services) as experts on the social life of subjugated peoples. But their expertise was never indispensable to the grand process of imperial power" (Asad 1991: 315).
48  Salemink 2003
49  Malinowski 1922
50  Malinowski 1922: 24–25
51  Malinowski 1929
52  See Harris and Sadler 2003 for one account of these espionage activities.
53  These four, Boas wrote, "have prostituted science by using it as a cover for their activities as spies. A soldier whose business is murder as a fine art…accept[s] the code of morality to which modern society still conforms. Not so the scientist. The very essence of his life is the service of truth" (1919: 797).
54  Chanlat 2014
55  Bateson 1958, Coon 1980
56  Benedict 1980
57  Valeriano and Bohannan 2008
58  "We need to know…whether there is a common set of circumstances under which left-wing and nationalist revolutions have occurred or have been attempted in recent years in Cuba, Algeria, Indo-China, Malaysia, the Philippines, Indonesia, Kenya, and Zanzibar. Are there any recognizable shifts in ideology or organization between these earlier revolts and the guerilla movements now taking shape in Guatemala, Venezuela, Colombia, Angola, Mozambique, Laos, Thailand, Cameroon, or southern Arabia? What are the types of peasantry and urban workers most likely to be involved in these revolutions; are these typologies of leadership and organization? Why have some failed and others succeeded? I may be accused of asking for Project Camelot, but I am not.

I am asking that we do these projects in *our* way, as we would study a cargo-cult or a kula-ring, without the built-in biases of tainted financing, without the assumption that counter-revolution, and not revolution, is the best answer, and with the ultimate spiritual and economic welfare of our informants, and of the international community, before us rather than the short-run military or industrial profits of Western nations" (Gough 1968: 23).

59 Engels 1984 [1845]

60 Morris 2015, Go 2016

61 Du Bois 1899

62 Du Bois 1903

63 Thomas and Znaniecki 1918

64 *The Polish Peasant* is "a neglected classic…[a] landmark because it attempted to integrate theory and data in a way no American study had done before" (Bulmer 1986: 45).

65 Bulmer 1986

66 Hull House 2010, Booth 1892

67 Lewis 2000: 188

68 "My vision was becoming clear.…The world was thinking wrong about race because it did not know. The ultimate evil was stupidity. The cure for it was knowledge based on scientific investigation. At the University of Pennsylvania I ignored the pitiful stipend. It made not difference to me that I was put down as an "assistant instructor" and even at that, that my name never actually got into the catalogue; it goes without saying that I did no instructing save once to pilot a pack of idiots through the Negro slums. The fact was the city of Philadelphia at that time had a theory; and that theory was that this great, rich, and famous municipality was going to the dogs because of the crime and venality of its Negro citizens, who lived largely centered in the slum at the lower end of the seventh ward. Philadelphia wanted to prove this by figures, and I was the man to do it. Of this theory back of the plan, I neither knew nor cared. I saw only here a chance to study an historical group of black folk and to show exactly what their place was in the community" (Du Bois 1940: 59).

69 "Park sought to understand the conditions that would allow the white man to rule the world. He argued that African colonization and American slavery were necessary because they provided the apprenticeships through which backward blacks advanced by being exposed to the white man's superior civilization" (Morris 2015: 222).

70 "While training his students, Park 'told them flatly that the world was full of crusaders. Their role instead was to be that of the calm, detached scientist who investigates race relations with the same objectivity and detachment with which the zoologist dissects the potato bug'" (Morris 2015: 114, quoting Park, Masuoka, and Valien 1975: 17).

71 "[T]he Chicago school – and indeed early mainstream American sociology in general – can be exposed for what it was: a parochial if not provincial body of thought that reflected little else than the worldview and groping aspirations of a handful of middling white men whose interests were tethered to the interests of the American empire" (Go 2016).

72 Even Du Bois, who placed so much faith in science to counter ignorance about race, wrote: "So far as the American world of science and letters were concerned, we never 'belonged'; we remained unrecognized in learned societies and academic groups. We rated merely as Negroes studying Negroes, and after all, what had Negroes to do with America or science?" (Du Bois 1968: 228, quoted in Morris 2015: 112).

73 Du Bois 1968: 222, quoted in Morris 2015: 135.

74 Du Bois 1968: 192, quoted in Morris 2015: 135.

75 "I did it [research for *The Philadelphia Negro*] despite extraordinary difficulties both within and without the group. Whites said, Why study the obvious? Blacks said, Are we animals to be dissected and by an unknown Negro at that? Yet, I made a study of the Philadelphia Negro so thorough that it has withstood the criticism of forty years. It was as complete a scientific study and answer as could have then been given, with defective

facts and statistics, one lone worker and little money. It revealed the Negro group as a symptom, not a cause; as a striving, palpitating group, and not an inert, sick body of crime; as a long historic development and not a transient occurrence" (Du Bois 1940: 59).

76  Anderson 1996
77  Duneier 1994, 1999
78  See, in particular, Duneier and Back 2006.
79  Leibow 1967, Stack 1974
80  Duneier and Back 2006: 549
81  Duneier and Back 2006: 547
82  Hasan 1999
83  Wacquant 2004b: note 20
84  Wacquant 2005a
85  Wacquant 2005a: 447
86  Duneier 2006: 148
87  Venkatesh 2009
88  "If we look at literature based on field work in the United States, we find a relatively abundant literature on the poor, the ethnic groups, the disadvantaged; there is comparatively little field research on the middle class and very little firsthand work on the upper classes. Anthropologists might indeed ask themselves whether the entirety of field work does not depend upon a certain power relationship in favor of the anthropologist, and whether indeed such dominant-subordinate relationships may not be affecting the kinds of theories we are weaving. What if, in reinventing anthropology, anthropologists were to study the colonizers rather than the colonized, the culture of power rather than the culture of the powerless, the culture of affluence rather than the culture of poverty?" (Nader 1972: 289)
89  Ehrenreich 2001
90  Wacquant 2004a: viii
91  Wacquant 2011, 2015
92  Pachirat 2011: 19
93  Mears 2011
94  Hamper 1986, Perkins 2004
95  See Gans 1962: 336–350 for a classic treatment of the continuum of participant-observer roles. See also the discussion of six degrees of researcher participation in Schwartz-Shea and Yanow 2012: 63–66.

# ACT FIVE: A NATURAL HISTORY OF FIELDWORK[1]

...the confusion of fieldwork, its inescapable reflexivity.

James Clifford, "Notes on (Field)notes" (1990: 54)

The field did to Maritya what the field always does: it scoured her and revealed the person underneath the encrusted layers of culture and ingrained habit and prejudice.

Mischa Berlinski, *Fieldwork: A Novel* (2007: 37)

## Scene

Lights come up on Piers Vitebsky, Karen Ho, and Timothy Pachirat walking with the wolfdog by the edge of Keuka Lake.

PIERS VITEBSKY: I'm so glad to be out of that barn. It was getting stuffy with all those ethnographers in there.

TIMOTHY PACHIRAT: It's gorgeous here.

KAREN HO: Yes, something so pleasant about the combination of water, light, and vineyards.

TIMOTHY: This whole turn of events has been a bit mind-blowing. It was bizarre enough to receive that letter from The Prosecutor inviting us to meet here for a trial, but then to have a talking wolfdog show up on top of it?

PIERS [bending to pick up a smooth pebble]: I know, it's certainly a strange set of circumstances to meet in.

[Skips pebble across the water. Wolfdog looks at the pebble skipping, then at Piers, and growls.]

TIMOTHY: She seems angry.

KAREN: Yes, she does. What's it like, Piers, to have an ethnographic informant travel all this way, to meet you, as it were, on your own territory?

PIERS: It's a nice reminder that the borders between our fieldsites and the rest of our lives are a lot more porous than we think they are. But I never thought I'd have that border crossed by a one-eyed wolfdog who can see the future!

TIMOTHY: I think it's perfect. I'm increasingly interested in interspecies and multi-species relationships, and I think it's fantastic that a very anthropocentric method, ethnography, is now faced with a crisis instigated by a future-telling canine.

KAREN [correcting him playfully]: *Lupus*-Canine.

TIMOTHY [repeating]: *Lupus*-Canine.

KAREN: So we only have a few hours to deliberate about the potion. Shall we get started?

PIERS [wearily]: Ah, I was hoping for some downtime. Candidly, I found a lot of our prior discussions a bit too abstract. Maybe I'm just romanticizing the past, but seems to me it used to be that ethnographers just went out and did their ethnographies. We didn't sit around for years and publish untold quantities of books debating the meta-level theory and the power implications of the method. We just went out and did it!

KAREN [laughing]: Yeah, I hear you Piers. But there were all kinds of dangers in that kind of "just do it" approach as well, not least of which is that novice ethnographers often had no idea at all what they were up to!

PIERS: But isn't that just it, though? Isn't that process of figuring it out as you go part of the initiation rite into ethnography?

TIMOTHY: I certainly went through it. And let me tell you, it wasn't enjoyable in the least.

PIERS: But what's the alternative? That we claim to be able to actually prepare students for the inexhaustible range of things they will encounter in the field? Hey, students! Take my seminar, do these readings, follow steps A through Q, and presto, you are prepared for ethnography!

TIMOTHY [shaking his head slowly]: No, I don't even think that's what's happening. I mean, it would be great if there were *more* opportunities for students to get a kind of practical, hands-on training. Not as a way of providing a formula, and not as a way of completely preparing them in some kind of ironclad sense, but in order to sensitize them to the kinds of enduring tensions they are likely to encounter.

KAREN: Right, a kind of condensed "natural history" of the ethnographic research process. And I agree with both of you, really. I do think, Piers, that what's been happening lately, in anthropology training at least, is that we've become engrossed with meta-theoretical discussions about ethnography, and less concerned, or less able to be innocently concerned, with the conduct of ethnographic field research itself. And so, you do get courses on ethnography now where the discussion centers on the colonial legacies of ethnography and the legitimacy of the method itself, but without any observation exercises that would allow students to experience something of the method before they do fieldwork for their dissertation projects. Ironic for a method and discipline that place so much value on the experience-near!

TIMOTHY: I think it signals the conflicted place that anthropology finds itself in.

PIERS: It seems actual methods classes are now more likely to be taught outside of the discipline of anthropology, in places like sociology and even political science!

TIMOTHY: I think that's accurate. In my political science graduate seminars on political ethnography, both at The New School and at the University of Massachusetts Amherst, a significant proportion of the students come from anthropology and sociology departments.

KAREN: Yes, I think there needs to be a balance, really, in any pedagogy about ethnography. It's absolutely important to convey the conflicted history and the theoretical concerns about ethnography, and it's also important to make sure that students have some experience of what it is to do immersive research. But it's also important to acknowledge—and I think this is your point, Piers—that there's no substitute for the actual conduct of ethnography itself and that much is often learned in the first full-bodied ethnographic research project that one undertakes, most often as a Ph.D. candidate.

TIMOTHY: It really is a central paradox of how ethnography is actually taught and reproduced, this sink-or-swim approach to training. Years of graduate coursework prepare students theoretically and conceptually for navigating the central questions of a discipline, but the actual *doing* of the ethnography is regarded as something of a make-or-break ritual, a coming-of-age, a trial by fire in which the researcher either *is* or *is not* successfully metamorphosed into an ethnographer.

KAREN: And in addition to the danger of failing to attain the coveted status of "ethnographer" in that trial by fire, there's always an opposite danger, so well captured by Mischa Berlinski's Martiya van der Leun in his lovely novel, *Fieldwork*.[2]

PIERS: Who?

KAREN: Martiya van der Leun. She's a fictionalized anthropology Ph.D. student at Berkeley who travels to Northern Thailand to do research on animist beliefs amongst the highland peoples there. She ends up becoming so immersed in her research world that she murders one of the American Christian missionaries who is trying to persuade her research subjects that they can overcome the demonic spirits that control their lives by converting to Christianity.

TIMOTHY: Ah, yes, she "goes native."

KAREN: Well, that's a really racialized and colonialist catch phrase—"going native." But, yes, the point is that she loses all perspective as a researcher. In essence, she gives up her positionality as a researcher.

TIMOTHY: In addition to the traditional trial-by-fire approach to fieldwork, with its attendant dangers of not quite being immersed enough and being overly immersed, there's yet another irony in how ethnography is taught and reproduced.

KAREN: What's that?

TIMOTHY: There's no time like graduate school for the kind of headlong, complete immersion required by an ethnographic project. Post-Ph.D. fieldwork—the increasingly rare one-year sabbatical notwithstanding—tends to be less prolonged, less extensive, and more amenable to the rhythms of a professionalized academic life, not to mention the constraints of non-academic adulthood. Thus, the paradox that it's one's first experience of extended ethnographic fieldwork that ends up being the most formative in its consequences for one's sense of self, reputation, and career.

PIERS: That's so true. But as you know, in the case of *The Reindeer People*, I spent twenty years off and on amongst the Eveny in Siberia. During this time, my personal life also continued. In fact, I dedicate an entire chapter, "Bringing My Family," to the experience of having my family live for a summer in one of the reindeer camps.

TIMOTHY: That's one of the reasons why I think you're an exception that proves this general rule, Piers.

PIERS: Yes, I was highly anxious about having my family there, but it was the only way I could continue to do immersive fieldwork and still be a part of their lives. More importantly, it represented a critically important opportunity to integrate two parts of my life. "My quest to understand the Eveny had taken me away from home for months at a time, year after year, and I felt that my family would be less likely to resent these people if they had lived with them.... Bringing together people from two separate parts of one's life also involved another kind of risk. Would the herders and my family like each other? Would they judge each other by inappropriate standards? How would I keep my family from becoming anxious or unhappy, and showing me up in a bad light? How would their more direct behavior find common ground with Eveny reserve, and how might this affect my future research? Having studied the lives of these people who opened up their homes to me, I would now have my own intimate life scrutinized, under very demanding conditions. Not only might my family reveal aspects of me that I may have wished to conceal, they would also see through any persona I might have developed in front of the herders. Perhaps I was even more concerned with the effect on our hosts than on my family. On this landscape, even the smallest group of helpless outsiders would put a strain on the resources of a camp; I could always reason with the family later."[3]

KAREN: It really is exemplary, Piers, what you did and how much of it you offer up to the reader, implicitly bringing in yet another set of eyes to watch you not only as an ethnographer, and not only as a father and a partner, but also as an ethnographer, father, and partner all at once! There is a lot of vulnerability in that chapter.

PIERS: I really didn't see a choice, Karen. Rather than give up ethnographic field-work or give up my family, I decided to try to integrate the two as much as possible, and to make that integration a further source of reflection in the finished ethnography itself.

KAREN: You learned all kinds of things, both about the Eveny and about your own family, that you couldn't and wouldn't have learned otherwise.

TIMOTHY: A contrarian might ask, why is it laudable? Why is it necessarily better to bring one's family to the field, much less to dedicate an entire chapter in your finished ethnography to that experience? But to me, those worries harken back to a fantastical mindset in which the ethnographer tries to be as unobtrusive and invisible as possible.

PIERS [chuckling]: An account, you could even say, enabled by an invisibility potion?

KAREN [laughing too]: Ha ha, good one, Piers! Way to stay on topic!

TIMOTHY [still deep in thought, as if the interruption hadn't occurred]: I'm not suggesting that all ethnographers should incorporate their intimate lives to this degree, but Piers shows that it can add immensely to the overall finished ethnography. And where one's so-called personal life is an unavoidable, obvi-ous reality of the fieldwork, I think it does often add to the persuasiveness of an ethnography for the researcher to make that a source of analytic reflection. It's not something I did very well in *Every Twelve Seconds*, but in retrospect I wonder how the book would have been different if I had included reflections on how my family experienced the research I was doing. I remember many days when I'd get home from a long day on the kill floor and my two daugh-ters, then six and two years old, would recoil in horror from the way I looked and smelled. How might reflecting on that have added to or complicated the book's analysis of distance and compartmentalization?

KAREN: You're not alone, Timothy. I would say it's a rare ethnography that even attempts this. Much of what we know about the intimate material and affective economies that provide the context for research comes from whatever fragments we can glean from book dedications and prefaces. In my case, for example, it was highly germane that my husband, Jeff, was a member of the investment-banking world I was studying. He'd often tell his colleagues, "Karen's studying us." And yet he makes an appearance only briefly in the preface. Jim Scott also writes only very briefly in *Weapons of the Weak* about having his family with him in the Malay village, although their perspectives certainly provided insights that he wouldn't have arrived at otherwise.

TIMOTHY: Yes, a careful reader of ethnography can discern traces of the autobi-ographical and the intimate and match them to various aspects of the research process—decisions made about where to do research, access questions in the field, whom one ends up spending time with in the field. The power of the autobiographical and the personal holds for all research methods, I think, but because ethnography involves such an intense degree of immersion, it becomes more visible, more unavoidable, than in other kinds of research.

KAREN: And attempts to erase the autobiographical and intimate contexts for research is a bit like forcing those parts of your life to swallow the invisibility potion, isn't it?

PIERS: Yes! And in *The Reindeer People* I wagered the opposite: why not draw on those parts of my life as a source of analysis?

[Karen and Timothy nod sympathetically.]

KAREN: But that's so counter to how we are implicitly socialized to think about rigor and objectivity in research and what it means to produce "valid" knowledge.

PIERS: It sure is.

KAREN: You know, I'm beginning to think this is a really useful way to proceed with the conversation during our walk.

PIERS: Talking about family?

KAREN: Not just family, but the actual practice and conduct of ethnography. Putting our heads together and drawing from our own experiences to craft a "natural history" of ethnographic fieldwork might bring us more clarity on what to do about the invisibility potion.

PIERS: That would certainly get us away from some of those important but quite abstract discussions we were having earlier in the barn. I like it.

TIMOTHY: Let's do it!

PIERS: So what are the stages in this natural history we're crafting?

KAREN: I don't think there's any series of clear, numbered steps that *every* ethnography takes. I tend to think of ethnography as unique amongst the family of methods precisely because it defies neat, linear "how-to" formulas.

TIMOTHY: I certainly agree. But I do think it's still possible to talk about a common lifecycle to most ethnographic projects. Laying it out that way might be a bit stylized, but it doesn't preclude the possibility of some stages overlapping with others, or even of a return to earlier stages and a skipping ahead to later stages.

KAREN: OK, I can go with that. So what are some of the stages, do you think?

TIMOTHY: Well, just speaking off the top of my head, I would say the major stages in an ethnographic life cycle, a kind of stylized natural history of an ethnography, if you will, include something like the following: negotiating a research question; defining "the field"; reflecting on the project's ethical considerations and gaining Institutional Review Board (IRB) or other ethics committee approval; gaining access; building relationships; navigating the field and dealing with improvisation, serendipity, and ambiguity; writing fieldnotes; and leaving the field.

PIERS [playfully]: Wow, Professor Timothy, you just rattled that off like you're giving a memorized lecture.

TIMOTHY [making a mock bow]: Thank you, Professor Piers, thank you. I actually do have it memorized because it forms the basis for a lecture entitled "Ethnography and Praxis" that I give in my graduate seminars.

KAREN: Listing the stages that way makes it sound like some sort of linear process. But you don't move from stage one to stage two to stage three, never looking back, do you?

TIMOTHY: Of course not. But, as a stylized arc, I think it's a pretty accurate reflection of the general process most ethnographers go through.

KAREN [playfully]: Well, Professor, I'd love to hear you walk us through each of the stages.

PIERS [laughing]: Yeah, me too, Professor.

TIMOTHY [incredulous]: Seriously? It seems a little elementary, and I feel ridiculous talking about it in the company of such accomplished ethnographers.

KAREN: Now, now. Don't be shy. It'll be fun.

TIMOTHY: OK, fine. But please jump in at any time with disagreements or clarifications.

PIERS: Of course!

TIMOTHY [taking a deep breath, then speaking in a playful, mock-lecture tone]: Well, students, thank you for signing up for this lecture series on ethnography. In last week's class, we talked about the ontological and epistemological foundations of ethnography. We distinguished method from methodology and talked about ethnography as a method that relates differently to the methodologies of interpretivism and positivism. We talked about how the method of ethnography can be used within a positivist methodological framework, albeit not without generating significant tensions that create a perceived need to "harness" ethnography to meet the demands of positivism so that it can be made to yield socially valid knowledge according to positivist standards. We also talked about the method of ethnography as it is used within an interpretivist methodology and identified several key areas of synergy between ethnography as a method and interpretivism as a methodology. These synergies included a socially constructivist approach to questions of truth and critical reflexivity about questions of power and positionality.

KAREN [still playfully]: That was a very helpful synopsis, Professor, especially since I skipped class for my interview with Goldman Sachs!

TIMOTHY [playing along]: You are most welcome. Please review it carefully as it is sure to be on the next exam.

PIERS [also playing along]: And what, dear Professor, will we be talking about today?

TIMOTHY: I'm so glad you asked. Today, we'll be talking about the praxis of ethnography, descending from the high altitudes of ontology and epistemology. And when it comes to practice and conduct, what better place to start than with the negotiation of the research question itself? We often talk about all research methods as if the research question were already in place, and yet it's one of the most important parts of the research process, and probably the one that's most difficult to think about in any systematic way.

PIERS: Where do good research questions come from?

TIMOTHY: Exactly.

KAREN [contemplative]: You are completely right. Most methods courses teach students how to *answer* a research question but not how to arrive at one. But that implicit sequencing doesn't account for the way different methods make some questions thinkable, and others not. And we need to ask: where do great ideas come from? What hones instincts for a good research question? We need to spend more time and emphasis in graduate school, and in academic life more generally, cultivating good questions and the qualities of mind—playfulness, imagination, omnivorous reading habits that take us far outside of our academic disciplines, and, indeed, out of academia altogether—

TIMOTHY [interrupting]: Reading habits that include poetry and fiction!

KAREN: Absolutely. We need to cultivate these qualities of mind, and we especially need to cultivate the practice of going through our everyday lives with an ethnographic sensibility. That's what's most likely to maximize our chances of coming across a good research question.[4]

TIMOTHY: I really like your list, Karen. Playfulness, imagination, wide reading, living life ethnographically.... I don't think they guarantee a good research question, but they certainly make one more likely.

PIERS: It was sad to me, going through graduate school and looking at my colleagues once I took a university position, how many of the people around me just lifted their research questions straight out of someone else's research program, out of the literature, or from what the government or some other funder was interested in.

TIMOTHY: I do think the literature is important.

PIERS: It's important as a springboard, but it more often serves as a straightjacket.

KAREN: Yes, it's true. So many of the most compelling ethnographies get started by accident, as it were, rather than solely through a studied approach to some faceless "literature."

TIMOTHY: By accident?

KAREN: Sure, or you could say by serendipity. Or you could say by the close observation of everyday life.

PIERS: Or you could say by a spark of chance that ignites the highly combustible combination of those things.

TIMOTHY: Meaning?

KAREN: Well, take Loïc's book on boxing, for example. The whole preface to that book is basically a hymn to the power of serendipity combined with the power of observation. Here's this French graduate student, living at the southern edge of the University of Chicago, and he's seeing, right in front of his face, the border that exists between the university and the rest of the city. He's seeing the private police force that works for the university, and the alarm boxes spaced every fifty yards, and the radical shift in basic infrastructural provisions that occur when you move across the line demarcating the university from the black neighborhood of Woodlawn. Now, most graduate students—the vast majority, even in anthropology and sociology—in that situation would fail to notice the importance of that observation. They would turn their backs on the poorer neighborhoods to the south. Not Loïc. The borders make him itch. To scratch that itch, he has to cross them, to explore them.

TIMOTHY: The ethnographic impulse.

KAREN: So here's this guy who grew up in a middle-class family in a small village in southern France, and he's at the University of Chicago crossing this border from his wealthy university to the poor neighborhood immediately next to it. And what does he find, with the help of another French friend who practices judo? He finds a boxing gym. It's full of black men, training. And what does he do? He joins the gym. So the fieldsite ends up being a matter of accident.[5]

PIERS: Yes, but enabled by curiosity.

TIMOTHY: Ethnographic gold. I'm reminded of the story of the origins of *The Polish Peasant*, the book that conventional histories of sociology credit with marking the beginning of ethnography in their discipline. Apparently, this book got its start when one of its authors, William Thomas, was very nearly physically hit by a pile of garbage that was being thrown out as he walked by. It turns out that this "garbage" was a bundle of letters written in Polish. These letters provided a window into the lives of Polish immigrants and their families that became the basis of *The Polish Peasant*.[6]

PIERS: Ha! I wonder how many thousands of academics would have dodged the "garbage" without ever looking into it, so to speak.

KAREN: Exactly. If you look under the surface of some of the greatest ethnographies out there, a deep, incorrigible, exploratory spirit motivates them. Even in the case of my own research on Wall Street, it was curiosity about the investment bank recruitment fairs at Princeton that led me to my research questions about how this world works and why there is such a superhighway between elite universities like Princeton and Wall Street.

TIMOTHY: Yes, I think that's right. You can see something of that spirit in your work too, Piers. It wasn't just intellectual or theoretical concerns that motivated you to spend entire seasons crossing the tundra in frigid conditions, right? And you see it as well in Anna's work on mushrooms and Mitch's work on booksellers in Greenwich Village.

KAREN: And you could certainly say it about your work on the slaughterhouse, Timothy.

TIMOTHY: Yes, that was an interest in crossing a different kind of border, a species border!

PIERS: Taken to an extreme, this sense of curiosity can be mistaken for voyeurism, as we just discussed with the larger group.

TIMOTHY: True. Another way of looking at Thomas's use of the letters is that he ended up snooping through other people's garbage to discover highly personal details about their lives.

PIERS: Sometimes ethnographers get charged as voyeurs, especially when racial and class boundaries are crossed in serious ways. That certainly happened with Loïc's book, for example. But taken to their logical extreme, those charges are also problematic. They suggest that no outsider ever has legitimacy when crossing a border to immerse in something other than their own pre-existing world.

KAREN: Yes, it's all in how it's done. So the question becomes, how do you teach that kind of spirit, that kind of sensibility to students.

PIERS: Well, I don't think you can actually teach it. All you can do is create an environment in which students who are already inclined to it can be nurtured, nourished, and encouraged to take risks.

TIMOTHY: That is so opposite the environment of a lot of graduate education in the social sciences, which produces a slow anesthetization through inducing timidity and safety.

KAREN: What does that look like, in practice?

PIERS: It's so hard to say, because every student is so different. I do know, though, that in addition to flourishing in conjunction with this kind of inquisitive and boundary-crossing spirit, ethnography also has another particular kind of relationship with the negotiation of a research question.

TIMOTHY: What's that?

PIERS: Well, I think that, with ethnography in particular, the research question is iterative, meaning it is never decided once and for all ex ante, but is constantly subject to change, even to radical revision, during the course of fieldwork.

TIMOTHY: Well, couldn't you say that about most methods?

KAREN: Maybe you could, but with ethnography the iterative nature of the research question is visible and foregrounded in a way that it's not in other methods.

And I would go further and say that ethnography celebrates the iterative nature of the research question where other methods actively suppress it, claiming that the question must precede the data, and that if the data reshape the question, then the research process is flawed.

TIMOTHY: Yes, I suppose you could think here of the move to encourage people to deposit their hypotheses online before they carry out their research.

KAREN: Doesn't that fly in the face of what Paul Rock calls "the prime ethnographic maxim"—that you can't know what you're exploring until it's been explored?[7]

TIMOTHY: Absolutely. But like everything we've been talking about, it can also be taken too far. There does have to be a balance between the field shaping the question and the ethnographer coming in with a set of interests, a set of questions, some of which might indeed be derived from her discipline or her reading of the literature.

PIERS: In fact, we heard a vociferous debate earlier between Mitch and Loïc about this tension between letting the field decide the research question and coming in with a set of predetermined theoretical interests.

KAREN: And as Mitch said in relation to the dilemmas inherent in all ethnographic work, rather than prescribing a single correct approach, it might be more productive to acknowledge a range of approaches, within ethnography, to negotiating and renegotiating the research question. At one end is "we cannot know what is being explored until it has been explored." From this perspective, research proposals are hardly the deductive exercise they are trumped up to be. They are really more an enabling fiction that is based on a hunch, or an instinct, or a desire to cross a particular boundary. And at the other end, where we might locate someone like political scientist David Laitin, ethnography is fit into a research design in a very tight and controlled way to address particular modes of data-gathering for pre-existing hypotheses that are not going to be altered and that have been derived from the literature in some way.[8]

TIMOTHY: Yes, and different disciplines have different tolerances for ambiguity or flexibility in the research question. As evidenced by Mitch and Loïc's argument, there can be strong disagreement even within the same discipline about this.

KAREN: True, but I think we can agree that ethnography tends to demand, as a method, more flexibility in the question.

PIERS: You could really go a step further and say that in good ethnographies, the research question of necessity changes as fieldwork is conducted. That it's a poor ethnography if the research question is not altered in any way as a result of the research process.

TIMOTHY: That makes ethnography a poor method for those who must define their research question in advance of data collection; or for those who must deposit their hypotheses online so that they can't be "fudged" later by the research findings.

KAREN: Well, that's one reason, I think, that folks like David Laitin talk about the need to discipline ethnography and to harness it within a positivist research paradigm if it's ever to produce scientifically valid knowledge.[9]

TIMOTHY: It doesn't help at all that many ethnographies are written as though the researcher had known from the start what the research question would be. It's as if their entire project has swallowed not only an invisibility potion, but also an amnesiac potion. This is why I am a big advocate of leaving up as much of the scaffolding in the finished ethnography as possible, to avoid this kind of immaculate conception fantasy of how the research question evolves.

KAREN: Yes, the virgin birth. This idea that research questions fall from the night sky, wrapped in little bundles dropped by storks.

TIMOTHY: I still think much more needs to be done to encourage students to cultivate the kinds of sensibilities that make original and exciting research questions more likely. As you said earlier, Karen, questions and methods co-constitute each other, and approaching every facet of one's life with an ethnographic sensibility means an openness to, a delight even, in being surprised. And surprise, in turn, often births exciting and generative questions.

PIERS: Not just surprise, but an entire range of emotions, including anger at injustice.

TIMOTHY: Yes. One of my favorite seminars in graduate school was taught by Jim Scott and Arun Agrawal and titled "Creativity and Method in Comparative Politics." Rather than assigning books on the philosophy of science or "how-to" methods articles, we read classic works in and outside of the social sciences, including Leo Tolstoy's *War and Peace* and Rachel Carson's *Silent Spring.* We asked how the author might have come up with the idea for their book in the first place. A kind of reverse engineering of the creative process that often pointed to surprise, wonder, and anger as starting points for truly original work.

KAREN: A nice idea!

[Piers nods.]

TIMOTHY [resuming mock tone of a lecturer]: So, students, I think we've now discussed quite a bit about the importance of making space for the negotiation of the research question, and about how, in ethnography, the research question is open to renegotiation in iterative conversation with the fieldwork experience itself. Once an initial research question has been negotiated, the next step in our stylized natural history of ethnography is what we might call "defining the field."

KAREN [laughing]: *Defining* the field. It sounds so, well, definite.

TIMOTHY: Yes, as I've said, this is a stylized representation of a typical ethnographic research process. I think we can only proceed with this natural history exercise with the big caveat that there is a lot of give and take in the actual research process itself.

PIERS: So true.

TIMOTHY: But with that caveat in mind, I do think it useful to talk about how we come to bound the field, both in time and space.

PIERS: There's so much variation in research projects that perhaps it's more useful to look at some actual examples of how researchers came to define their fieldsite.

KAREN: That's a great idea. Piers, you and I are quite similar in this respect.

TIMOTHY: Similar? Piers was in Siberia studying nomadic people and you were in lower Manhattan studying investment bankers!

KAREN: True, but both of us conducted ethnographic fieldwork that was multi-sited rather than being bound to and by a single location. For you, Piers, it was moving across reindeer camps, especially between camps seven and ten. For me, it was moving between lower Manhattan investment banks. It's quite striking to compare the maps we produce of our fieldsites. The scale of our maps is so vastly different: yours would be about 22 miles per inch, while mine is 0.75 miles per inch, and yet they both convey how much movement was involved in our research.[10]

TIMOTHY: Yes, I've actually given a lot of time and thought to comparing the maps produced by the different ethnographers in our gathering.

PIERS: Why?

TIMOTHY: I love maps! And maps, when presented/reproduced in ethnographies, provide a nice shorthand for how the ethnographer is bounding her fieldsite.

KAREN: So, what did you learn by comparing the maps of the people gathered for the trial?

TIMOTHY: One of the most striking observations is the enormous variation in the scales of the maps. Séverine's map covers the entire globe and shows the primary site of her fieldwork along with secondary sites and sites where she had worked before starting on her research.[11] Piers's map, which ranges across hundreds of square miles of land, also has an enormous scale.[12]

The smallest scale, perhaps, is my map, which is of the division of labor and space on the kill floor of an industrialized slaughterhouse that is perhaps only a few hundred yards wide.[13] Close to this kind of small scale is Mitch's map, which is of a few city blocks in Greenwich Village. What's interesting in Mitch's map is that he populates it with photographs of the men and women whom he studied, placing them on the map in the approximate places where they set up their book-vending tables. He also includes photographs of people who work for the Business Improvement District and influence much of the city's policies and policing of public space.[14]

Jim's map is of the households in the village of Sedaka, where he conducted his fieldwork, showing their distribution along a major footpath that lies off a surfaced road, along with the locations of their rice fields, palm and fruit trees, and the village coffee shops and sundry stores.[15] And Anna's map, from *In the Realm of the Diamond Queen*, a book based on her earlier ethnography in Kalimantan, Indonesia, shows the movement of swidden agriculture fields for one family unit across a twenty-eight-year time period in the village of Rajang. Her map is not only of distribution in space, but also of movement across the passage of time.[16] What's more, she also includes a map of the spiritual world drawn by Induan Hiling, the Diamond Queen after whom her book is named.[17]

PIERS: Yes, like Anna, I also have maps not just of the physical world, but also of the spiritual worlds depicted on mummies of reindeer herders; and I have maps of the distribution of wild and domesticated reindeer in Russia, as well as a map that shows how a reindeer herd moves in response to perceived danger.[18]

KAREN: Scale is not the only way to parse these maps. In Piers's and Anna's cases, we have the difference between maps of material, empirical reality and cosmological realities. Their fieldwork was multi-sited not just in a physical sense, but also in the sense of crossing between material and spiritual worlds.

PIERS: And species worlds!

TIMOTHY: Yes, and then we have incredibly detailed maps of very small spaces, such as my map of the kill floor. Because I worked in three different jobs on the kill floor, I too would describe my ethnography as multi-sited.

PIERS: How so?

TIMOTHY: Well, insofar as I moved between very different locations and jobs on the kill floor, my fieldwork could be compared to the fieldwork you did, Piers, in following nomadic reindeer herders, or that Karen did in researching different investment banks in downtown Manhattan.

PIERS: I wonder if this might not apply to the other ethnographies we've been discussing as well, so that the question is not whether an ethnography is multi-sited, but rather *how* it is multi-sited. Even the smallest and most geographically contained of fieldsites, as Timothy's was, contains multiple locations and vantage points within them.

KAREN: It definitely applies. Take Jim's work in Sedaka, for example. At first glance, you might say his ethnography was single-sited rather than multi-sited, because he immersed himself in a single village in Malaysia.

PIERS: Right. He might have compared a rice farming village in Malaysia, such as Sedaka, with a rice farming village just over the border in Southern Thailand.

KAREN: But on closer examination, we learn that Jim's work was also multi-sited in that a central crux of his argument revolves around careful, painstaking attention to what the poorer people in Sedaka did in and outside the presence of the rich in the village, and vice versa. So you could say, in fact, that, analytically speaking, Jim conducted fieldwork in at least four different sites, all within Sedaka!

TIMOTHY: Yes, that's exactly what I was getting at. There's a parallel there with my three sites: liver hanging, which put me at a maximal distance from the killing on the kill floor; chute work, which put me at a minimal distance to it; and quality control work, which made me a player in the slaughterhouse's power hierarchies. I used the contrasts to arrive at some of my central conclusions about how concealment and visibility work in concert on the kill floor of the slaughterhouse. We might even say that there is a similar dynamic at work even in very character-driven research of the kind that we get in Mitch and Katherine's work.

It's telling, for instance, that my map of the kill floor locates anonymous workers according to their spatial location in a division of labor, whereas Mitch has photographs of actual people, their names, and where they are located in a small radius around Sixth Avenue and Greenwich Avenue in Manhattan. I use roles and their spatial and labor divisions as my frame, whereas Mitch uses actual people as his. And yet even with Mitch's work, it is possible to talk about a multi-sited ethnography insofar as he utilizes what he calls an extended-place method that gets at structures of power by interviewing officials in the Business Improvement District and a similarly situated, although racially different, family of Christmas tree vendors. So although Mitch's map is character-driven, it also illustrates the structures of power that shape the social situations he studies. Similarly, Katherine conducts research in a single Mumbai slum, and yet she, too, might be said to have a multi-sited study insofar as it is the fault lines of conflicts amongst families and generations in that slum that drive her narrative in *Behind the Beautiful Forevers.*

KAREN: So is there really no such thing as a single-sited study?

TIMOTHY: I would say that when we pay close attention to how settings are defined in ethnographic work, all studies reveal themselves to be multi-sited, even to researchers who initially imagine and define their fieldsite as a single site.

PIERS: Some studies are designed very explicitly to be *multi* in a comparative sense. We would here think of Clarissa Hayward's ethnography, *De-Facing Power*, which explicitly compares two elementary schools in Connecticut, one in an affluent suburb and one in an impoverished urban area.[19] Then there are other studies, which, particularly at the outset, may understand their sites to be more or less singular or unitary. I imagine Jim thought of his research in this way when he settled into Sedaka, or that you, Timothy, thought of your research in this way when you gained access to the kill floor of a single slaughterhouse.

KAREN: So, for Jim, it becomes very apparent that the poor and the rich are giving him very different accounts of themselves and each other depending on who is around, or that for Timothy it becomes unavoidably obvious how working in the cooler produces a vastly different experience of killing than working in the chutes or as a quality control worker.

TIMOTHY: Well said. But so far we have been talking more or less about how we bound our fieldsites in space. There is also another important dimension—time.

KAREN: Yes, most ethnographies focus primarily on the present while, perhaps, offering some historical context.

TIMOTHY: But then there are other ethnographies in which the past or a past event plays a central role. An exemplary ethnography in this regard is Diane Vaughan's study of the Challenger explosion, through which she develops a method that she calls historical ethnography.[20]

KAREN: Vaughan's work is an important caution for ethnographers to avoid the fallacy of the ethnographic present, the mistake of taking whatever one encounters in the field and universalizing it across all time periods, past and present.[21]

PIERS: Indeed. My own work, for example, took place just at the cusp of, and continued well beyond, the dissolution of the Soviet Union. Falling into the trap of the ethnographic present would have been almost impossible for me because of those seismic changes in the macro power structures surrounding the Eveny reindeer herders.

TIMOTHY: These questions about time are also related, albeit on a different scale, to the importance of paying attention to the date, time, and duration of the ethnographer's fieldwork. If you are doing research on agricultural communities, for example, but you only conduct your fieldwork during the summer months when you don't have academic obligations, you are going to get a very different understanding of your fieldsite than if you also include fieldwork that spans winter and fall.

And in other contexts, temporalities other than seasons might be more important. If you are conducting research on the Department of Motor Vehicles, for example, but you only do fieldwork on Monday mornings because that is what your schedule allows for, you are going to get a very different sense of what happens than if you were also there on Friday afternoons or Wednesdays at noon. Similarly, if you only spend thirty minutes in the waiting room each time you visit, you'll develop a very different sense of the rhythms of the day than if you spend four hours on site. Persuasive ethnographies tell their readers not only how the fieldsite was defined, but also about the date, time, and duration of the researcher's access and how this might matter to the researcher's interpretations.[22]

PIERS: That's part of the scaffolding that we were talking about earlier.

TIMOTHY: Before we move on to the next phase in our stylized natural history of ethnography, I think we should also talk about how, in practical terms, ethnographers come to choose their fieldsites in the first place.

KAREN [laughing]: I heard a rumor from somewhere that Jim chose Sedaka because he happened to be traveling through there at sunset and the mountain directly to the south was beautiful.

PIERS: Now that's some serious case-selection logic!

TIMOTHY [laughing]: That's funny, but not entirely true. Jim also had other criteria. For example, he chose to do his fieldwork in the Muda region of Malaysia in part because peasants there were relatively well off compared to others on the peninsula.

PIERS: Wait, doesn't that make it less likely that he would find open class conflict?

TIMOTHY: Exactly! Jim wanted to find a hard case for class conflict. If there was conflict in the Muda region, he reasoned, then it would also be likely to exist in places where peasants were much worse off.

KAREN: But what about his selection of the village of Sedaka specifically?

TIMOTHY: That was informed, in part, by the fact that an earlier researcher had lived there, in the early 1970s, providing him with time-series information on the village.

PIERS: So the sunset and beautiful mountain case-selection logic is just a myth?

TIMOTHY: No, he writes that the sunset and the mountain view were also important. The point, I think, is that, at least for Jim, fieldsite selection involved systematic criteria, like finding a hard rather than an easy case, and favoring a place where earlier research allowed him to make comparisons across time. But within those criteria, serendipitous factors like sunsets and mountain views also mattered.[23]

KAREN: What about you, Timothy? How did you end up in that particular slaughterhouse in Omaha? A nice sunset perhaps?

TIMOTHY: Ha. No sunsets or mountain views inside a slaughterhouse, Karen! My fieldsite selection also combined systematic criteria with serendipity. "Once I had decided on industrialized slaughterhouses as a research site, I began by ruling out poultry slaughterhouses because the physical uniformity of chickens allows for an automated killing process in which humans are largely absent. This left either hog or cattle slaughterhouses as possible research sites. My next step was to compile data from the Food Safety Inspection Service of the United States Department of Agriculture (USDA), which publishes a directory of all federally inspected slaughterhouses in the United States. Since the focus of my study was on large-scale industrialized slaughterhouses, I limited my search to those employing five hundred workers or more.

"Using these data, I mapped the geographic location of each of these slaughterhouses and isolated specific areas where they are clustered. Because no guarantee existed that I could gain access to a particular slaughterhouse (or to any slaughterhouse at all, for that matter), I sought a location with a number of slaughterhouses within a small geographic area. Additionally, given my interest in the production of social invisibility—in how the slaughterhouse is constructed as a place that is 'no place'—I wanted to find a slaughterhouse in an urban location.... Slaughterhouses are socially invisible, it could be argued, because they have for the most part moved to rural locations out of the sight, sound, and smell of the vast majority of meat consumers. By choosing an urban or semi-urban location, I was able to examine some of the tensions and paradoxes that arise when the signs of an activity that is meant to be invisible are exhibited in plain sight.

"Filtering the USDA data on industrialized meat production plants employing five hundred or more persons through these criteria, I identified Omaha as a potentially fertile location for my field research.... Within the city limits of Omaha and Council Bluffs, Iowa (which lies just across the Missouri River), there are several industrialized slaughter and fabrication operations, employing more than six thousand workers.... In terms of density of slaughterhouses within and around a major urban area, Omaha appeared to be a location with exceptional promise."[24]

KAREN: That seems very deductive to me.

TIMOTHY: I don't think deductive is quite the right word, Karen. I would call it systematic. Deductive implies that there was a linear movement from theory to hypothesis to data. The final selection of my fieldsite was anything but linear. And yet, I agree that you could say I was very systematic in defining criteria for my fieldsite, from the type of animal killed, to the number of workers employed, to its rural or urban location.

PIERS: What is striking about the way both you and Jim decided on your fieldsites is the particular combination of a systematic approach with a decision that, at the end of the day, turned out to be equally reliant on improvisation and serendipity. I mean, as you write, Timothy, you really had no guarantee at all that you would get hired in any slaughterhouse, much less a particular one that you moved across the country in the hopes of getting into.

TIMOTHY: That so much of what happens in the field relies on serendipity, or what others might just call luck, doesn't change the fact that there are systematic preparations that can be made that make it more likely that this so-called luck will strike.[25]

KAREN: How do you teach new ethnographers to think about defining their fieldsites in ways sensitive to both systematicity and serendipity?

TIMOTHY: I often recommend "The Power of Example," a chapter in Bent Flyvbjerg's wonderful book *Making Social Science Matter*. There, he writes about using information-based case selection and thinking carefully about the work that one's case is likely to be able to do.[26]

KAREN: Say more.

TIMOTHY: Flyvbjerg divides all cases into two broad categories: randomly selected cases that purport to be representative and therefore generalizable to a larger population of cases; and information-based cases selected because of the researcher's sense of the kind of analytic work the case might do in relation to her questions.

PIERS: And most ethnographic research would consider a prospective field through an information-based case-selection strategy?

TIMOTHY: Yes. Ethnographic field sites are not typically chosen using a random-sampling strategy, but rather on the basis of specific information that is already known or suspected about the possible fieldsite.

KAREN: So what are the different kinds of analytic work that information-oriented cases can do?

TIMOTHY: There are what Flyvbjerg calls "extreme or deviant cases," which are unusually good or unusually bad cases of something, where "good" or "bad" is defined in relation to something of specific interest to the researcher. In-depth exploration of these kinds of extreme or deviant cases is especially good at illuminating relationships, dynamics, and processes that might also be operative in less visible ways in other, less extreme cases. One example might be Shamus Khan's selection of St. Paul's School as an extreme case of the stratification of wealth and privilege in high school education.

KAREN: That's his book *Privilege*, right? An excellent book and another example of studying up.[27]

TIMOTHY: Indeed. And then there are what Flyvbjerg calls "maximum variation cases," which, as the name suggests, are two or more cases that differ in some maximal way along one dimension of interest. Researchers who want to conduct comparative ethnographies sometimes use this type of strategy. One of the students in my Political Ethnography graduate seminar, for example, conducted fieldwork on prenatal classes in two hospitals in Brooklyn: one hospital served largely lower-income communities of color, while the other served largely white, affluent New Yorkers. The student found that both the pedagogical style and the messaging around parental responsibility were radically different in the two hospitals.[28]

PIERS: *De-Facing Power*, the book by Clarissa Hayward we discussed earlier, would be another example of defining the field through maximum variation.

TIMOTHY: Right. "Critical cases," another kind of information-based case, speak to particular questions or problems in ways that strategically allow logical deductions to be made about other kinds of cases. Flyvbjerg notes that one way to think about critical cases is to ask most and least likely questions. Where are you most and least likely to find X? If you were interested in the ubiquity of negative disciplining strategies in public schools, for example, you might seek out a place where you would think it least likely to find those strategies at work, as does Clarissa Hayward when she conducts fieldwork in a wealthy, privileged, suburban public elementary school in Connecticut. Or, if you were interested in the possibility of democracy, for example, you might ask where democracy seems most likely to be possible. If you could show that even there, democratic processes are not followed and democratic values are discarded, then you might argue that the case demonstrates how much less likely it is to find democracy in other settings.

KAREN: Wait, but didn't you just say Clarissa Hayward's cases were maximum variation cases?

TIMOTHY: Yes, I did. A single case can do more than one kind of work. The way Hayward defined her fieldsites in her study of disciplinary power in two public schools utilized a logic of maximum variation *and* a critical case logic.

Or, to take my work as another example, we could think of the modern industrialized slaughterhouse as a kind of extreme or deviant case of everyday, or normalized, violence. Where else does deliberate mass killing occur on the scale of billions per year? Thinking of the slaughterhouse as an extreme case allows us to demonstrate the potential ubiquity of violence in our society. At the same time, the slaughterhouse also presents us with a kind of "least likely" critical case. What I found on the kill floor, the physical site where we would least expect violence to be hidden from the participants in that violence, is that the compartmentalization of space and labor continue to hide the violence, even from those who directly participate in it. So if violence is hidden here, where it is least likely to be hidden, we have good reasons to strongly suspect that this violence will also be hidden in other areas of society as well.

And finally, my movement through different jobs and locations in the slaughterhouse also demonstrates what serendipitous unfolding can achieve. In my first job on the kill floor, I was located a maximum distance from the place of killing, hanging livers. In my next job, I was put at a minimal distance to the site of killing, as a chute worker driving live animals into the kill box. And finally, in my third job, I became imbricated in the vertical hierarchies of the plant, allowing me to observe and participate in relations between the United States Department of Agriculture meat inspectors and the kill floor managers. So, without knowing in advance that my research would unfold across these different sites, and despite it ostensibly being a "single" case, my research led me through a series of maximum variation cases, and that variety tells us a lot about how experiences of killing are processed by the participants depending on where they are located both physically and hierarchically in the kill floor's finely divided chains of labor.

In other words, my "single site" study generated cases of all three types—extreme, critical, and maximally variable.

PIERS: It sounds like where a fieldsite fits within Flyvbjerg's typology really depends quite centrally on how the ethnographer is thinking about the research problem.

TIMOTHY: I think here about Nelson Goodman's example of baggage at an airport. If we look at a big pile of luggage, Goodman asks, how do we decide which ones are most similar? A general person might sort the luggage by size, shape, and color. A baggage handler would say that the bags heading to the same destination are the ones that are the most similar. And a pilot might say that the bags that weigh the same are the ones that are the most similar.[29]

KAREN: So it's the research questions we ask and our prior ordering schemas that determine what kind of case something is.

TIMOTHY: That's it: there is no quality inherent to the case itself that renders it one or another kind.

PIERS: Are those all the kinds of cases?

TIMOTHY: No, Flyvbjerg also describes one final type of case, which he calls the "paradigmatic case." It's the kind of case that catches fire and takes on a metaphorical resonance that is capable of establishing entire new schools of thought. He offers two examples: Foucault's panopticon and Clifford Geertz's Balinese cockfight.[30]

PIERS: Well, we could really add a third, I think, and one drawn from our own ranks. At least in the social sciences, Jim's Sedaka has become something of a paradigmatic case in that it turned a lot of conventional theories about the nature of domination and resistance upside down. It's exactly that kind of case—one that opens up an entire area of study.

KAREN: I still sense a deep paradox here in the way we've been talking about defining the field.

TIMOTHY: What do you mean?

KAREN: On the one hand, we're talking about the different kinds of cases and analytic leverage that cases might be able to provide in very precise terms. On the other hand, we've spoken a lot about ethnography as a process of discovery, a process where the research question is constantly being renegotiated in response to what is encountered in the field. We've noted the ethnographic maxim that ethnographers can't know what there is to explore until after it's been explored. How does this tension get reconciled?

TIMOTHY: You know, that's such an excellent question, and such a difficult one. There is no formula to resolve this tension. As we were discussing with the larger group earlier, it's an inherent part of living "among wolves." As is so often the case with ethnography, we end up invoking experience, learning by doing, practice, and the feel of things.

KAREN: But isn't this a strike against ethnography in comparison with other methods which might be more clear-cut?

TIMOTHY: I don't think so. With any method, no matter how step-wise and linear it appears in the presentation, there is always an element of skill, of sensibility, that cannot be coded and that cannot be taught abstractly or even be made explicit linguistically. Drawing on Bourdieu, we might say that every method has a habitus.[31] Or, if you prefer Michael Polanyi, that every method draws extensively on an unspoken and in many ways unspeakable wellspring of tacit knowledge.[32] I do think, however, that ethnography is unique in the degree to which it underscores and calls attention to these dimensions of habitus and of tacit knowledge. For better or for worse, other methods have become much more adept at disguising, hiding, or driving underground the existence of their own tacit knowledges.

PIERS: Wow, that's a pretty radical claim, if you think about it.

TIMOTHY: In an interview Flyvbjerg conducted with Herbert Dreyfus, Dreyfus said to him, in essence, that you can't come up with rules for deciding in advance what makes something great. He gives the example of Cezanne as a paradigmatic modern painter and says that this judgment relies, ultimately, on intuition. Dreyfus is saying, in essence, that the most important research decisions—for example, how to define the boundaries of the field or determine the case in ethnographic research—depend ultimately on intuition. And he goes further and says that while public reasons can be offered for decisions made based on intuition, they won't be the real reasons.[33]

PIERS: There are a lot of places that I'd get in trouble for saying this, but I'll say it anyway. I happen to agree with Dreyfus.

KAREN: Really?

PIERS: Yes, but I think there's responsible intuition and then there's reckless intuition. I think responsible intuition requires all the due diligence the researcher can muster. It requires weeks in the library tracking down the location of every slaughterhouse in the United States that employs over 500 people, as in Timothy's case. It is not simply an abandonment of attempts to reach for cases that have utility as critical cases, or extreme cases, or maximum variation cases, as some versions of reckless intuition would have us believe. It's not: "Oh, I'm relying on intuition, so I don't need to justify how I've defined the boundaries of my field, and I don't need to think about what kind of work my case might be doing analytically. It's just all my intuition that's driving this, after all!"

TIMOTHY: I've had students who come to me with that attitude of reckless intuition. It's as if, in realizing that ethnography cannot be bound by any set of strict, step-wise rules, they swing wildly to the opposite end of the pendulum and become gods and goddesses of their own worlds.

KAREN: Yes, but that approach is ultimately doomed to fail. There is judgment, and there is evaluation. The judgment of the success of a case depends ultimately on evaluation by one's peers in the academic community, and also possibly on evaluation by the larger society.[34]

PIERS: Timothy, I like the distinctions Flyvbjerg makes between different kinds of cases, but I don't think it should be an absolute rule that one has to be able to locate their fieldsite within his typology. If I had applied it to the Eveny reindeer herders, for example, I might never have gone to Russia. Certainly, I could not have anticipated the collapse of the Soviet Union when I began formulating my plans for that research. So what I would say to the aspiring ethnographer is, Yes, go ahead and use Flyvbjerg's typology as a tool for thinking through how you define the field. But also realize that there is a lot that won't immediately fit, or that you can't and should not be able to make sense of. Learn to develop, hone, and trust a responsible intuition for what is likely to make a terrific case.

TIMOTHY: Well said!

KAREN: I'm reluctant to leave this lofty terrain of intuition and creativity, but perhaps we should move on to the next stage of our natural history.

TIMOTHY: Yes, and the next stage is...[mimics drumroll] ethics review committees, like the Institutional Review Board (IRB), and ethics!

KAREN [sighs]: Ah, the IRB and ethics. Or really, the IRB and *not*-ethics!

PIERS: What do you mean by that?

KAREN: I just mean that there's this bad tendency these days, at least in the social sciences, to equate review committees with ethics, as if the two were synonymous. In fact, they are not.[35]

PIERS: And why is this the next stage in our natural history?

TIMOTHY: The reason I put it here, at this stage, is because many states, including US federal policy, now require ethics committee approval before research that involves human subjects and is intended to produce systematic knowledge is conducted by anyone at a university or elsewhere.

PIERS: Anyone?

TIMOTHY: Anyone. Faculty, graduate students, sometimes even undergraduate students. The only exemption is for students conducting research for coursework when it is not intended to result in generalizable knowledge.

PIERS: I see. So once the research question has been negotiated, at least in a preliminary sense, and once the field has been defined, at least in a preliminary sense, then the next step would be to seek IRB approval for the proposed research?

TIMOTHY: Exactly. Technically speaking, IRB approval is required before any research begins at all, meaning before the ethnographer even accesses the field. Research Ethics Committee policy in the UK, in fact, as implemented on several campuses, prohibits researchers from doing any exploratory "legwork" prior to getting the research approved.[36]

PIERS: How does this square with the notion that in ethnography one doesn't know the field until one enters the field?

TIMOTHY: That's one of the big problems, Piers. Most IRB applications that I am aware of require the researcher to specify in advance the population he or she is going to be interacting with in the course of the research, what the nature of those interactions is going to be like, and even what kinds of questions the researcher is going to be asking. They also often require a written consent form to be signed by everyone the researcher interacts with. The form has to state the topic of the research, the expected benefits and harms of the research to the participants, and even the amount of time the interaction with the researcher is expected to take. All this disfavors ethnographic projects in at least two ways. One is what we've already discussed, again evoked in the ethnographic maxim that one cannot know what is being explored until it has been explored. Each of us can imagine how impossible it would have been, prior to any exposure to our fieldsites whatsoever, to specify in advance the populations with whom we would be speaking, for how long, on what exact topics. Many of us would not have even been able to specify a precise or exact research question, waiting to allow that to develop in the course of the fieldwork itself! Keep in mind that in a biomedical and experimental model of research design, which historically has served as the framework for IRB policies, researchers specify "populations" in advance of the study and then recruit from them, sampling for purposes of generalizability. But in ethnographic fieldwork, a large part of the research process—to translate into terminology not typically used by ethnographers—is about discovering who the relevant "populations" are and how they matter. It is not a question of sampling!

KAREN: Yes, I see what you mean. But I think we're getting a bit ahead of ourselves with this kind of critique. It's important to look at what the IRB is intended to do before we pick apart what it actually does. Let's remember that the IRB grew directly out of an ugly history of people being used, wittingly and unwittingly, in various research experiments and projects that ended up causing them significant harm. We can think here of the experiments performed by Nazi doctors on Jewish and other prisoners during the Second World War.

And, there have been plenty of problems here in the United States too! Perhaps most infamous is the US Public Health Service Study at Tuskegee University, in which a nearly all-white cadre of doctors and medical staff employed by the United States Public Health Service recruited approximately 400 black men with late-stage syphilis in Macon County, Alabama. They concealed their research purpose, which was to chart the trajectory of untreated syphilis. Promising the men medical treatment, the doctors gave them only aspirin and iron tonic. Additionally, the doctors recruited another 200 syphilis-free black men as "controls," giving them the same treatment. This study lasted for four decades, beginning in 1932. During these forty years, the doctors published results from their studies in prestigious medical journals while an untold number of the men passed their disease on to their partners and children before dying, some of them of causes related to untreated syphilis. The study ended only in 1972 after one of the investigators revealed the story to an Associated Press reporter. The resulting press generated public outrage. Subsequent Congressional hearings led to the crafting of federal regulations governing research involving "human subjects"—today's IRB policies.[37]

TIMOTHY: As you recount this history, Karen, I'm struck by how central a role race plays in it. I'm also struck by the absolute power of the researchers over their research "subjects."

PIERS: Yes, me too. But what's also interesting to me is that this history is centered in abusive practices in biomedical research, not social science research.

KAREN: Well, there are plenty of examples of abusive social science research as well. Perhaps the three most infamous, the ones that keep being invoked regarding the legal regulation of social science research, are Stanley Milgram's *Obedience to Authority* experiments, Phillip Zimbardo's Stanford Prison Experiment studies, and Laud Humphreys's studies of homosexual behavior in *Tearoom Trade*.[38]

PIERS: Well, again, I would note that Milgram's and Zimbardo's studies were conducted as controlled experiments within a laboratory setting. Only Humphreys's research qualifies as a type of fieldwork. So, again, we see the enormous influence of experimental research on regulations that end up impacting ethnographic and other non-experimental researchers.

TIMOTHY: And I would also say, drawing on a nuanced analysis made by Dvora Yanow and Peregrine Schwartz-Shea, that these three cases have taken on a kind of mythology of their own as representing the "bad boys" of unethical research in the social sciences.[39]

KAREN: The "bad boys?"

TIMOTHY: Yes, Yanow and Schwartz-Shea show how these three examples have become ciphers for unethical research; ciphers that are circulated and recirculated in textbooks and lectures as examples of what to avoid and as rationales for why we need legal regulation of social science research, with very little nuanced analysis of what, precisely, is unethical about them. I know I've been guilty of doing this myself.

KAREN: So what's Yanow and Schwartz-Shea's argument? Are they saying that the studies were not unethical?

TIMOTHY: They are trying to move away from a kind of moral absolutism that creates stark categories of "ethical" vs. "unethical" and, in particular, a kind of moral absolutism in which a lack of informed consent always necessarily means that a project is unethical.

KAREN: Say more.

TIMOTHY: Well, one of the valuable things they do is to distinguish between covert research and deception. In covert research, participants—and they use the term participants rather than subjects because it better reflects the non-laboratory setting and the ethics of ethnographic work—are not told that research is being conducted. In deceptive research, participants are told that research is being conducted, but they are deliberately misled about the intentions of the research.

KAREN: I see. So Stanley Milgram's *Obedience to Authority* experiments were not covert, but they were deceptive, since he told the participants—

TIMOTHY [interrupting]: Well, I think it's more appropriate to call them subjects, since they were in an experimental lab, a setting which Milgram controlled.

KAREN: OK, subjects then. Milgram's study was deceptive because he told the subjects the research was about teaching and learning when, in fact, it was about their willingness to obey authority even if it meant inflicting violence on another human being.

TIMOTHY: Right. And it was further deceptive since he tricked his subjects into believing in the realness of the electric shocks they were inflicting on other people whom they thought were subjects just like themselves, but who in fact were actors paid by Milgram.

KAREN: Right, and so the claim is that Milgram's experiments were unethical because they caused potential psychological damage to the people participating in them who had not been told the real purpose of the experiment.

PIERS: Damaged because the experience made them see themselves as bad people?

KAREN: That, and the stress that they experienced when, seeing or hearing the play-acted effects of the fake electric shocks—which they believed to be real—on another person, they faced their responsibility for causing that injury.

TIMOTHY: Yes, but Yanow and Schwartz-Shea argue in their paper that the evidence of actual harm is very weak; indeed, how the subjects themselves reacted after the experiments—many by expressing gratitude about what they had learned about themselves—differed remarkably from how some of Milgram's fellow academics critiqued his study as unethical on its face because of the deception involved. In the absence of demonstrable harm from the deception, Yanow and Schwartz-Shea argue that we should also assess the ethics of the research not by a morally absolutist standard that all deception is necessarily wrong, but by the important knowledge that it produced—itself a central principle ensconced in ethics theory and practice since the post-World War II statements, such as the 1964 Declaration of Helsinki. In this case, Milgram's work taught us about the capacity of hierarchy and authority to foster compliance, even when it enabled violence.[40]

KAREN: Interesting. That account of Milgram runs so counter to the standard story that's told about how unethical his experiments were! I'll have to think about it more.

PIERS: After we eliminate all of the biomedical abuses and the controversial laboratory-based research in psychology, what's left that relates directly to ethnographic field research?

TIMOTHY: It's a good point, Piers. Arguments for bureaucratic regulation of ethnographic fieldwork often get made by referencing real and perceived histories of abuse in biomedical and experimental research, rather than by examining the fieldwork research record itself.

KAREN: Laud Humphreys's book, *Tearoom Trade*, was definitely based on fieldwork, and it generated an enormous amount of controversy, with some members of his own department demanding that his doctorate be rescinded.

PIERS: Wow. What did he do?

KAREN: Humphreys was interested in "deviance" and how it was targeted and punished by authorities like the police. In the first phase of his research, he offered his services as a lookout in public restrooms where men engaged in sexual activity with other men.

TIMOTHY: And he did this without informing the men that he was conducting research, which would make it a covert research project in Yanow and Schwartz-Shea's distinction between covertness and deception.

PIERS: Well, it's hard to imagine how he could have done the research if he had informed the men. The act of informing them itself might have caused them a great deal of anxiety and fear.

TIMOTHY: This is exactly part of Yanow and Schwartz-Shea's argument.

KAREN: Wait, there's more. He also recorded the license plates of many of the men involved in those activities. Later, he used that license plate information to retrieve their names and addresses. A year after his covert research in the public restrooms, he altered his appearance and visited the homes of some of the men he had traced, this time as a survey researcher conducting a second, legitimate survey. Through this subterfuge, he was able to get detailed personal information about the family status, occupations, incomes, etc., of the men he had observed in the public restrooms. All this research allowed him to develop a novel profile of men who engaged in sexual interactions with other men.

TIMOTHY: So Humphreys's research was both covert and deceptive, depending on the phase.

KAREN: Yes. And on that basis, it's often referenced as a key example of unethical fieldwork and as a rationale for why we need a regulatory system that requires informed consent.

TIMOTHY: But as with Milgram, Yanow and Schwartz-Shea urge us to take a more nuanced approach than simply condemning all covert and deceptive research as unethical. In particular, they note that there is no evidence that any of Humphreys' participants were ever harmed by his research. Quite to the contrary, his work is widely recognized within the LGBTQ community for its importance in shifting conversations and perceptions of homosexuality and the actual policing of "deviance."

PIERS: The positionality of the researcher seems to be a big part of this conversation. In biomedical and psychology experiments, researchers hold an enormous amount of power over their subjects. In ethnographic fieldwork, by contrast, researchers are often interested in situations of power imbalance, where they not only do not hold power over their participants, but both they and their participants may be contending with structures of domination or oppressive power.

TIMOTHY: That's exactly right, Piers. And yet ethics review committees often think through issues of informed consent without attention to the nuances of context. Even though there are provisions that allow for waivers, informed consent is often seen as an uncontested good, while covertness and deception are characterized as categorically bad.

KAREN: So part of the argument here is that standards of ethics imposed by state ethics bureaucracies, like the IRB, might draw on a logic that differs from how impacted subjects and participants themselves evaluate the ethicality of the research?

TIMOTHY: Yes. And, in fact, that the IRB is really geared towards a set of legal requirements, not towards ethics per se. Historian Zachary Schrag underscores this point in his superb history of the IRB and its relationship with the social sciences, aptly titled *Ethical Imperialism*.[41]

PIERS: That's the moral absolutism that Yanow and Schwartz-Shea warn against, I guess.

TIMOTHY: Yes, and it's a formulaic absolutism in the name of ethics that, ironically, can short-circuit serious thinking about ethics. Yanow and Schwartz-Shea draw attention to an alternative way of thinking about these questions developed in the 2010 revision to Canada's Tri-Council Policy (TCP) statement on "Ethical Conduct for Research Involving Humans." That revision allows for the possibility of covert research conducted on centers of power, such as governments and corporations, under the logic that requiring informed consent from these groups can often mean that critical inquiry will be silenced or shut down. TCP specifically gives the examples of research on institutional sexual abuse or dissident scientists.[42]

PIERS: I can see why you would like those guidelines, Timothy. Didn't you conduct covert research for *Every Twelve Seconds*?

TIMOTHY: Yup.

KAREN: Wouldn't many people say that's problematic on its face? That because you didn't seek informed consent from the slaughterhouse and its workers, your research is unethical?

TIMOTHY: Yes, some people have said that. But, much like Canada's Tri-Council statement, and in keeping with the arguments put forward by Yanow and Schwartz-Shea, I think it's crucial to look at the underlying contexts of power when we think about how to conduct ethical research. I don't think there is a single, ethically pure way to conduct research. All research involves ethical trade-offs. The responsibility of the researcher, in this view, is not to clear some set of bureaucratic requirements that certify the research as "ethical," but rather to be as aware and reflexive as possible about the ethical trade-offs that all research necessarily requires.

KAREN: I don't know. It sounds like a slippery slope to me. Frankly, I don't really trust the individual researcher to make the right decision in the midst of the intensity of fieldwork. I think the better course of action is to reform ethics committees, to make them specific to the social sciences, or, better yet, specific to ethnographic research in particular.

TIMOTHY: Accountability is important. But I think what's most important is that we don't confuse any kind of "accountability structure" for actual ethics. I would argue that an external system of bureaucratic control, no matter how reformed, can never truly engage all of the relevant ethical questions, or even the most important ones. What we really need is more serious ethics education in graduate programs, where ethics is not conceived of as a set of rules or the sacralizing of a few moral absolutes, but rather the development of a sensibility and a reflexivity that can adjudicate responsibly between the competing ethical demands present in any research project. And this sensibility should orient itself around the relationship between the researcher and her participants, rather than around a desire to protect academic institutions from controversy or legal challenges.

KAREN: But does that then mean that we shouldn't have external systems of control at all? I fear the consequences of that.

PIERS: It's unlikely that we'll reach complete agreement on this question. What do you say we move on?

KAREN: Sure. What's the next stage in our natural history?

TIMOTHY: Looks like it's gaining access.[43]

PIERS: Gaining access. Such funny language. What are we talking about? A fortress? A bank vault?

KAREN [laughing]: Fieldsites, Piers, fieldsites.

PIERS: It's so militarized. So espionage-like, this fieldwork that we do.

TIMOTHY: Didn't we already have a three-hour conversation about that?

KAREN: We did. Let's not repeat it.

PIERS: OK, fine. But it is worth pointing out these resonances, these historical echoes. I mean, look at the origins of this invisibility potion we've all been summoned here to discuss. It was funded by the Department of Defense!

TIMOTHY: I hear you. But I also think there is universality in ethnographic fieldwork to that moment of entry.

KAREN: I would call it more of a process than a moment.

TIMOTHY: Fair enough.

KAREN: But I do agree that there's something universal about the experience of moving from outsider to insider.

PIERS: Yes, but once you're in, you of course realize that there is no single in. Just lots of ins. And more ins. Which means lots of outs too.

TIMOTHY: In other words, there's no single moment of access. Just lots of moments of access.

KAREN: Deep. But all subsequent moments of access begin with a single, first moment of access. It's that moment we're talking about here.

TIMOTHY: I like the way John Van Maanen thinks about this. He argues that any notion of neutrality in fieldwork is purely illusory, and that in the field the ethnographer is inevitably caught up in webs of power and cannot be neutral.[44]

KAREN: I think the important point here is that decisions made by the researcher about how to access the research site can have major implications for the perspectives and information available to the researcher during the course of the research.

TIMOTHY: Yes, I think that's the key point here. Just as there is no "neutral" role in the fieldsite, as Van Maanen points out, there is no "neutral" mode of access.

PIERS: I suppose the invisibility potion could change that?

TIMOTHY: Maybe it could, but, at least for me, one of the exhilarating things about access in ethnographic research is that there's never any taking it back. There's never any hitting the reset button and trying again. It all occurs live, as it were, with no retakes.

PIERS: Exhilarating is one word for it, Timothy. You can never enter the same research site twice, so to speak. Still, others might describe it as anxiety-provoking. Because, more often than not, there's also the reality that so many factors are beyond the ethnographer's control.

KAREN: Unlike a regression analysis, which you can run again and again and again with different variables! We keep returning to the same themes over and over in this conversation about the practice of ethnography: the impossibility of total control, the need to work in real time, the need to improvise in response to the situation in the field.

TIMOTHY: Exactly what makes ethnography so thrilling!

PIERS: Or unacceptably anxiety-provoking and out of control, depending on your tolerance for risk and ambiguity.

KAREN: Does good science require total control? I think that's the question for ethnography.

TIMOTHY: Ha, to the contrary. Can science conducted under an illusion of total control in a nonlinear dynamic world ever be good?[45] I think that's the question.

It's as if ethnography, in trying to get as close to the phenomenon of interest as possible, seeks out and welcomes uncertainty, whereas most other methods use every possible trick to impose an illusion of certainty and control.

PIERS: Fighting words!

TIMOTHY [laughing]: Yes, but not in this company.

KAREN: We're right back to living among wolves again, aren't we? OK, have we said all there is to say about gaining access?

PIERS: No, probably not, but let's keep this moving. What's next?

TIMOTHY [looking down at list]: Looks like it's building relationships.

PIERS: So just to review where we are now in this natural history of ethnography: we've negotiated a research question, however provisional; defined the time and space parameters of our fieldsite or sites; and gained access in some way to that site or those sites. That's where we are?

TIMOTHY: Yes, that's where we are. And now we're going to try to build relationships in our fieldsites.

PIERS: I have a favorite story to share about this.

KAREN: From your own fieldwork?

PIERS: No, actually, from another anthropologist, Paul Rabinow.

KAREN: What's the story?

PIERS: So here's Rabinow, right, a young Ph.D. student from the University of Chicago, conducting fieldwork in Morocco in the late 1960s. Like a lot of other Ph.D. students doing fieldwork, he's really heavy on theoretical training and light on fieldwork training. So here he is, on site, and he's beginning to develop informants.

KAREN: Informants?

PIERS: Yes, informants. That's literally what he—and other ethnographers in that era—calls them.

TIMOTHY: There's something refreshingly honest about that.

KAREN: Depressingly honest.

PIERS: So, anyway, here's this one guy, Ali, whom Rabinow gets to know, I think at a tea shop or something. And Rabinow actually really doesn't like Ali very much at all. He finds him annoying.

KAREN: Why?

PIERS: Who knows? It's just one of those things that happens between people sometimes. Annoyance, irritation, dislike. Nothing concrete you could nail down, but just a sense of exasperation around this person.

TIMOTHY: As the saying goes, someone you don't like could pick up their fork "wrong" and you'd be outraged, but someone you like could dump their entire plate of food in your lap, and it would be immediately overlooked or forgiven.

PIERS: Exactly. So here's Rabinow and Ali. Rabinow doesn't much care for Ali, but it's early in his fieldwork and Ali is the best thing he's got going for him, informant-wise. And then Ali invites Rabinow to this wedding party in a faraway village.

KAREN: I guess Ali must have liked Rabinow enough to want to invite him to a party!

PIERS: Not necessarily! You see, Rabinow has a serious asset that makes him valuable as an acquaintance. Rabinow has a car.

TIMOTHY: Ah yes, the superiorly equipped ethnographer gaining friends through their resources.

KAREN: Like paying someone for doing an interview with you, except subtler.

PIERS: Definitely more subtle and complicated. And blurry, as with our real-life friendships. I mean, we expect friendship, in some idealized sense, to go beyond instrumental value. I think that's good. I think that's noble. But most friendships also contain some element of exchange of value as well, whether it's obviously material, as in lending someone money, or relational, as in helping someone find a job or make a connection through your networks, or even symbolic and status oriented, as in playing the implicit role of being the "diversity" element in someone's group of friends. Anyway, so Ali is inviting Rabinow to this party and Rabinow quite frankly doesn't really want to go. He doesn't like Ali much. He's tired and not feeling great. The village is far away. But he's doing ethnography so he figures he better not turn down this opportunity. And so he goes.

KAREN: What happens?

PIERS: Things start out fine. There is dancing and merriment. Rabinow observes and participates. He gets to know more of Moroccan rural culture. It's ethnographic fieldwork. He's fulfilling his role as the Ph.D. student ethnographer. But as the evening wears on and it's getting later and later, Rabinow's stomach starts getting sicker and sicker. He's tired. Exhausted, actually. He wants to go home.

KAREN: But not Ali?

PIERS: Exactly. Ali is showing no signs of losing steam. He's dancing. He's laughing. He's completely in the moment. Rabinow waits for as long as he can. Then he politely asks Ali if they might go back to town soon. Ali laughs and says yes, yes, but not now. Rabinow waits. He waits some more. Then he goes back to Ali and tells Ali he is feeling sick and would like to return home. Ali says yes, in a moment. At this point Rabinow has stopped doing official fieldwork. He waits at the edge of the celebration. The night is late. Ali shows no signs of flagging. Rabinow's stomach hurts. He needs to go home. Another hour passes. It is close to three in the morning. Finally, Rabinow walks up to Ali and tells him he is leaving. Ali says he is not ready to leave. Rabinow says he is leaving anyway.

KAREN: What happens?

PIERS: Ali gets in the car, but they start fighting. Rabinow has snapped. He is no longer in fieldwork mode. He is not a researcher. He is not a Ph.D. student. He is not an ethnographer. He is just Paul Rabinow, and "Paul Rabinow" wants to be home, in bed. The fighting continues. Rabinow thinks he should stop fighting, thinks he is ruining this relationship, and with it his ethnography and his fieldwork. But he can't contain his pent-up frustration and irritation any longer. Informant or not, Ali is behaving like a selfish, self-centered narcissist, and Rabinow tells him exactly that. Ali, offended, threatens to get out of the car unless Rabinow backs down and apologizes. They are in the middle of nowhere. It's dark. It's miles and miles from town. Rabinow does not apologize. Instead, he pulls the car to a stop by the side of the road and tells Ali to get out if he wants to.

TIMOTHY: Oh, man, that sounds bad.

PIERS: There they are, eyeball to eyeball. Neither blinks. Ali gets out of the car and starts walking. Rabinow drives home, gets into bed, and falls asleep. The next morning, though, he is full of regret. He contemplates packing up his things and flying back to Chicago. He feels that he has completely blown it as an ethnographer. He's not suited to the research. He can't contain his true feelings about people. It's over.

KAREN: Does he go home?

PIERS: No, but then a few days later, he visits Ali. After some initial aloofness, Ali completely warms up to Rabinow. There is a new respect that wasn't there before. In turn, Rabinow doesn't find Ali nearly as irritating. Their relationship improves and expands. Rabinow goes on to complete his fieldwork, write a dissertation, and become a professor.[46]

TIMOTHY [laughing]: And everyone lives happily ever after. But seriously, I do love the story. We can't erase who we are as ethnographers. We can't erase the fact that we will like some people and find others annoying. It's not even ideal to erase those things about ourselves. By presenting ourselves as completely bland, we can even lose the respect of those we are doing fieldwork among.

PIERS: Yeah, I think it's definitely context-specific, though. I can see other situations where Rabinow losing his cool like that could really alienate other people. So I don't think this is a recommendation to get mad at people and abandon them on lonely roads in the middle of the night. But I do think it's a valuable lesson in the importance of not letting go of who you are when you do fieldwork. It isn't about erasing or altering your personality in order to "build rapport" with people, but rather taking your full self into the field with the intention of building rapport.

KAREN: I like the story too. But I think it also points to a caution about the very phrase "building rapport," which gets repeated endlessly in descriptions of ethnographic fieldwork. You said, Piers, that Rabinow went into the field with the "intention of building rapport." But the rapport part was only instrumental to his real intention, which was to conduct research. His primary goal was not to build friendships and rapport; he did those things in order to support his primary research goals.

PIERS: I think I see what you're saying, but I think of building rapport as being equal parts gaining people's respect and, occasionally, their genuine affection as well. It's not a popularity contest that you try to win through flattery or by making yourself all things to all people. It's about being humble enough to learn while still having enough of a sense of yourself to offer something in return.

KAREN: OK, I agree with much of that. But I would suggest that we replace this phrase "building rapport" with something like "forming relationships." Rapport is not an emotionally neutral term. It suggests a positive regard between the people in the relationship, a genuine liking even. So when it's used in the context of ethnographic fieldwork, which always has as its primary intention the research itself, it can connote a kind of sliminess on the part of the ethnographer. I know that's not how you mean it, Piers, but the risk of the connotation is there. If we talk about what ethnographers do in the field as forming relationships, it helps us avoid some of this baggage. Forming relationships is a more straightforward description of what ethnographers do; it doesn't specify the emotional content of those relationships. They may be intimate and positive, leading toward genuine friendship, as was the case between you and many of your participants, Piers. Or it may be emotionally neutral, a relationship of mutual convenience rooted more in what each party sees as instrumentally useful in the other. Or it may even be conflictual, as were Timothy's relationships with some of his other co-workers in the slaughterhouse.

TIMOTHY: What a provocative point, Karen. I like it. Saying that our goal is to build rapport, as I have often done, also suggests that if we do not form relationships with positive emotional valences with all of our participants, then we have failed in some way. But if we take Van Maanen's injunction that there is no such thing as neutrality in fieldwork seriously, then it's simply not possible that we can conduct fieldwork in a way where everyone "likes" us. And while I really like the story Piers told about Rabinow and Ali, I think it's useful to place it alongside the ethnographic fieldwork conducted by Kathleen Blee, who had to form relationships—to use Karen's suggested term—with people whose values she found unequivocally abhorrent.

PIERS: In what way?

TIMOTHY: Well, she conducted ethnographic research with neo-Nazi, skinhead, Klu Klux Klan and other women participating in white supremacist hate groups.[47]

PIERS: Whoa.

TIMOTHY: Right, whoa. Blee creates a nice contrast to Rabinow here because she knew from the start that she was deeply unsympathetic, even overtly antagonistic, to the worldviews of the people she would be conducting ethnography among.

KAREN: So does it even make sense to talk about Blee "building rapport" among white supremacists? Or would it make more sense to talk about her "forming relationships" with them?

TIMOTHY: Blee herself uses the term "rapport" to describe her relationships with these women, even as she describes the ways in which the context of her research made the very notion of rapport deeply problematic. My sense is she would not object to the replacement of rapport with a notion of forming relationships.

PIERS: Why did these women even want to talk to her in the first place?

TIMOTHY: She notes a variety of motives, including a sense of being flattered that a professor wanted to listen to their views, a desire to generate publicity for their groups and their causes, and wanting someone to be a recorder of their lives.

KAREN: But it must have been tough for Blee herself.

TIMOTHY: Yes, she writes insightfully about the emotional side of forming relationships, describing feelings of fear, revulsion, and even—to her own dismay—a kind of voyeuristic thrill at having gained the confidence of people participating in a secretive and widely despised social movement. And, interestingly, she writes about the way her own shock and horror at the horrific things she was hearing in her interviews dulled as her fieldwork progressed, until it got to the point where her unstructured life history interviews with these women began to feel like business transactions, with the interviewer and the interviewee negotiating to get the most favorable terms possible. The emotional dulling affected Blee so deeply that she had to take a break of several years after the completion of the fieldwork before being able to return to the material with the same sense of urgency that animated the project originally.

PIERS: Well, I wonder if it's really dulling, or if it's more a feeling of being overwhelmed by the horror of what she was hearing and experiencing.

TIMOTHY: I certainly felt overwhelmed during my fieldwork in the slaughterhouse. And, like Blee, I found that I had to take a break from my fieldnotes before I could return to them with an ability to write about them analytically.

KAREN: So the ethnographer performs a lot of emotional labor in this process of building relationships with people in the field.

TIMOTHY: Yes, and that emotional labor can be very challenging as well as analytically insightful. All the more reason to take detailed fieldnotes on this aspect of fieldwork, something I hope we'll talk about when we discuss writing fieldnotes.

PIERS: Placing Blee's story alongside Rabinow's helps me better appreciate your objection to the phrase "building rapport," Karen. In one case, we have a new ethnographer who has a simple personality conflict with one of his potential research participants. In the other, the ethnographer knows from the beginning that she finds loathsome the political and personal views of the people she will be working with. But in both cases, there is an importance and centrality to forming relationships, demonstrating that these kinds of ethnographic relationships are neither about rigidly maintaining the boundaries of self-identity nor about losing one's identity in the field.

KAREN: Every ethnographer's situation will be different, of course, depending on the context. But what is certain is that because ethnography is such a deeply relational enterprise, this element of forming relationships in the field is a central requirement of ethnography.

TIMOTHY: And I would add that it is a central modality as well. Meaning, it is not just a requirement in the sense that all ethnographers have to do it. But also that the initiation, negotiation, deepening, and, sometimes, ending of relationships constitute one of the primary ways that we develop ethnographic knowledge in the field. It would not be too much of a stretch to say that ethnography is centrally about creating and building relationships.

PIERS: I like that very much. In my case, those relationships grew and deepened over the course of decades until by the end of the project it seemed natural, even required, to write and think about them as friendships.

[Wolfdog turns suddenly and snarls. Piers jumps back, frightened.]

KAREN: I'm not sure the wolfdog agrees, Piers!

[Wolfdog locks eyes with Piers for several moments before turning back.]

TIMOTHY: I'm not sure what's going on with the wolfdog, Piers, but I don't think it's necessary to think of those we encounter in fieldwork as friends. Kathleen Blee is really a great example here. I don't think she would ever call any of the women in her ethnography her friends.

PIERS: No, I don't think so either. In fact, I'm irked when I hear ethnographers referring to their relationships as friendships when that depth, trust, and mutual regard clearly has not been developed. In those situations, I much prefer the more honest use of "informants," as Rabinow deploys it, or of "participants." None of the terms we use to describe the people ethnographers study— subjects, informants, participants, interlocutors, friends, natives—is perfect. Each of them illuminates different aspects of the unavoidable tensions when research is conducted primarily through the medium of human relationships.

TIMOTHY: Right. As in life, relationships formed in ethnography can span an enormous continuum, from purely instrumental ones in which the terms subject and informant seem more applicable, to deep relationships of trust and emotional reciprocation in which the term friend is appropriate.

KAREN: Yes, and the ethnographer's task is to enter the field open to relating, ready for all the surprises, joys, frustrations, and antagonisms that relationships imply.

TIMOTHY: That's well said, Karen.

[Momentary lull in conversation.]

Let's move forward, shall we? Next in our natural history is navigating the field and the value of improvisation, serendipity, and ambiguity.

KAREN: That sounds fun.

TIMOTHY: I have a story from my fieldwork in the slaughterhouse that illustrates this nicely.

PIERS: Let's hear it.

TIMOTHY: Well, we've already talked a little bit about the role of serendipity in my getting into the slaughterhouse.

PIERS: Right, how even though you exercised a lot of care in terms of selecting a range of possible fieldsites, there was still a huge element of the unknown about where you would, or *if* you would, actually gain entry into a slaughterhouse.

TIMOTHY: Exactly. I didn't get hired at the first slaughterhouse I applied to, so I went to apply at a different slaughterhouse. I didn't get hired there either, so I returned to the first slaughterhouse again and again. Only after repeated returns was I hired.

PIERS: I can see how that story highlights how serendipity, improvisation, and a tolerance for ambiguity are important in the process of getting into the fieldsite, but what about their importance after you are inside the fieldsite and trying to navigate it?

TIMOTHY: Once hired, I had no idea where the slaughterhouse was going to place me. Remember, it's not like I had any control over this, aside from marking on my application that I want to be in "slaughter," as opposed to "fabrication" or "warehouse" or "sanitation."

This dynamic of serendipity and improvisation replays time and time again throughout my fieldwork. It comes up in interactions I have within each job I perform in the slaughterhouse. What do I say to co-workers during lunch breaks? What do I do when a liver cart tips over in the cooler and scatters the livers across the floor? What do I do when I see workers failing to sanitize their knives as required? How do I interact with the front office staff when I go there for training? And improvisation also plays a key role in my transitions between my different slaughterhouse jobs. I can't foresee and control the moments of transition, but I improvise when I sense them happening.

KAREN: How so?

TIMOTHY: Well, my first job is hanging livers in the cooler. I'm there for two months. It stretches on and on. The monotony is unbearable. I'm down in the freezing basement of the cooler memorizing poetry, playing pranks on my co-workers, wondering how the heck I am going to write a dissertation based on doing nothing but hanging livers for an entire year.

PIERS: An entire year?

TIMOTHY: Well, that was my rough sense of how long I would spend working in the slaughterhouse. So there I am, hanging livers, day after day, with no apparent end in sight. Then, everything changes one day. Just like that, without forewarning. The slaughterhouse loses a liver contract with someone and there is no more need for the liver hangers. All the cattle livers will now go straight down the chute into the pet food room. My co-worker Ramón and I are out of our liver-hanging jobs. I begin the next chapter of the book with the words my supervisor greeted us with that morning: "Guys, no more livers next week."[48]

KAREN: Disaster! Were you out of a job?

TIMOTHY: I could have been, but this is where the improvisation comes in. Rather than see it as a loss, as a "No," I responded with improvisation's central refrain: "Yes, and...."

KAREN: Yes, and?

TIMOTHY: Right, the key in improvisation is never to shut something down, never to say no. It is to take whatever you are given and ~~build on it, to have the response of~~ "Yes, and...." When the liver hanging job ends, I use it as an opportunity to gain access to a completely different part of the kill floor. Anxiously waiting in the hallway for a new job assignment, I proactively approach one of the kill floor managers and remind him that I have previous experience working on a cattle ranch. Perhaps I could work in the chutes with the live cattle, I suggest. And that's where I end up for my next job in the slaughterhouse, allowing me to experience not only the work of killing at a distance, in the cooler hanging livers, but also the work of killing at close range, in the chutes, where the live cattle are driven into the kill box to be shot.

KAREN: Obviously, you could never have planned that.

TIMOTHY: Yes, but neither was it entirely the result of chance or dumb luck. It's tempting, in retrospect, to read my book and other ethnographies as continuous narratives that unfold in some sort of planned or inevitable fashion. But none of this felt continuous or planned to me at the time. Hanging livers, day after day, for two months—that was the entirety of my experience. I had no idea that I would or could ever be moved to a different work position. Some ways of writing ethnography, like some ways of writing history, have a way of erasing all the contingencies, all the uncertainties, the multitude of ways things might have been otherwise. That's why, when I'm teaching my students about the importance of serendipity, improvisation, and ambiguity, I encourage them to write their finished ethnographies in ways that preserve rather than erase the deep contingencies of fieldwork.

KAREN:  It's something like Machiavelli's Fortuna, half in human hands, half out of our control. The question in ethnography, as in political life the way Machiavelli understands it, is how to educate oneself, how to train one's sensibilities, to be able to seize the opportunities that Fortuna offers and thereby take full possession of the half that is under the control of human hands.[49]

TIMOTHY:  I like that very much, Karen! It's a nice way of talking about the centrality of serendipity and improvisation in navigating the field. And seizing the opportunities offered by Fortuna is something that's demonstrated again and again during my fieldwork in the slaughterhouse. It happens again, for example, when I seize an opening created by the firing of one of the quality control workers in the slaughterhouse and apply for that position. Once promoted to quality control, I suddenly have complete access to the entire physical space of the slaughterhouse—not just the dirty and clean sides of the kill floor itself, but also the fabrication department and the front office. This physical access is what allows me to create detailed maps of the division of labor and space in the slaughterhouse and to create the appendix that describes in vivid detail the job of each worker on the kill floor line.

And serendipity is at play not only in the obvious transitions from job to job in the slaughterhouse, but also in other moments that occur, detonation-like, unplanned and unbidden. The cattle escape that opens my book, for example, struck me like an epiphany in the middle of my fieldwork. Here I was, more than a month into the deadening monotony of hanging livers in the cooler, and six cattle escape from a slaughterhouse just up the street from the one I'm working in. Incredibly—one might even say serendipitously—this escape occurs during the ten-minute afternoon break when I and a bunch of other workers are outside getting some fresh air and sunshine. We watch the Omaha police, who have been alerted to this escape and are in hot pursuit of one of the cattle, trying to herd her into a waiting trailer. When she won't comply, they open fire on her with shotguns and kill her.

KAREN:  Whoa.

TIMOTHY:  Yeah, whoa. The next day in the lunchroom, the workers are upset about the shooting. Disgusted and angry at the police for killing the animal, they express solidarity with her. One worker even says, "They shot that cow just like they shot an unarmed man from Mexico last year. You know if you are Mexican in this country, the police will do anything to you."[50]

KAREN:  In no universe could this kind of thing be planned or anticipated. A cattle escape. A killing by the police. Worker reactions of horror and disgust. You didn't select the event. The event selected you.

TIMOTHY:  Exactly, Karen. But I had to be present—not just physically, but also intellectually—in order to be selected by it. And as indicated by my placement of the cattle escape story at the opening of the book, this unanticipated event became an organizing lens for the entire project. It allowed me to experience and witness, in real time, the tension between what happens when something occurs at a distance versus when that distance is collapsed. As ethnographers, we make ourselves available, we hone our sensibilities, we do the hard, grinding labor of being present, day-in and day-out. And, if we have eyes to see and ears to hear, events will select us that will draw all of the unruly strands of our observations into intelligible tapestries. So, Karen, you are right that ethnographic research is very much like Machiavelli's Fortuna in that way.

Moments like the cattle escape, the police killing, and the responses of the slaughterhouse workers.... As ethnographers, we cannot predict and control them—an impossibility, since we are not in control of what happens in the field in the same way a laboratory scientist is in control of a chemical experiment, or even in the same way that Milgram was in control of what his subjects knew and didn't know about his experiment. No, our task as ethnographers is to show up, day-in and day-out, and to do the hard, often repetitive work that allows us to recognize those moments of surprise when they do occur. And that is where serendipity and improvisation meet to produce ethnographic magic.

KAREN: Sounds dreamy.

TIMOTHY: Yes, but the actual experience of it can be anxiety-provoking. This is why taking advantage of serendipity and improvisation depends crucially on another quality in ethnographic fieldwork: tolerance for ambiguity.

KAREN: Say more, please.

TIMOTHY: Ethnographic fieldwork, and in particular the work of navigating the field, requires a strong stomach for *not* knowing, or only partially knowing, how things are going to turn out, and for trusting your sensibilities and instincts to recognize and take advantage of key moments and openings when they occur. Ethnography is not for those who need to have a high level of control over their projects from beginning to end.

PIERS: Add to that a further irony, that the costs in time and preparation are so high in ethnographic fieldwork that the temptation is surely to become anxious at the lack of control. You can spend years learning a language and move across the world to get to your fieldsite, but all that doesn't guarantee any particular outcome. And you can't go in trying to strong-arm your fieldsite into producing results for you. The best results come from this mix of serendipity and improvisation, this capacity to work with rather than against Machiavelli's Fortuna. And for that, you need patience and an ability to be comfortable with ambiguity.

KAREN: That's very powerful.

TIMOTHY: And now we should turn to a stage in our natural history very much under the researcher's control: writing fieldnotes!

PIERS [faking enthusiasm]: Woohoo! Writing fieldnotes!

KAREN: Sarcasm noted.

PIERS [chuckling]: Look, it can definitely feel like a chore, especially after a long day riding a reindeer in −80-degree weather. But in all seriousness, fieldnote writing is the lifeblood of ethnography, the process that takes the messiness of the field and inscribes it into words.

KAREN: I wonder sometimes about that metaphor of inscription, as if the fieldsite were an amorphous, constantly shifting landscape, and the task of the ethnographer is to fix it, to inscribe that landscape into the permanence of words before it shifts again and disappears forever.

TIMOTHY: Clifford Geertz also uses the word inscription to describe what happens when ethnographers move from fieldwork to fieldnote writing.[51] But even Geertz doesn't think that inscription fixes these raw moments of fieldwork, preserving them for later study. He underscores that moments of observation, inscription, and analysis are not as discrete as they may seem.[52]

KAREN: So one implication is that even the act of writing fieldnotes is itself already interpretive. There is no moment prior to the inscription which is non-interpretive and which can then later be subject to interpretation or analysis.

TIMOTHY: Precisely.

KAREN: Well, I suppose that's really where a positivist and an interpretivist might part ways on what fieldnotes are about. There are some positivists who really do believe in not just the possibility but also the necessity of capturing "mere reality," whether it is in fieldnote form or in the form of survey responses or coded variables. So, for a positivist, this kind of answer from Geertz is deeply discomfiting. It suggests that data are not reliable, not replicable, and if data are not reliable and not replicable, then what is the science in our enterprise of scientific knowledge production really all about, anyway?

TIMOTHY: Better to acknowledge that than to live in denial of it. We don't gain anything by creating an alternate universe in which data are declared to pre-exist interpretation. So an interpretivist response to these positivist concerns is that they are hardly unique to ethnography as a method. It's just that ethnography calls attention to the inescapable inevitability of interpretation in ways that other methods do not.

KAREN: Back to the wolves again.

[Piers howls playfully. Wolfdog cocks an ear.]

PIERS [in a playful tone]: Look, what fieldnotes "are" has been a longstanding topic of debate in anthropology. Some say they are inscriptions. Others say transcriptions. Still others, translations. And others, narrations. And still others say they are textualizations. Each of these metaphors captures something different about the power relations inherent to conducting ethnography.[53] Then there was the whole critique of "culture as text" that reached its high-water mark in anthropology with the publication of James Clifford and George Marcus's *Writing Culture*.[54] And now we have a turn to re-theorizing ethnographic fieldnotes in our digital era of the internet, cell phones, and social media.[55]

But I like to keep it simple. What I tell my students is this: if you didn't write it down, it didn't happen. There are huge, enormous chunks of your fieldnotes that will never end up in your finished ethnography: by definition, the finished ethnography is a curation of your fieldnotes. And that curation, in turn, highlights certain themes or key narrative arcs that are themselves put into more or less explicit conversation with existing theory or with "the literature."

TIMOTHY: And there's no way of knowing beforehand which fieldnotes are going to be highlighted and selected in that curation process and which are not.

KAREN: Exactly. And it's possible to write many ethnographies out of a single set of fieldnotes.

TIMOTHY: Another claim that might sound radical to positivist ears.

PIERS: The point is, if something—a characterization, an event, a site description, a direct quote—is not included in the fieldnotes, then it is likely to be lost to the finished ethnography.

TIMOTHY: That's a great point. I'd like to expand on it a little by drawing on an analogy from digital photography. Now, I realize this analogy is problematic in its intimation that the ethnographer is like some kind of recording device, capturing everything objectively as it happens.

KAREN: No worries there. I think we are all sufficiently sophisticated to realize that even cameras must be aimed somewhere and their shots framed by someone, that their so-called objectivity is anything but objective. And also that, as with fieldnotes, digital pictures can often serve to catalyze a whole series of memories that surround, but are not directly referenced by, the photograph itself.

TIMOTHY: OK, good. Because what I want to say is that writing fieldnotes is a bit like playing with the number of pixels in a digital camera. Some digital cameras can capture higher resolution images than others. Anyone with a digital camera knows you can zoom in on a photograph, but only to a certain point before the image becomes pixelated, broken down into a blur.

KAREN: How is that like fieldnotes?

TIMOTHY: Well, when I'm exhausted after a long day of fieldwork, and when I'm finally sitting down to write fieldnotes, I'm often tempted to gloss or to summarize. But I try to remember, even in the midst of exhaustion, that I want my descriptions to have the highest resolution that I'm capable of producing. In the later finished ethnography, I can always zoom out, but I will never be able to zoom in with more focus than what I have evoked in my original set of fieldnotes.

KAREN: I like it. So there is something of an imperative for the ethnographer to capture as much as possible in fieldnotes and with the highest level of detail possible.

PIERS: That's quite a task.

KAREN: It is. And it can feel overwhelming, especially in the early stages of a fieldwork project.

TIMOTHY: Why especially in the early stages?

KAREN: Well, because it's at that stage that absolutely everything is new. Nothing can be taken for granted, nothing can be relegated to the background. In fact, you don't even know yet, as a researcher, what should count as background and what should count as foreground.

PIERS: Right. Later in a research project, as certain themes, ideas, or narrative arcs emerge in your fieldnotes, you can begin to focus your fieldwork along certain lines of sight.

KAREN: Always open to interruption, of course.

PIERS: Interruption, and even radical reversal. But overall, there is an iterative, funnel-like process in which your notes are at their widest aperture at the start of a project and gradually become more focused throughout the project.

KAREN: Fieldnotes written during those initial fieldwork moments are also crucial because those are the moments when so much is happening around your positionality, around how you are presenting yourself in the field, and around how others are reading that presentation. They are the early days of a relationship in which so much is being set for how the interactions that follow will proceed.

PIERS: But it's also important because you really need to be paying attention to what stands out to you, what surprises you. As you spend more time in a fieldsite, you begin to take more and more for granted. By necessity of operating, of maneuvering in the fieldsite, certain routines and actions become habits. But initially, it is the strangeness of those routines and actions that needs to be textualized in the fieldnotes.

TIMOTHY: This is exactly what makes jottings so important.

KAREN [taking on mock voice of a student]: Professor, what are jottings?

TIMOTHY [playfully]: Well, Eager Student, jottings are real-time, contemporaneous bits of fieldwork that you capture as it is unfolding by scrawling down certain key words or phrases or descriptions in your notebook, or on a scrap of paper, or on your smartphone: fragments you can later use to recreate a more extended scene or conversation or characterization.

PIERS: I like to use mnemonic devices in my jottings. So, for example, I might enter a room or a setting and quickly compress the key color schemes around me into a short mnemonic. Take the lake around us, for example. The things that immediately strike me about it are that it is narrow, long, and the water sounds like a lapping dog, and that it turns obsidian black when the clouds pull across the sun. So, in my jottings I might quickly write, "Keuka = Narrow, Long, Dog, Obsidian." Or, if I wanted to compress it even more, I could write, "K=NOLD."

TIMOTHY: And you could remember that later when writing your fieldnotes?

PIERS: Yes, as long as I returned to write my fieldnotes as soon as possible after each specific fieldwork episode—something that I have found to be absolutely critical in creating vivid fieldnotes. I really see the fieldnote writing as a kind of cathartic outpouring. I try not to be too critical of what I'm writing. I just want the sentences to come as fast as possible, as I try to inscribe the fieldwork experience on the page. In fact, my family sometimes laughs at me because when I am in the field I refuse to discuss my day with them until I've sat down and written my fieldnotes first. I want the page to be the first expression of the day's emotional and experiential vividness.

KAREN: "K=NOLD." Now I will always remember Lake Keuka a certain way.

PIERS: Yes, and the point is that each of those things—narrow, long, dog-lapping sound, obsidian color—is not meant to be the totality of my description of the scene, but rather a placeholder to jog my memory about even more detailed and vivid descriptions. So, it's not just that the lake is long, but that it's long in a Y-shape, with ragged edges where bits of forest or rock protrude. And it's not just that it's narrow, but that it's narrow enough for me to be able to see someone's white apron fluttering in the wind on a laundry line on the opposite shore. And so on. None of these details are important in and of themselves, but taken together they could serve an important function in the finished ethnography, not least by helping to establish that sense of verisimilitude—that sense of "being there"—that is so key to persuading the reader of an ethnographer's ethnographic authority.

TIMOTHY: Of course, all of this attention to detail requires an enormous amount of time and effort. It's critically important to remember that a few moments in the field can actually take hours to write up later as fieldnotes. One of the biggest mistakes I made as a new ethnographer was to spend too much time in the field relative to the time I could give to writing fieldnotes. Now I am much more disciplined about reducing my time in the field in order to create more time for writing fieldnotes daily. There's this sense of excitement that's generated by being in the field, especially initially, where things are happening so fast. It's euphoric. And it's easy to get swept up by the fieldwork and to think, "Well, I can always write about this later." But I think it's critically important to remember that fieldnote writing is a part of fieldwork, an indispensable part of it, and it's not possible to conduct good ethnographic research without taking the time to write good fieldnotes. So wherever the ethnographer has control over how she spends time in the field, I always recommend that she set aside two to three times the amount of fieldwork time for writing fieldnotes.

Sometimes, of course, it's not possible for the ethnographer to control how much time she spends in the field. For example, if she's doing fieldwork where she's required to volunteer a certain number of hours every day with the organization she's studying, or where she's employed as a worker, then she will have much less control over fieldwork time. In those instances, I suggest that the fieldnotes be sculpted around a certain portion of the day that can shift as the days go on. So the first set of fieldnotes from the first day might focus on the morning. The second set from the second day might focus on the afternoon, and so on. But regardless of the specifics, the main point here is that there needs to be a conscious allocation of time between fieldwork and fieldnote writing. It's an easy and seductive mistake to spend too much time conducting fieldwork and too little time writing the fieldnotes that inscribe that fieldwork in text.

PIERS [in playful mock tone of a student]: Professor, that's some great advice in terms of managing the balance between fieldwork and fieldnote writing. Of course, it's a little hard to follow when you're out in the middle of Siberia crossing the tundra on the back of a reindeer with another seven hours of travel ahead of you. You can't exactly say, "Oh, wait, stop this reindeer. I've completed my participant observation quota for the day, and now it's time for fieldnote writing.

[Everyone laughs.]

TIMOTHY: Well, isn't that one of the things that makes ethnography so thrilling, Piers? It is we, the researchers, who must adapt ourselves to the worlds we study, rather than forcing that world into neat, controllable robots that we line up and march like foot soldiers through our research designs.

KAREN: I was struck earlier, Piers, when you were talking about seeing a white apron fluttering on a laundry line on the opposite shore of Lake Keuka, by how much you sound like a poet. And I do think ethnographers should share a poetic sensibility, insofar as that means rendering concrete, specific detail in original ways that invite the reader into a certain world.[56]

TIMOTHY: I find joy in this element of fieldwork, that beauty can be evoked or created even in the most mundane description or moment of interaction. Not that the thing being described or the interaction being recounted is necessarily beautiful itself—don't forget I did fieldwork in a slaughterhouse— but that there is an art in evoking it, in calling it forth with vividness.

PIERS: But it takes practice. And it's a lot more difficult than it seems.

TIMOTHY: Yes. The five senses become crucially important in creating these kinds of lush ethnographic fieldnotes. We rely so heavily on sight, and to some extent also on hearing, that we often neglect our other senses: smell, touch, taste. Depending on where I'm doing fieldwork, I sometimes like to spend several concentrated days developing rich descriptions based on a single sense. What is everything that I can taste in my fieldsite? That I can smell? What are the ways in which my skin is making contact with others, with the air, with the clothing that I'm required to wear in the fieldsite? It helps to focus my attention on things that might otherwise go unnoticed or remain in the background. And I find that it allows me to create much more vivid scenes in my finished ethnographies than I might otherwise.

KAREN: That's fantastic advice. When it comes to the sense of hearing, one thing that I really try to focus on in my jottings is getting down as much verbatim language as possible. I think it's so easy to paraphrase what we think we hear someone saying or the gist of what we think they mean, but my fieldnotes, and my finished ethnography, are much more powerful when I work to capture word-for-word dialogue in my jottings and then translate those into my fieldnotes.

PIERS: Yes, I completely agree with that. And not only to capture verbatim language, but also to capture the body language and the facial expressions and the tone and cadence of voice that accompany that speech.

TIMOTHY: Right, exactly! Like the way you just gestured with your left hand, as if releasing a dove into the air, when you said "body language," Piers.

PIERS [laughing]: And the way your eyebrows just furrowed playfully and your eyes twinkled a bit when you said, "Right, exactly!" Timothy.

[All laugh.]

KAREN: Another thing I really try to pay attention to in my jottings is my own reactions. What's going on with me. I think that's an important component of being self-aware and reflexive in my fieldwork. If I myself am the primary instrument of research, then I think it's important for me to give some attention in my jottings to what is going on with me.

TIMOTHY: I do that in my jottings too. And I usually distinguish those kinds of self-reflective observations from my other jottings by putting them in a different column in my notebook or by drawing a triangle around them or something.

PIERS: What do you mean by paying attention to your own reactions?

TIMOTHY: Well, for me, it's about noting when I'm feeling anxious or upset or when I'm especially drawn to or irritated by someone. Or noting how others seem to be interpreting my presence. Just notes on what is happening with me as I am in the field.

KAREN: Yes, and for me those kind of jottings also include meta-observational things, like me noting that I can't quite keep up with a rapid flow of conversation or that my hand is really hurting or that I'm spending too much time trying to make sure my sound recorder is still working. Things that help me know later what conditions were shaping my fieldwork at that moment.

PIERS: I also include those kinds of observations in my jottings, but I don't necessarily distinguish them from my other observations. They kind of all flow together.

TIMOTHY: Yeah, I don't think there's any one right way to do this. It's all about what kinds of jottings, what techniques of jottings, really work for you in terms of creating the most vivid set of fieldnotes later. But one of the benefits of visually distinguishing this element of reflexivity in jottings—whether by creating a separate column for it or putting a triangle around it—is that it helps me to see with just a glance how much attention I'm giving to description and how much to reflexivity. I've had students who are all reflexivity all the time, and others who are so focused on description that they erase their presence altogether.

KAREN: I'm curious to know how you two organize your fieldnotes while you're writing them?

PIERS: This is actually a surprisingly complicated question. Often people who haven't done fieldwork or written fieldnotes think of writing up fieldnotes as a fairly simple and straightforward process. You go to the field. You observe and maybe participate. You jot. Then you come home and write about what you observed and participated in. End of story.

But it's so much more complicated than that! Writing fieldnotes entails so many choices. We often make them implicitly, but I've found that the more explicitly aware I am of my writing choices, the higher the quality of my fieldnotes. Here, I've found Emerson, Fretz, and Shaw's terrific book *Writing Ethnographic Fieldnotes* especially helpful.[57]

TIMOTHY: What are some of those choices, Piers?

PIERS: I think one of the most important choices is point of view. It's not at all self-evident what point of view fieldnotes should be written from. I think the most intuitive point of view for a lot of ethnographers is the first-person point of view. That's how I write most of my fieldnotes, especially when I'm directly participating in the situation I'm studying, as was the case for most of my research for *The Reindeer People*. But sometimes the first-person point of view can be limiting, too self-involved. Sometimes I think it's better to use a third person or a third-person-focused point of view, especially when I'm sitting back and more closely observing what is going on around me. I have an entire set of fieldnotes written from the third-person-focused point of view, for example, where I follow the grandmother in one of the reindeer herder's camps for an entire day from dawn until nightfall, doing nothing but taking jottings on her movements and later converting those jottings into a set of fieldnotes in which she is the sole central character. So I might write something like:

> Grandma began stirring under her blankets of reindeer hides just as the sky changed from black to the color of a bruise. Coughing loudly, she sat up and was still for a long moment before rising with a loud sigh to her feet and moving across the hut to the embers of the fire, barely flickering with orange from the night before. She took two ends of a rope strung through the handle of the blackened and dented cooking pot and, in a rapid, easy motion, folded the left end over the right end, then twisted both in a circular motion before folding the right end back over the left and hanging the rope onto a stout metal tripod above the embers. Outside, one of the reindeer made a clicking sound, "Chok-chok-chok." "Oh, little Bill Clinton," Grandma said, "it's too early in the day for you to be seeking a mate. Go back to sleep."

KAREN [laughing]: Little Bill Clinton?

[The wolfdog, far ahead of the three humans, turns and snarls again, her fangs glinting in the light reflected off the lake. Engrossed in their conversation, the humans neither see nor hear her.]

PIERS [also laughing]: Yes, the Eveny named one of their more promiscuous reindeer after Bill Clinton. But you can see how in those fieldnotes, I deliberately excluded the first-person point of view, allowing me to focus intently on the grandmother and her perspective. In doing so, I gained insight into things that might have otherwise escaped me: the knots being tied for particular purposes and the calls used for different reindeer, for example.

TIMOTHY [taking up a mock student tone]: So, Professor Piers, are first and third person the only two choices when it comes to adopting a point of view in fieldnotes?

PIERS [playing along]: Why no, Student Timothy, there's also third-person omniscient point of view, which I sometimes like to utilize as an exercise to keep me humble.

KAREN: What do you mean?

PIERS: Well, third-person omniscient is that point of view you sometimes encounter in novels—take Tolstoy's *War and Peace*, for example—where the narrator somehow is able to follow multiple characters in contemporaneous time and is able to describe not only their actions, but also their internal thoughts and emotions.[58] It is a kind of "god's eye view from nowhere," to borrow a felicitous phrase used by Donna Haraway and others.[59] So, adopting this writing stance about the same set of fieldnotes, I might write, for example:

> *Grandma began stirring under her blankets of reindeer hides just as the sky changed from black to the color of a bruise. Her dream—a nightmare about two reindeer herders being caught in a blizzard and riding blindly over the edge of a cliff—only heightened her anxiety about the late return of her two sons from the tundra. "They should have been back two days ago," she thought to herself, "and now this dream." Coughing loudly, she sat up and was still for a long moment, willing the anxiety into a manageable container before rising with a loud sigh to her feet and moving across the hut to the embers of the fire, barely flickering with orange from the night before. "If my sons had been here, they would not have allowed the fire to die down so low in the night," she thought, "unlike this tall white man who calls himself an anthropologist but is almost no help to me in the camp." She took two ends of a rope strung through the handle of the blackened and dented cooking pot and, in a rapid, easy motion, folded the left end over the right end, then twisted both in a circular motion before folding the right end back over the left and hanging the rope onto a stout metal tripod above the embers. Outside, one of the reindeer made a clicking sound, "Chok-chok-chok." The familiar sound made her smile and finally freed her completely from the ominous tendrils of her dream, thrusting her fully into the*

*realness of the day ahead. "Oh, little Bill Clinton," she said, "it's too early in the day for you to be seeking a mate. Go back to sleep."*

KAREN: Why does that keep you humble? It seems like the opposite—that you'd need to be incredibly arrogant to be able to adopt that point of view in your fieldnotes.

PIERS: But that's exactly it. The sheer absurdity involved in me getting inside her head—knowing what she dreamt the night before or what she is silently thinking and feeling in a given moment—is an apt reminder not to project internal feelings and states of mind onto others in my fieldnotes. It reminds me how much I don't know about what's going on, and it helps me keep my writing focused on descriptions of what I am observing rather than evaluative labels. It helps me remember to write, "She sighed as she moved to the fire," instead of, "the weight of her worry for her sons was nearly crushing."

Playing with a third-person omniscient narrative voice in my fieldnotes keeps me anchored to the centrality of the intersubjective element in all social interaction and it gives the lie to claims, sometimes implicit in other methods, that to conduct research is to play the role of omniscient narrator.

KAREN: That's a great idea. I'm going to try it out in my next set of fieldnotes.

PIERS [continuing]: Third-person omniscient is essentially permission to engage in all of those things we try to avoid as good fieldnote writers—generalizations, evaluative judgments, telling rather than showing—creating these little moments throughout fieldwork where we intentionally try to commit all of those sins as brazenly as possible really helps to bring home why we strive to avoid them in most of our fieldnotes. But the main point here is really that point of view is an important decision that we make each and every time we sit down to write fieldnotes. Implicitly, we often fall into one or another point of view in our fieldnotes, but it's important to try to purposefully vary this, if for no other reason than to keep our writing fresh.

KAREN: In addition to choices about point of view, there are also deliberate writing choices about time that we make in our fieldnotes.

TIMOTHY [taking on mock tone of student]: Time?

KAREN: Yes! Namely, the choice between writing our fieldnotes in real-time or end-point time.

TIMOTHY [continuing with playful tone]: What do you mean, Professor Karen?

KAREN: Well, think about it this way. If we were each to go back after our stroll and conversation this afternoon and write a set of fieldnotes about it, there's a very basic choice that we'd each need to make about how to deal with chronology in our notes. Should we write the fieldnotes chronologically, recounting the conversation and what we learned about each other and the lake as it unfolded? That would be writing from the perspective of real-time.

Or should we start the fieldnotes by giving some overview information at the outset, information that in reality we only picked up bit by bit along the way? For example, starting the fieldnotes with an overview of the different topics that we covered in the conversation, or with the names of everyone in the conversation, or even with the name of the lake we were walking along, things that we ourselves may not have learned until the middle or the end of the actual fieldwork session. That would be writing from the perspective of end-point time.

TIMOTHY: I see the choice involved. For me, it has been tempting to try to recreate everything in real time, to reveal bit by bit what I learned and experienced. But that can be so time-consuming. End-point fieldnote writing allows for an initial concentrated overview of the key points of information, and that can then enable notes that are more directed, more focused.

KAREN: It seems, then, as with so many of the choices facing an ethnographer, that this really isn't a question of which approach is always better, but rather a question of how the ethnographer wants to use both in a strategic way.

TIMOTHY: Yes. And I think the overarching goal, regardless of whether using real- or end-time chronology is to show, rather than tell.

PIERS: Show rather than tell?

TIMOTHY: Yes. For example, one of the important elements in fieldnote writing that I try hard to focus on is creating rich, complex, rounded characters instead of relying on stock or flat characters with very little depth. Consider: if I were writing a set of fieldnotes about this walk with you and Karen, a flat or stock way of characterizing each of you would simply be to call you academics or ethnographers. That would be *telling* the reader about you, and I would be using the role to stand in for your personality, what you look like, your outlook on life, and so on.

Alternatively, I could write down specific details that would create a richer, more rounded characterization of each of you. For Karen, I might include, verbatim, some of the jokes she's told and describe her facial expressions as she told them. This would *show*, rather than tell about, her sense of humor. Or Piers, I'd want to maintain the possibility of sharing with eventual readers of my ethnography the way you described, verbatim, the setting around us. By including this kind of detail, my fieldnotes would enable me to later *show* readers how sensitive you are to the play of light and color in your surroundings, rather than simply *telling* them that you have acute observational skills. And then there are still other things that I am sure to learn about you in the days ahead that would continue to help me in my quest to characterize you as richly as possible.

KAREN [making a funny face]: My sense of humor, huh?

[Simultaneous laughter.]

But joking aside, it seems to me that this emphasis on showing rather than telling signals one of the distinguishing characteristics of an ethnographic sensibility more broadly, and not just in the writing of fieldnotes.

PIERS: Meaning?

KAREN: Well, as we approach the complexity of the social world, the ethnographic sensibility cautions us not to create "stock characters" out of that world; not to summarize and simplify when we can evoke and complicate.

TIMOTHY: That's a really important point, Karen. There's a homology here between the ethnographic imperative to "show not tell" in fieldnotes and a larger intellectual and political sensibility about how to approach and understand the social world.

PIERS: It's a homology that really makes ethnography the odd one out in the overall privileging of parsimony and simplicity in much of the social sciences.

[A small pause as all consider this point.]

OK, so we make writing choices about point of view and how to handle time. But how do we structure the actual fieldnotes?

TIMOTHY: When I teach ethnography, I ask students to physically divide their fieldnote pages into three separate columns. The first is labeled "Description," the second, "Reflexivity," and the third, "Analysis." Using Piers's notes on his morning with Grandma for content, my tripartite fieldnote structure might look something like this:

[Draws in sand; Table 5.1 is projected onto back wall of stage.]

As I've taught ethnography over the years, I've noticed that some of my students, most often the theoretically inclined ones who want to include some empirical component in their work, have one or two terse descriptive observations and then pages and pages of theoretical engagement. I remember one student who wrote, "There is a surveillance camera located on the street corner," followed by four single-spaced pages of Foucault-inflected reflection on discipline and surveillance in modernity. Then, there are students who skimp on description and analysis, but fill page after page of their fieldnotes with reflections on how they are feeling and what is going on internally for them. And then there are students who are masters of description, but never reveal anything reflexive. So asking them to use this three-column format makes their tendencies more visible and suggests where to further develop their fieldnotes.

KAREN: Ok, but I would just add that this is a diagnostic, not a prescriptive, technique. I think ethnographers vary in terms of the emphasis they want to put on description, reflexivity, and analysis. We shouldn't be striving here for some kind of formula, although self-awareness is helpful.

TIMOTHY: Well, I'm glad you see the value of the three-column format. I have a lot of students and a few colleagues who find it too formulaic or constrained. They say it disrupts the flow of their writing.

**Table 5.1** Fieldnotes

| Description | Reflexivity | Analysis |
| --- | --- | --- |
| March 30, 1992 Observations—from dawn until dusk Fieldnote writing—that evening (from jottings) | Woke up so f-ing tired and still sore from slipping by the stream yesterday. Will I ever get the rest I need out here in the camp? | Today, I'm experimenting with a third-person-focused, real-time writing technique. Because there's not much happening while the men are out on the tundra, it's a good opportunity to focus more directly on Grandma and her routines. |
| Grandma began stirring under her blankets of reindeer hides just as the sky changed from black to the color of a bruise. Coughing loudly, she sat up and was still for a long moment before rising with a loud sigh to her feet and moving across the hut to the embers of the fire, barely flickering with orange from the night before. She took two ends of a rope strung through the handle of the blackened and dented cooking pot and, in a rapid, easy motion, folded the left end over the right end, then twisted both in a circular motion before folding the right end back over the left and hanging the rope onto a stout metal tripod above the embers. Outside, one of the reindeer made a clicking sound, "Chok-chok-chok." "Oh, little Bill Clinton," Grandma said, "it's too early in the day for you to be seeking a mate. Go back to sleep." | At this point, I felt the same discomfort about being alone with Grandma in the camp that I felt last night. I wonder if it's because I feel like I'm a burden on her in a way that isn't true when the other men are around to help. Watching her knot the rope with such dexterity, I'm reminded again of how clumsy I feel doing anything out here on the tundra. I've gotten to the point where I could tell it was a reindeer sound, but it feels like I'll never be able to identify specific reindeer from the sounds they make. Is it even possible to learn this skill as an adult? Is it hopeless for me? | This is the first time I've seen Grandma sitting so still after waking up. She's usually a blur of activity from the first moment the sky lightens. Perhaps she is getting sick, or perhaps she is worried about the prolonged absence of her sons. If the right opportunity arises, I should find a way to broach these topics with her. The alacrity with which she identified Bill Clinton just from a few vocalizations is astounding. The technical vocabulary that the Eveny have to describe reindeer is growing daily (see ongoing dictionary project for reindeer terms). But equally impressive is the familiar intimacy—is it going too far to call it love?—that individuals like Grandma exhibit for specific reindeer. This could be the beginning of an analysis of the intimacies of mutual reindeer–human domestication on the tundra. |

PIERS: Not at all! I think this is one of those cases where structure can aid rather than dampen creativity.

KAREN: I noticed one other structural element in this sample fieldnote, Timothy.

TIMOTHY: What's that?

KAREN: The use of a standardized heading that records the date, time, and duration of the fieldwork itself, as well as the time that's elapsed from the fieldwork session to the fieldnote writing and whether I used jottings, recordings, or other aids to help me with writing up the fieldwork.

TIMOTHY: Those headings really help me to track, across fieldwork sessions, certain patterns that might be emerging that I wouldn't otherwise be aware of. Am I only visiting my fieldsite on certain days, for example?

KAREN: This brings us to our earlier discussion of the importance of paying attention to the time parameters of our fieldsite and fieldwork.

PIERS [playing the student]: I really like all of these suggestions a lot, Professors. I am going to start putting some of them into use in my next ethnographic project.

TIMOTHY [also playing]: Yes, me too. And thank *you* as well, Professor Piers, for all of your insights.

But [growing serious] I think it's important not to lose sight of the larger goal here. These techniques for fieldnote writing are not an end in and of themselves. They exist to enable us to create thicker, richer, lusher fieldnotes, to inscribe, transcribe, translate, narrate, and textualize [raises eyebrows and hands in mock praise of himself for remembering all of those terms] the experiences of fieldwork in ways that create as much immediacy as possible for our ultimate readers. As *Writing Ethnographic Fieldnotes* reminds us again and again, we want more concrete detail and less generalization; more sensory imagery and less evaluative labels; more immediacy and less detachment; more distinctive qualities and less visual clichés. All of these techniques are useful insofar as they help us to accomplish that in our fieldnotes.

KAREN [laughing]: Ha. Well, then, with that benediction proclaimed on fieldnotes, shall we move on to the next item on our natural history of ethnographic fieldwork?

PIERS: We shall indeed. Timothy, what's next?

TIMOTHY: Exiting the field!

KAREN: This is complicated.

PIERS [cavalierly]: Complicated? What could be easier than leaving the field!

KAREN [with mock horror]: Piers!

PIERS [laughing]: Kidding, Karen, kidding. I'm so glad we've listed it as one of the stages of fieldwork. We don't talk very often about leaving the field, do we?

KAREN: It's such an essential part of the ethnographic research process.

TIMOTHY: My big question for you two is: how do you know when it's time to leave the field?

PIERS: When your funding runs out, when your romantic partner threatens to leave you because they haven't seen you in so long, or when you are under pressure to finish your thesis or your book in order to get or keep a job.

KAREN [laughing]: Hilarious.

PIERS: Well, seriously. We often give some sort of intellectual answer to this question, but the fact is that everyday life concerns often have as much impact on our ethnographic research decisions as intellectual concerns.

TIMOTHY: True. And it's also true that my question about how you know when it's time to leave the field is misleading in situations where the timing of your exit is not under your control. There may be a shift in the power dynamics in the field, or an event might occur that necessitates you leaving the field, even if you don't feel ready to.

But, those caveats aside, I still do think it's also important to think about how you would know, in an ideal world where there were no real-life constraints, how long to spend in the field.

PIERS: Well, I think you all know I spent twenty years researching *The Reindeer People*, so I'm probably not a good person to ask this question. I mean, were it up to me, I would still be in the field!

KAREN: I can certainly understand that. But twenty years just isn't going to be realistic for most people.

TIMOTHY: Much less two years!

KAREN: The traditional answer from anthropology has been a year. Like the word *field*-work itself, I think that the implicit expectation of "a year" of fieldwork relates to the rural locations of the first ethnographies in anthropology. A year allowed those ethnographers to experience their fieldsites across an entire cycle of wet and dry seasons or growing and resting seasons or fertile and fallow ones.

TIMOTHY: Thinking again about your fieldwork on Wall Street, Karen, it might mean that an ideal amount of time would have allowed you to experience a complete boom and bust cycle, or, barring that, at least an entire tax or accounting cycle.

PIERS: Right, I think the central idea here is that of the cycle. Are there recurring rhythms that circle back on each other in your fieldsite, and if so, how can you identify them and try to experience them in their entire duration?[60]

KAREN: With the enormous caveat, of course, that sometimes ethnographers can't know what the relevant cycles are until after they've started their fieldwork!

TIMOTHY: Another rule of thumb I like to use for when a researcher can start thinking about whether it's time to leave the field is when nothing, literally nothing, really catches her by surprise anymore. When there aren't any serious new discoveries being made.

KAREN: That's a good answer. But how do we know that the ethnographer hasn't simply been completely "captured" by one way of seeing? Or that her sense of curiosity hasn't been dulled by the repetition of fieldwork? And then, what about the people who continue to marvel and learn and be surprised every day, no matter how long they've spent somewhere?

PIERS: That was definitely true for me among the Eveny. I mean, even after I felt like I had a pretty good grasp of the textures of Eveny life, there were always dynamic changes in the relationships between people and between people and reindeer. There was always more to learn.

KAREN: Hence your twenty-year fieldwork stint!

PIERS: Exactly.

TIMOTHY: So perhaps another possibility is that the ethnographer exits the field only after exerting the effort to discover things that might overturn or discredit or cast suspicion on the interpretations they've formed throughout the fieldwork. The duration of fieldwork shouldn't just be about coming to a point where you feel like you have an excellent grasp on what is happening in the field, or where you have reached some analytic insights or conclusions that seem theoretically generative. It should really also be about an active searching, on your part, for things that might complicate or call into question some of the knowledge or the theoretical lines of sight that you've developed.

KAREN: Yes, I think it's true that after a certain point of immersion and exposure, fieldwork needs to contain active attempts to unsettle the conclusions you seem to be arriving at.

PIERS: Yes, I'd agree with that. But, you know, deciding when to exit the field isn't just about when it's good from the researcher's point of view, or good from the point of view of the theories and knowledge being generated by the researcher. It's also about how to negotiate a big transition in the relationships that have been formed in the field. As we've been emphasizing all along, ethnography is about relationships. So leaving the field is also about leaving, or at least significantly altering, relationships that are likely to have become very important to both the researcher and the people she's interacted with.

TIMOTHY: Say more.

PIERS: Well, for me, leaving the field was extremely difficult. I came to consider many of the Eveny reindeer herders my friends, and the act of leaving put our research relationship back into the spotlight.

KAREN: But leaving the field is not necessarily synonymous with ending relationships that have been formed in the course of fieldwork. There is a transformation of those relationships, most obviously in that the ethnographer is no longer actively researching those in the field and is perhaps also no longer physically present in their lives. But transformation is not the same as termination.

PIERS: Exactly. The ethnographer still has responsibilities to those in the field, even after the fieldwork has ended.

[Wolfdog snarls.]

KAREN [looking up suddenly]: Did anyone else notice that it's starting to get dark?

PIERS: Um, no. Lost in conversation like typical academics.

TIMOTHY: You're right, Karen. It's going to be night out here pretty soon.

KAREN: As fun as this conversation has been, we still don't know what to do about the invisibility potion!

PIERS: I think we should destroy them. Both the potion and the formula.

[Wolfdog turns and stares at Piers, her mouth forming an agonistic pucker. She can barely be seen in the fading light.]

TIMOTHY: Destroy them?

PIERS: Yes, destroy them.

[Wolfdog growls menacingly, hackles raised. The three ethnographers look at each other with concern and some fear.]

KAREN: You know, I agree with you, Piers. Given everything we've been saying about the importance of embodiment to ethnography...

[She is interrupted when the wolfdog, her growl turning into howling, takes off in a full sprint toward the barn.]

TIMOTHY, PIERS, AND KAREN: Whoa!

[All three start to run.]

KAREN: We better catch her before she gets back!

[Lights fade to darkness.]

## End of Act Five

## Notes

1 This title is inspired by a subheading in Paul Rock 2001: 32
2 Berlinski 2007
3 Vitebsky 2005: 331–332
4 Mills 2001, Pader 2006
5 "I landed in the Woodlawn boxing gym by default and by accident" (Wacquant 2004a: viii–x).
6 Thomas and Znaniecki 1918, Bennett 1981: 123, Duneier, Kasinitz, and Murphy 2014: 3
7 "The textbooks and colleagues sometimes give one a heroic image of the ethnographer as a man or woman with clear eyes and a penetrating vision who can, from the first, see ahead and understand what is to be seen, who can plan and act purposefully, striding out into the field like Indiana Jones. One's own experience tends to be quite different. It is of an initial confusion and muddle, a lack of purpose and direction, no sense of one's bearings but a reluctance to say so. One begins with very little useful knowledge of the research problem and the research site, only a sense acquired at some point that there might be something interesting to be found. The *prime ethnographic maxim* is that one cannot know what one is exploring until it has been explored" (Rock 2001: 33, emphasis added).
8 Laitin 2003, Schwartz-Shea and Yanow 2012
9 Laitin 2003
10 Ho 2009: 8, Vitebsky 2005: 64
11 Autesserre 2014: 11
12 Vitebsky 2005: 64
13 Pachirat 2011: 44
14 Duneier 1999: front matter
15 Scott 1985: 88
16 "This trail of remembered fields marks the landscape for the founders of this umbun (family unit). The neighborhood becomes not just a forest with scattered current fields but also a landscape of umbun movement over time, a life history remembered in regrowing forest" (Tsing 1993: 164–165).
17 "The complex drawing…presents a complete ritual performance—a curing ceremony. [Induan Hiling] has drawn not only the mountain-vegetation opposition described above, but also the shaman who brings together tradition and inspiration. On each side of the drawing are rocks; the triangles dominating the landscape are mountains. On the rocks and mountains grow vegetation: at the peak of the darkest mountain is a wild fig tree; a wild palm grows on the mountains to its left, and herbs and grasses, including the plant that appears to have drifted off the top, are found near that mountain's summit. At the left of the picture, Induan Hiling has drawn the dreamer in the form of an airplane. The airplane-dreamer energizes and experiences the dream landscape. Meratus commonly describe airplanes as vehicles of spiritual travel. Here, the representation of spiritual travel empowers the drawing as a shamanic ritual. Induan Hiling's sister, who was suffering from leprosy, kept this picture as an aspect of her cure. The drawing is not meant as a reminder of a shamanic performance; it is itself a curing ritual" (Tsing 1993: 241).
18 Vitebsky 2005: 10, 22, 93
19 Hayward 2000
20 Vaughan 2004
21 Sanjek 1991
22 Schwartz-Shea and Yanow 2009
23 Scott 1985: 63–64, 90, Munck and Snyder 2008: 373
24 Pachirat 2011: 281–285
25 On the "legwork" phase of fieldwork, see Wilkinson 2014.
26 Flyvbjerg 2001: 79

27  Khan 2013
28  Thomson 2009
29  Goodman 1972: 444–445. My thanks to Fred Schaffer for leading me to this example.
30  Flyvbjerg 2001: 80
31  Bourdieu 1977
32  Polanyi 1966, Nicolini, Gherardi, and Yanow 2003
33  "Heidegger says, you recognize a paradigm case because it shines, but I'm afraid that is not much help. You just have to be intuitive. We all can tell what is a better or worse case—of a Cezanne painting, for instance. But I can't think there could be any rules for deciding what makes Cezanne a paradigmatic modern painter.... [I]t is a big problem in a democratic society where people are supposed to justify what their intuitions are. In fact, nobody really can justify what their intuition is. So you have to make up reasons, but it won't be the real reasons" (Flyvbjerg 2001: 80). See also Yanow and Tsoukas 2009.
34  "The scholarly community is built on the exercise of judgment. Whether it is assessing a dissertation, evaluating a manuscript in the peer review process, or judging a research proposal for funding, scholars sit in judgment of others and, likewise, submit their own scholarship to such judgment. There are consequences of these judgments: some proportion of graduate students fails to receive degrees, some manuscripts are never published, and many research proposals go unfunded" (Schwartz-Shea 2014: 122).
35  IRBs, for example, "largely focus on complying with the regulatory details of the federal policy, fostering a thin, compliance, or checklist ethics rather than a more substantive engagement with issues arising in the actual conduct of political scientific, sociological, and other field research" (Yanow and Schwartz-Shea 2016: 278).
36  Dvora Yanow, personal communication (May 24, 2017). The following discussion draws on the most current IRB regulations in existence at the time of publication. However, in 2015 the US federal government initiated the formal process for changing the regulations that govern human subjects protection policy. The review process is ending as this is being written; the new rules are scheduled to go into effect in January 2018 unless stopped by the current administration. See also Yanow and Schwartz-Shea 2016: 277.
37  This recounting draws on Susan Reverby, *Examining Tuskegee: The Infamous Syphilis Study and its Legacy* (2013). Reverby's superb history details not only the Tuskegee study itself, but also the collective memory about Tuskegee and the continued work that "Tuskegee" does in shaping narratives of race relations and research ethics in the United States.
38  Milgram 2010, Zimbardo et al. 1972, Humphreys 2009
39  For a sophisticated and nuanced analysis of ethics in these three studies that challenges the simple, mythological narrative that they were unethical on their face, see Yanow and Schwartz-Shea 2015. The discussion that follows draws heavily on that analysis. For another, recent reassessment of covert participant-observation research, see Roulet et al. 2017.
40  See Brannigan, Nicholson, and Cherry 2015 for an alternative, and critical, assessment of Milgram's contributions to knowledge.
41  Schrag 2010. For ethnographically informed studies of the wide variability in how local ethics committees actually function, see Gray 1981, Fitzgerald 2005, van den Hoonaard 2011, Stark 2014.
42  "Research in the form of critical inquiry, that is, the analysis of social structures or activities, public policies, or other social phenomena, requires an adjustment in the assessment of consent. Where the goal of the research is to adopt a critical perspective with respect to an institution, organization or other entity, the fact that the object of the research may not endorse the research project should not be a bar to research receiving ethics approval. Where social sciences or humanities researchers seek knowledge that

critiques or challenges the policies and practices of institutions, governments, interest groups or corporations, researchers do not need to seek the organization's permission to proceed with the proposed research. If institutional approval were required, it is unlikely that research could be conducted effectively on such matters as institutional sexual abuse or a government's silencing of dissident scientists. Important knowledge and insights from research would be forgone" (Canadian Institutes of Health Research, Natural Sciences and Engineering Research Council of Canada, and Social Sciences and Humanities Research Council of Canada 2010: 35).

43 Feldman, Bell, and Berger 2003

44 "...neutrality in fieldwork is an illusion. Neutrality is itself a role enactment and the meaning of such a role to people will, most assuredly, not be neutral. Only by entering in to the webs of local associations does the field-worker begin to understand the distinctive nature of what lies within and without these webs. The field-worker's initial tasks involve finding out what classes of people are present on the scene and trying to figure out the cleavages that operate within these classes. There is unlikely to be much of a honeymoon period in fieldwork, for in short order the field-worker will have to decide which of the inner circles and classes to accept as his or her own" (Van Maanen 1991: 39–40).

45 Agar 2013

46 Rabinow 2011: 40–49

47 Blee 2003

48 Pachirat 2011: 140

49 Cruikshank 2016

50 Pachirat 2011: 2

51 "[A] piece of anthropological interpretation consists in: tracing the curve of a social discourse; fixing it into an inspectable form. The ethnographer 'inscribes' social discourse; he writes it down. In doing so, he turns it from a passing event, which exists only in its own moment of occurrence, into an account, which exists in its inscriptions and can be reconsulted. 'What does the ethnographer do?' – he writes" (Geertz 1973b: 452–453).

52 "...the view of anthropological analysis as the conceptual manipulation of discovered facts, a logical reconstruction of mere reality, seem[s] rather lame. To set forth symmetrical crystals of significance, purified of the material complexity in which they were located, and then attribute their existence to autogenous principles of order, universal properties of the human mind, or vast, a priori *weltanschauungen*, is to pretend a science that does not exist and imagine a reality that cannot be found. Cultural analysis is (or should be) guessing at meanings, assessing the guesses, and drawing explanatory conclusions from the better guesses, not discovering the Continent of Meaning and mapping out its bodiless landscape" (Geertz 1973a: 20).

53 For a summary, see Emerson, Fretz, and Shaw 2014: 16. Sanjek 1990 offers a more in-depth treatment.

54 Clifford and Marcus 1986, Keesing et al. 1987, Wedeen 2002, 2009, 2010, Sanjek 1990

55 Sanjek and Tratner 2015

56 "....to remember dialogue and movement like an actor; to see colors, shapes, textures, and spatial relations like a painter or photographer; and to sense moods, rhythms, and tone of voice like a poet. Details experienced through the senses turn into jottings with active rather than passive verbs, sensory rather than analytic adjectives, and verbatim rather than summarized dialogue" (Emerson, Fretz, and Shaw 2014: 35).

57 Emerson, Fretz, and Shaw 2014. Much of the conversation below derives from this now-foundational "how to" text.

58 Tolstoy 1920 [1869]

59 Haraway 1988

60 Thanks to Dvora Yanow for helping me think through this point.

# ACT SIX: THE TRIAL

At the heart of this controversy [over Alice Goffman's book] are the fundamental limitations of ethnography as a mode of inquiry. Ethnography can look like an uncomfortable hybrid of impressionistic data gathering, soft-focus journalism, and even a dash of creative writing.

Leon Neyfakh, "The Ethics of Ethnography" (2015)

That those flaws [in Alice Goffman's book] managed to go unnoticed for so long reflects a troubling race-related blind spot among academic and media elites. The failure of *On the Run* is not only the failure of an individual book and an author, but of the system that produced them.

Paul Campos, "Alice Goffman's Implausible Ethnography" (2015)

In Alice's desire to kill a rival 4th Street Boy, she exposed not only herself to harm, but also Mike...and the children, women, and men back on 6th street....The book reflects a disconcerting cognitive bias within the academic community that praises the hunting of a Black man with murderous intent.

Michele Goodwin, "Invisible Women: Mass Incarceration's Forgotten Casualties" (2015)

[W]hat [Goffman's] book fails to grasp and what much of sociology cannot account for even as it reproduces its logic is that the violence everywhere and everyday enacted by the state on black people is the grammar that articulates the "carceral continuum of black life." All black life, on the street and on the page.

Christina Sharpe, "Black Life, Annotated" (2014)

There's no risk-free, ethically insuperable way to get a close-up view of the kind of social world Alice was studying, where bravado and posturing, and the dramatization of destructive intent, are part of the fabric of everyday life.

Jack Katz, "Email Communication with Eugene Volokh" (2015)

We live in a world of weapons-grade fraud, hoaxes, and exaggeration in both the so-cial and physical sciences, so the idea that ethnography is especially flawed is absurd.

David Perlmutter, "In Defense of Ethnography" (2014)

Qualitative "research" is useless because there is no way to tell if what is claimed is a reflection of reality or simply the "researchers" [sic] gullibility and biases, or even if it's all a fabrication.... At least [quantitative research] can be put to the test in replication studies, as is increasingly done in social science. To use a book like Alice's as a guide to understanding social problems is to put enormous trust in her judgment and honesty—even when she openly admits to being a politically motivated advocate. There's no way to verify many of her claims.

Anonymous comment, *Marginal Revolution.com*

Almost all the topics that sociologists study, at least those that have some relation to the real world around us, are seen by society as morality plays and we shall find ourselves, willy-nilly, taking part in those plays on one side or the other.

Howard Becker, "Whose Side Are We On?" (1967: 245)

I am an invisible man. No, I am not a spook like those who haunted Edgar Allan Poe; nor am I one of your Hollywood-movie ectoplasms. I am a man of substance, of flesh and bone, fiber and liquids—and I might even be said to possess a mind. I am invisible, understand, simply because people refuse to see me. Like the bodiless heads you see sometimes in circus sideshows, it is as though I have been surrounded by mirrors of hard, distorting glass. When they approach me they see only my surroundings, them-selves, or figments of their imagination—indeed, everything and anything except me.

Ralph Ellison, *Invisible Man* (1952: 7)

## Scene

Cut back to the closing of Act Four: the sound of a motorcycle engine gradually grows louder and soon a cloaked, hooded figure can be seen in the background approaching the barn on a Harley Davidson, the folds of his cloak flowing dra-matically in the air. A long wooden staff is strapped to the back of the motorcycle. The motorcycle approaches the barn and The Prosecutor dismounts as Séver-ine Autesserre, Katherine Boo, Mitchell Duneier, Alice Goffman, James C. Scott, Anna Tsing, and Loïc Wacquant gather in a semicircle around him.

ALICE GOFFMAN: The Prosecutor, I presume?

THE PROSECUTOR: Hello, Alice. I'm late because I was just wrapping up another case in Virginia. The jury deliberations took longer than expected.

[Voice grows menacing.]

But, of course I emerged victorious. Yet another win for the facts against shoddy, anecdotal, so-called scholarship.

[Looks around at the group.]

And hello, Séverine, Katherine, Mitch, Jim, Anna, and Loïc.

ANNA TSING: You know our names?

THE PROSECUTOR: I make it my business to know all the facts. And let's dispense with niceties, shall we? Where are Karen, Timothy, and Piers?

KATHERINE BOO: They're outside with the wolfdog.

THE PROSECUTOR: The what?

JAMES C. (JIM) SCOTT: When we arrived here, we found a wolfdog who had run all the way from Siberia with an invisibility potion found in an icy high mountain pass. The wolfdog had dreamed…

THE PROSECUTOR [interrupting]: This is nonsense. There is no invisibility potion, no wolfdog, and no dreaming. What is wrong with you ethnographers? We live in a real world of hard facts, as I shall demonstrate as soon as we get this trial underway.

JIM: No, really, there…

THE PROSECUTOR [interrupting again]: Stop! We are here to deal with facts not fantasy.

[Looks around impatiently.]

I had hoped to also include Karen, Timothy, and Piers in this trial, but I don't have time to waste waiting on them. I have many more miles to travel today, for there are many other scientific pretenders who also need to be put on trial. So many trials, so little time.

LOÏC WACQUANT [cutting]: It is we who have just spent hours waiting on you! What is the meaning of this rude…

THE PROSECUTOR [pounding his staff on the floor]: Enough! We are here for one purpose only, and that is the ethnographic trial of Alice Goffman's book, *On the Run*. Public interest and the integrity of science demand it! Let's move upstairs and begin.

[Cut to the upper barn on Lake Keuka. The room is bare and austere, with wrinkled gray wood for floors and walls. Cracks in the back wall allow in piercing rays of angled afternoon sun, casting the room in a spotted patina of light. Standing or seated in a pattern loosely suggesting a courtroom are Katherine Boo and Séverine Autesserre (judges); The Prosecutor; Alice Goffman (defendant); Anna Tsing and James C. Scott (counsel and assistant counsel for the defense); and Loïc Wacquant and Mitchell Duneier (witnesses).]

KATHERINE [in a serious voice]: I am Judge Katherine Boo.

SÉVERINE AUTESSERRE [also serious]: And I am Judge Séverine Autesserre.

KATHERINE: Judge Séverine and I do hereby open the trial of The Prosecutor v. Alice Goffman.

SÉVERINE: As you know, The Prosecutor summoned us all here to hold an ethnographic trial of Alice's book. Initially, we all thought the idea ludicrous, but as news of The Prosecutor's victories against other young ethnographers accumulated, we each agreed to take time out of our very busy summers to be here. After all, if The Prosecutor is going to assume the mantle of "the public interest" and "the integrity of science," we thought we should have at least some say in how those things are understood.

We've all consented to play our roles in this trial to the best of our abilities, and we should do so with seriousness of purpose. Just to review, the roles we've agreed on are as follows: Alice, as the defendant and the author of *On the Run*, you will, of course, play yourself. Mitch, since you served on Alice's dissertation committee, we have recused you from any official role to avoid conflict of interest. However, we will be calling you as an expert witness to clarify a few contentious issues related to standing. Loïc, at your request, you will also be called as a witness. The Prosecutor, of course, will play the role of prosecutor.

THE PROSECUTOR [interrupting animatedly]: Role? It's not a role!

[Shouting and holding his staff above his head.]

  I. Am. The. Prosecutor!

SÉVERINE [calmly]: You will refrain from any further outbursts of this type or we will throw you out of our courtroom.

[The Prosecutor lowers his staff and sulks.]

SÉVERINE [continuing]: Anna and Jim, you will serve as counsel and assistant counsel for the defense respectively. And, as we've already noted, Katherine and I will serve as judges, our primary purpose being to try to keep the proceedings as fair as possible and to rule on any procedural questions. Originally, Karen, Piers, and Timothy were slated to form an ad hoc jury, but as they are presently away assisting the one-eyed wolfdog, we shall have to proceed without a jury.

THE PROSECUTOR [muttering]: A likely story, this fantastical wolfdog. What are they, afraid of me? Couldn't they have come up with a better excuse to skip my trial?

KATHERINE: It's not your trial. We are all here of our own accord, and we can leave at any time.

LOÏC [emphatic]: Whoever's farcical trial this is, I would like to state my objection to it in the strongest possible terms.

KATHERINE: But you came, did you not?

LOÏC: Only as a witness so that I could express my objections.

SÉVERINE: Very well. What are they?

LOÏC: The idea of an "ethnographic trial" is the very negation of social science, which by constitution should follow the Spinozist dictum, "Do not laugh, do not mock, do not judge."[1] Social scientists are not moralists, and even less judges. As ethnographies of courtrooms show, a trial is *everything but* an inquiry in search of truth. Its procedures are designed to establish guilt according to legal statutes, categories, and precedents. Now, American sociology is full of guilt—racial in particular—toward subordinate categories, but that's not a reason to erect guilt mongering to the level of method![2]

THE PROSECUTOR: That's a highly ironic position, given that the very idea of a trial derives from an essay by one of your fellow sociologists [looks at Mitch] entitled "How Not to Lie with Ethnography" in which he advocates for ethnographic trials.[3]

LOÏC [under his breath]: You would make an enormous error to lump all of us together in that way.

MITCHELL (MITCH) DUNEIER: Well, on this point Loïc and I are agreed. This trial is a terrible idea. It's an agreement rich with irony, I admit, given the typical tenor of our exchanges.

[Looks at Loïc and smiles.]

But who knows, maybe this could be the start of a less prosecutorial relationship between us, Loïc?

[Loïc grunts noncommittally.]

THE PROSECUTOR [looking at Mitch]: If this trial is such a terrible idea then why did you write an essay encouraging ethnographers to imagine that they are standing trial for ethnographic malpractice?

MITCH: Your Honors, may I respond at length?

KATHERINE: Certainly. It is in keeping with your role as an expert witness on questions of standing.

MITCH: The main point of my essay "How Not to Lie with Ethnography" was to encourage ethnographers to seek out what Max Weber, in "Science as Vocation," called "inconvenient facts"; that is, perspectives, opinions, and even potential participants in an ethnographic project that might call into question the ethnographer's interpretations and conclusions. Since The Prosecutor has invoked it in support of this trial, I would like at this time to read selections from that essay into the record.

[Holds a printed article up to catch the light so that he can read it.]

In the section of that essay subtitled "The Ethnographic Trial," I write:

*One of the ways I can accustom myself to inconvenient phenomena is to imagine that I will stand trial for ethnographic malpractice. An attorney has brought a claim against me on behalf of my study's readers. The trial will be held at a courtroom near the site of the study, and witnesses who know about my subject will be called. The important thing about these witnesses is that they will be the ones I most fear hearing from because what they know is least convenient for the impressions I have given the reader. They may also have been the least convenient for me to get to know.*

*In such a trial, we are not interested in the rights of the community under study or even the rights of any of the people being called to the witness stand, but the reader's right to a reasonably reliable rendering of the social world.*[4]

LOÏC: Once again, I state my objection to the application of a legal framework, a trial framework, to social science. I think the exhortation that ethnographers imagine themselves accused of ethnographic malpractice is misguided, since trials are not places where truth is adjudicated.

MITCH: I could not agree more with this point. The ethnographic trial envisioned in my essay was intended solely as a thought experiment that ethnographers might apply to their own work, a dramatic device to encourage ethnographic researchers to think carefully, and hard, about whom they build relationships with in the field and about how the shape and direction of these relationships might make it less likely that they will hear conflicting viewpoints and experience conflicting perspectives. What The Prosecutor is doing with the essay—zooming from trial to trial in his flowing black cloak and celebrating his legalistic victories over scholars—contradicts both the substance and the spirit of the essay in every way.

LOÏC [irritated and interrupting]: Be that as it may, you certainly let the evil genie out of the bottle with this one, Mitch.

MITCH [glancing at Loïc]: Well, so much for a less prosecutorial relationship.

[Turns back to the judges.]

As I was saying, Your Honors, my point in this short essay, which is really quite simple, is that one way to counterbalance some of the potential biases of ethnography, particularly its tendency to locate the researcher in one particular place in the social worlds and power hierarchies she studies, is to imagine what the most theoretically inconvenient evidence or occurrences or people might be—evidence, occurrences, and people who might challenge some of the theories or arguments being developed by the ethnographer. As my essay further states:

[Holds the article back up to the light and continues reading.]

*A primary task of ethnographers is to help their readers recognize phenomena that are inconvenient for the line or theory that has emerged from their fieldwork. Ethnographers well into their studies could, as a matter of course, ask a few simple questions: Are there people or perspectives or observations…whose existence is likely to have implications for the argument I'm making? Are there people or perspectives of phenomena…that, when brought before the jury, would feel they were caricatured in the service of the ethnographer's theory or line of argument?*[5]

An imaginary trial, as a thought experiment that an ethnographer applies to herself and her own work and [looks hard at The Prosecutor] *not* to anyone else, seemed to me to be one effective way to ask these questions in the service of creating a reasonably reliable account of the social world under study.

ANNA: Interesting. But even that gets into some pretty complicated ideas, don't you think?

MITCH: Like what?

ANNA: Well, it raises huge questions about what we mean by reasonably reliable, as well as about whether it ought to be the aim of an ethnographer to represent all the viewpoints in the social world she studies accurately and fairly.

JIM: Yes, and I also have some questions related to how you think about sampling, validity, and ethnographic work in that piece.

MITCH: Well, Jim, I was really doing some work of translation there. The essay was published in a highly positivist, quantitative methods journal, and the language of sampling allowed me to convey these ideas in ways legible to that particular audience.

JIM: I sympathize. Sometimes I feel like getting lost in translation is all I do anymore.

ALICE [impatient]: Your Honors?

SÉVERINE: Yes, Alice?

ALICE: This conversation seems to be getting a little off track, and as the "defendant" in this exercise, I would like to say a few words.

KATHERINE: Of course, Alice!

ALICE: I agree with both Mitch and Loïc that the framework of a trial has no place in how social scientists should judge one another's work. I do think that as a thought experiment that ethnographers apply to themselves, the idea can be helpful. But to take it to the level of an actual, staged trial is ludicrous.

SÉVERINE: Well, would you like us to call the whole thing off? I think you have a right to do that, since we are all here voluntarily, and The Prosecutor has no actual power to force us to hold this trial.

THE PROSECUTOR [indignant]: I have the power of the public interest and of the integrity of science!

LOÏC [scoffing at The Prosecutor]: Yes! I think we should call this whole thing off!

SÉVERINE: The court was asking Alice, not you.

ALICE: Let's just call this entire thing off! That was indeed my first reaction when I received the summons from The Prosecutor. If we don't stage the trial, we deny The Prosecutor his power.

[Looks at The Prosecutor and pauses. Prosecutor scowls.]

But then I began to think of it in different terms. It's important that people know that *On the Run* already has and continues to be subjected to a trial in the court of public opinion. Various academic and public critics have both defended and attacked the book on multiple fronts.[6] Indeed, it's surprising how many of the public discussions of my work are titled in ways that derive directly from courtroom language. One review is entitled, "The Trials of Alice Goffman,"[7] and two authors of completely separate essays about my work both use "Ethnography on Trial"[8] as their titles.

Even more specifically, I find it telling that some of the most sustained critiques of *On the Run* have been produced by law professors who are clearly invoking legal standards and procedures in their evaluation of my work specifically, and of ethnography more broadly.[9] Indeed, I believe one of them, Northwestern University professor of law Steven Lubet, even has a forthcoming book entitled *Interrogating Ethnography: Why Evidence Matters*. According to an announcement that's circulating about a conference on the book, Professor Lubet's *Interrogating Ethnography: Why Evidence Matters* is "a significant volume discussing the role of evidence in ethnography from the standpoint of a specialist in trial advocacy."[10]

So, yes, reflecting on the ubiquity of courtroom tropes in both the public and academic treatments of my book, the figure of The Prosecutor does seem an apropos way of synthesizing all of these critiques in a single person and of asking whether a legal framework is an appropriate one for the judgment of ethnographic work, and of scholarly work more broadly.

THE PROSECUTOR [glowering]: I'm no synthesis! I'm an actual person who rides an actual motorbike and carries an actual staff of justice and tries actual scholars in actual trials in which they are found actually guilty.

[Pauses.]

I do agree, however, that I'm apropos. I'm always apropos.

ALICE [continuing without acknowledging the interruption]: So, yes, as I was trying to say, despite my objections to the framework of a trial and its misapplication of standards of guilt and innocence to scholarly work, I think we should move forward with this particular trial of my book. After all, in many of the published critiques of my work, it is not just my book but the entire enterprise of ethnography that is called into question.[11]

THE PROSECUTOR [gleefully]: Ha ha! There you have it! She agrees!

KATHERINE: Please stop interrupting!

ALICE [continuing]: As I was saying, staging this trial may allow me to get feedback from a jury of my peers, that is, my fellow ethnographers. And, I also think that the trial will allow us to explore some really important questions not only about my work, but about ethnography more broadly, in a concrete way.

JIM: Your Honors?

KATHERINE: Yes, Jim?

JIM: Before we continue, let me just say that while I'm generally in favor of this kind of role-playing, I think it's important not to lose perspective. We've all been more or less randomly assigned to these roles for the purpose of this exercise, right?

KATHERINE: Yes, with the exception of The Prosecutor and Alice.

JIM: OK, but my main point is this. Alice, don't take it too personally when one of us either attacks or defends you. It's all for the sake of the exercise, OK?

ALICE [uncertainly]: Yes, I get it.

SÉVERINE: Also, regarding roles, we should note that there's some fluidity here. Because we are only a small group, we will be conducting an abbreviated trial by asking the prosecution and the defense each to make their most compelling cases in extended statements. And, as we've already noted, we do not have a jury.

KATHERINE: Right, so the point of this is not to render a single verdict of guilty or not guilty, but rather to create a structured space for a spirited conversation.

THE PROSECUTOR [pounding his staff on the floor]: That's unacceptable! I am here to obtain a guilty verdict.

SÉVERINE: You should be thankful we've agreed to respond to your summons at all!

KATHERINE: As judges, we would like to make one last point of clarification before we continue. Mitch, your essay states pretty strongly that the goal of an imagined ethnographic trial is not to protect the rights of the research subjects or the rights of the real and imaginary witnesses who have been called to testify at the trial, but rather to protect the rights of the reader.

MITCH: Correct. But that point serves to underscore, once again, the conscribed way in which I meant to deploy the conceit of a trial as a highly limited thought experiment that the ethnographer would apply to themselves to help with only one among many of the considerations important to ethnographic work. Of course, in broader terms, the entire corpus of my work demonstrates in the strongest possible way a concern not just for the "rights" of research subjects, but also for their dignity as human beings as well.[12]

KATHERINE: Thank you for clarifying that, Mitch. Given the breadth of the public critiques against Alice, we as judges don't think the scope of this trial should be limited only to the rights of the reader.

THE PROSECUTOR: Good! Because I have prepared a lot of charges against *On the Run* that have nothing to do with the rights of the reader.

SÉVERINE [severely]: Please do not interrupt the court!

KATHERINE: As I was saying, the court thinks the rights of the research participants are also extremely important here. Indeed, we wonder if in some way the rights of the research participants and the rights of the reader aren't inextricably linked, such that research that violates the rights of the research participants would also make the rendering of the social world in the ethnographer's account less reliable.

ANNA: Again, big questions about what exactly we mean by reliability.

KATHERINE: Questions that we hope may get addressed as the trial unfolds.

[Long pause. The Prosecutor shifts about on his feet while expectantly fingering his staff of justice.]

ALICE: Shall we begin?

THE PROSECUTOR: It's about time!

KATHERINE [with gravity]: The prosecution may offer its statement.

THE PROSECUTOR: Gladly, Your Honors. Our first set of charges—and I use the plural here to indicate that the charges I bring derive from a synthesis of published, public critiques that have been made of Alice's book—is brought on behalf of readers who have the right to a reasonably reliable rendering of the social world that Alice writes about. These charges are:

First, data fabrication.[13] On behalf of the readers of Alice's book, we charge that Alice fabricated data in her book, including entire interviews that, according to the chronology provided in her book, could not possibly have happened when she said they happened. For example, in chapter seven of her book, Alice reports verbatim an interview she conducted with Mr. George on the second-floor porch of his home. Alice writes that she spoke with Mr. George immediately after visiting her research subject and friend Chuck in county jail. In the course of this interview, Mr. George talks about the recent election of Barack Obama, which occurred in the fall of 2008. Thus, it is reasonable to assume that the interview took place no earlier than the fall of 2008. However, the reader learns two pages later that Alice's research subject and friend Chuck was killed in the summer of 2007. So, as readers we are left to wonder which was fabricated: Chuck's death, the date of Chuck's death, the interview, the date of the interview, or all four?

Another example of fabrication concerns claims by Alice that she spoke with Philadelphia police officers at a hospital who told her that the Philadelphia police department routinely checks hospital visitor logs and runs the names of visitors against a list of local residents with outstanding arrest warrants.[14] This practice, alleges Alice, keeps residents from going to the hospital to visit sick family members or even to get treated themselves, out of fear of arrest.

However, conversations by several different researchers with the Philadelphia police department and Philadelphia public defenders inquiring about this allegation have all resulted in the same response from the Philadelphia police: no, there is no such practice of checking visitor logs.[15]

Second, data destruction.[16] Alice destroyed all documentary evidence of the fieldwork on which her research was based, making it impossible to verify, corroborate, or otherwise cross-check her book even against her own notes. No different from other researchers, ethnographers like Alice have an ethical and scientific responsibility to make the information they have extracted from the social world available to anyone who would like to see it. Indeed, Your Honors, other disciplines like political science are rapidly moving toward procedures specified by guidelines like Data Access and Research Transparency (DA-RT) that strongly require all researchers, regardless of methodology or method, to post their data to online repositories so that other interested parties can use them to verify the analysis and conclusions reached by the researcher or to develop their own analyses. In the case of ethnographers, guidelines developed by DA-RT strongly encourage depositing to a repository all "source materials [including data from interviews, focus groups, or oral histories; fieldnotes (for instance from participant observation or ethnography); diaries and other personal records…]."[17] Now, DA-RT requirements do allow exceptions in the interests of human subjects protections, but the prosecution wishes to underscore here that not only did Alice fail to deposit her source materials in a widely accessible database, she deliberately destroyed them! It is hard to think of anything that could do more to rouse the suspicions of a reader than the deliberate destruction of all possible evidentiary bases for the claims that an author is making.

On this point, the prosecution would like to acknowledge Alice's stated reason for the destruction of her fieldnotes. In essence, Alice feared that her notes would provide law enforcement or other interested parties with the means of identifying and prosecuting her research subjects for illegal activities. We will address the effectiveness of this reasoning further when we turn to charges that can be brought against Alice on behalf of her research subjects, but for now we would simply like to note that—whether with the motive of protecting research subjects or not—the destruction of fieldnotes violates the rights of the reader of her ethnographic work because it removes any possibility of corroborating Alice's finished book *even against her own recorded fieldwork.* This holds true not only for an outside party, but, more strikingly, even for Alice herself, who, given the destruction of her fieldnotes, has only her memory and her already published accounts to rely on.

The destruction of fieldnotes—not to mention the anonymizing of the research subjects—might also do more to protect the researcher than those being researched. Your Honor [gesturing to Katherine], as you yourself stated in an interview about *Behind the Beautiful Forevers,* a work that shares many structural similarities with Alice's in terms of working with vulnerable, racialized, and policed populations:

[Pulls out and reads from a sheet of paper.]

*All of us who do nonfiction work must expect that our work is going to be scrutinized. One of the reasons I use so many documentary tools is because I hope when someone says one day, "that didn't happen," I'll be able to say, well, look at this and here's the tape of my fact checking, to have a kind of body of evidence for what's in my book. Often in writing about poverty, you'll see a line that says names and details have been changed, and I think that more often protects the writer more than it does the low-income people.*[18]

From this contrast between Your Honor's approach and Alice's, we can easily see why critics of her book say that ethnography has lower standards for truth-telling, documentation, and fact-checking than journalism![19]

Third, severely contradictory post hoc explanations that bring into question the basic trustworthiness of the researcher and, therefore, of the research itself.[20] Alice ends her book with an account of driving her armed research subject and friend Mike around in a car so that they could look for, and exact revenge on, the person who killed Chuck, another of Alice's research subjects and friend of both Alice and Mike. The prosecution would like to read into the record the relevant passage from Alice's book:

[Thumbs through a copy of *On the Run* and finds his place.]

*...I don't believe that I got into the car with Mike because I wanted to learn firsthand about violence, or even because I wanted to prove myself loyal or brave. I got into the car because, like Mike and Reggie, I wanted Chuck's killer to die.... I stopped seeing the man who shot [Chuck] as a man who, like the men I knew, was jobless and trying to make it at the bottom rung of a shrinking drug trade while dodging the police.... I simply wanted him to pay for what he'd done, for what he'd taken from us.*[21]

Later, when Northwestern law professor Steven Lubet noted that this passage constituted an admission of guilt on Alice's part that she had engaged in a conspiracy to commit murder—a serious felony offense[22]—Alice wrote this public response:

[Pulls out another sheet of paper and reads.]

*[L]et me say as plainly as possible: at no time did I intend to engage in any criminal conduct in the wake of Chuck's death. The passage in question comes at the end of a methodological appendix, in which I was describing the community reaction to this death as well as my own reactions in this difficult period. The summary account in the book does not include significant points that are relevant to the claim that I was engaged in criminal conspiracy. Most important, I had good reason to believe that this night would not end in violence or injury.... Talk of retribution was just that: talk.... These drives seemed to satisfy the feelings of anger and pain; they were a way to mourn a dear friend, and showed people in the neighborhood that Chuck's friends were doing something.*[23]

Your Honors, at this point, the prosecution is not concerned with whether or not Alice indeed committed a felony, as Steven Lubet alleges. That is a question of law for another kind of court. Rather, the prosecution's concern is with what appears to be a clear and blatant contradiction between the account Alice gives in the book and the later, post hoc account she gives in response to Steven Lubet's critique. Who is the reader to believe? The prior Alice of the book, who wanted Chuck's killer to die and who did not care that he, too, was another impoverished man on the run from the police, or the Alice looking back on her own book, who understood all along that the car ride was purely performative and ritualistic, with no actual possibility of murder or physical harm being inflicted on anyone?

The problem of contradictory post hoc explanation is further exacerbated by the later Alice's reference to a series of "significant points" that were omitted from the "summary account" given in the book. Because Alice has destroyed her fieldnotes and any materials that might allow her to go back in time and review what those missing significant points might be, her explanation presumably relies entirely on her memory and recollection of those significant points, a memory and recollection now subject to the pressure of an accusation of criminal conduct. Thus, the destruction of field-note data exacerbates the problem of contradictory post hoc explanations. Had Alice posted her fieldnotes to an online repository (as strongly encouraged, for example, by DA-RT), readers could check that repository to see for themselves what, if any, "significant points" Alice left out of her "summary account."

To make matters worse, Alice's admission that her account was a "summary" one that neglected entirely to address the performative, ritualistic nature of the car ride further erodes any confidence and trust a reader might have in her ethnographic writing.[24] The persuasiveness of ethnographic writing derives in large part from its thickly descriptive qualities. If Alice is leaving out "significant points"—including an analytically and theoretically important insight about the performative nature of rituals of violence in the neighborhood she studied—only to reference them later, after the publication of the book and as a way of extricating herself from charges of criminal conduct, then how is the reader to trust that any of the other accounts in the book are not similarly plagued? In short, the contradiction between Alice's book account and her post hoc account create a situation in which the reader is led to question her ethnographic credibility.

Fourth, prejudicial bias.[25] The passage from Alice's book just read into the record demonstrates how prejudicially biased Alice became in the course of her research. This bias not only extends to how Alice viewed and wrote about the police in her book, but also to how she wrote about others in the same or adjacent social worlds as her primary research subjects and friends. Alice so took on the point of view of those specific individuals that she wanted to "see die"[26] another individual who was similarly situated to her research subjects in every way except for the street that he lived on. Moreover, as Amy Wax and Michele Goodwin have each outlined, Alice privileges the perspectives and experiences of Chuck, Mike, and their friends over the perspectives and experiences of other similarly situated black men from the same neighborhood who chose to keep themselves off the streets and out of trouble with the law, as well as over the perspectives and experiences of black women in the same neighborhood. Importantly, these perspectives and experiences might have led Alice to a different series of conclusions than the ones that she arrives at in her book, which, as the prosecution understands it, is precisely the reason why Mitch would have ethnographers imagine themselves undergoing an ethnographic trial in the first place.[27]

There is a direct parallel here to Mitch Duneier's critique of Clifford Geertz's famous essay, "Deep Play: Notes on the Balinese Cockfight." Duneier critiques Geertz for, essentially, advancing a huge set of generalized claims about the community and culture he was studying based on his relationship with one very specific family in that community, without attempting to reach out to others who might have been in conflict with that family or who come from a different social class than theirs. In the same way, we might say that the prejudicial bias, or shall we say murderous bias....

ANNA: Objection, Your Honor!

KATHERINE: Sustained! Counsel, please watch your language.

THE PROSECUTOR: Yes, Your Honor. The prejudicial bias exhibited in Alice's work towards the police, towards other residents of 6th Street, towards women in the neighborhood, towards similarly situated residents of other adjacent neighborhoods—this prejudicial bias all stems from her deep empathy, an empathy she herself describes as friendship, with this one specific group of males on 6th Street. And this prejudicial bias calls into question Alice's reliability and trustworthiness as an ethnographer. It calls into question, for the reader, the trustworthiness of her account.

[Turns and looks pointedly at Alice. Then back at the judge.]

That, Your Honors, summarizes the charges the prosecution would like to bring on behalf of the right of the reader to a reasonably reliable rendering of the social world that Alice studied.

SÉVERINE: Is the prosecution finished with their opening statement?

THE PROSECUTOR: Not yet, Your Honor! Given that Your Honors have explicitly widened the scope of the trial beyond the rights of the readers to also include the rights of the communities and participants in the research study, the prosecution would also like to bring a series of charges on behalf of the communities and specific individuals Alice studied.

KATHERINE: You may proceed. But please keep the remainder of your opening statement concise.

THE PROSECUTOR: Certainly, Your Honor. With respect to the rights of the research subjects in *On the Run*, the prosecution would like to bring the following charges:

First, that Alice actually intended to physically harm—indeed, kill— someone who could plausibly be understood to be her research subject.[28] Your Honors, we are not engaging here the question raised by Steven Lubet about whether or not, according to prevailing *legal* standards in the United States, Alice committed a felony in the course of her fieldwork. Far more straightforward, and far more simple from the perspective of protecting the rights of her research subjects, is the undeniable fact that Alice became so entwined in her specific situation as a friend of Chuck, Mike, and other members of her immediate neighborhood, that she was willing to assist Mike in hunting for and killing another similarly situated individual who lived in a nearby neighborhood. This individual, no less than Chuck, Mike, or anyone else who comprised part of the racialized, relatively impoverished population, very much qualifies as one of Alice's "research subjects." Indeed, it is hard to think of a more direct and egregious violation of the central value of the protection of research subjects than Alice's outright admission, and publication, of her desire to see one of her research subjects dead.

Second, that despite destroying her fieldnotes and other research materials, Alice failed to adequately protect the anonymity of her research subjects.[29] In the wake of Lubet's critique of *On the Run*, several journalists and academics made attempts to locate the 6th Street neighborhood that Alice conducted research in, as well as the specific people she did research with. In one case, Jesse Singal from *New York Magazine* identified Alice's neighborhood through a simple internet search, then showed up in the neighborhood with a photograph of Alice and a box of Munchkins from Dunkin' Donuts. As he tells the story, it was not long before he was sitting in the living room of Ms. Linda and then meeting Josh at a bar for drinks.[30] Similarly, Paul Campos, a professor of law at the University of Colorado, conducted "cursory online research" and was able to identify with reasonable certainty the real identities of Chuck and Mike, as well as pull up their complete police records.[31] It seems that if the motive behind Alice's intent to destroy her fieldnotes was indeed to protect her research subjects, she might have done a better job of concealing or disguising their identities in her published book.

Third, by virtue of her research, Alice opened up the 6th Street community and other communities like it to even more intensive modes of surveillance and control. By revealing to law enforcement and the general public how fugitives and the social structures around them operate—including, for example, revealing how urine samples are bought and sold to pass probation-related drug tests—Alice actually further subjects these hyper-policed communities to the aggression of law enforcement.[32]

And fourth and finally, Alice reinforces a long relationship of domination and exploitation of impoverished neighborhoods that exist in close proximity to the University of Pennsylvania and other prestigious schools, such as the University of Chicago. As a privileged white woman, Alice reenacts and reinforces a dynamic whereby, as Christine Sharpe eloquently puts it:

[Takes out sheet of paper and reads.]

*The black communities of 4ᵗʰ and 6ᵗʰ Street continue to be laboratories in which Alice and other student and faculty researchers at the University of Pennsylvania do fieldwork. With its frisson of 'authenticity,' On the Run may have a long and varied life ahead (a mini-series? feature film?) shaping misperception and abetting black narrative and material subjugation. I already know that this book will be chosen for First Year common reading programs and that all over the US, historically white colleges and universities with small black undergraduate and faculty populations will read and then reproduce as truth On the Run's ethics and methods; which is to say, its relations and practices of power. In the neoliberal 'engaged' university, On the Run is sure to be a primer for how to do immersive 'urban' ethnography. And so continues, into the next generation, what Sylvia Wynter has called our black narratively condemned status.*[33]

That, Your Honors, sums up our case against Alice and her book, *On the Run*.

[The Prosecutor takes a self-satisfied step back with a dramatic flourish of his staff.]

KATHERINE: Very well. Let us now turn to a statement from the counsels for the defendant.
ANNA: Thank you, Your Honors. We would like to begin by making a simple, but important, distinction in the face of all of these charges brought by the prosecution against our client, both the charges on behalf of readers who have a right to a reasonably reliable rendering of the social world and on behalf of those who participated in Alice's study by virtue of being observed by her or by entering into a social relationship with her.

This is the distinction between applying evaluative criteria *external and foreign* to the type of interpretive ethnographic project that Alice was engaged in and applying criteria consistent with that type of project.

Your Honors, attention to the kinds of terms deployed by the prosecution in their charges against Alice on behalf of readers signals immediately that they are working within a decidedly positivist conception of the world. Most ethnographers working within an interpretivist logic of inquiry would not be so quick to characterize their research as being about the *extraction* of *information* from the social world and the subsequent analysis of the *data* byproducts of this extraction, but would instead speak about the co-constitution of intersubjective knowledge in collaboration with the social world.[34]

Indeed, the D in the political science DA-RT project referenced by the prosecution stands, of course, for data. It is this underlying and unexamined assertion—that *all* evidence-based social science is about the *extraction* of *information* that is then subsequently processed and analyzed as *data* in order to produce social science *knowledge*—which most clearly signals that the framework being applied to Alice's work is not the proper, appropriate one.

The prosecution has suggested, for example, that many of the problems of credibility in Alice's work might have been prevented if she had posted to a repository the fieldnotes, diaries, and other personal records written or recorded in the course of her fieldwork. But, Your Honors, we wish to ask the prosecution this: why stop with requiring ethnographers to post their fieldnotes, diaries, and personal records? Why not also require Alice, or any other ethnographer, to wear 24-hour, 360-degree Visual and Audio Recording Technology (VA-RT) that will be digitally live-streamed to an online data repository and time-stamped against all fieldwork references in the finished ethnography? Would the time-stamped, 24-hour, 360-degree VA-RT then constitute the raw "data" that transparently verify both Alice's "data" and her interpretation and analysis of those data?

VA-RT—while an exaggeration—dramatizes a mistaken view that Alice's or any other ethnographer's fieldnotes, diaries, and personal records constitute a form of raw "data" that can then be checked against any "analysis" in a finished ethnography. In our view, Your Honors, the fallacy underlying the mistaken proposal that ethnographic fieldnotes, diaries, and other personal records should be posted to an online repository derives from at least three places.

The first is an extractive ontology inherent in a view of the research world as a source of informational raw material, rather than seeing knowledge as resulting from a specifically relational and deeply intersubjective engagement. Fieldnotes—and even a VA-RT—will always already contain within them the intersubjective relations and the implicit and explicit interpretations that shape both the substance and the form of the finished ethnographic work. Quite simply, there is no prior, non-relational, non-interpretive moment of raw information or data to refer back to. What this means is not only that there are no prior raw "data" to reference, but that any attempt to depersonalize and remove identifying information from fieldnotes in order to comply with confidentiality and human subjects concerns will render the fieldnotes themselves unintelligible, something akin to a declassified security document in which only prepositions and conjunctions are not blacked out.

Second, fieldnotes, far from being foundational truth-objects upon which the "research product" rests, are themselves texts in need of interpretation. Making them "transparent" in an online repository in no way resolves or obviates the very questions of meaning and interpretation that interpretive scholars strive to address.

And third, neither fieldnotes nor VA-RT offers a safeguard "verification" device regarding the basic veracity of Alice's or any other researcher's claims. The researcher produces them, and, in the end, they are dependent on the researcher's trustworthiness. Even though we are not aware of the existence of such research misconduct, we must admit that it would not be impossible for a researcher to fabricate fieldnotes or to stage performances or otherwise alter a VA-RT recording.

Now, this is not to say that there is therefore no framework at all that can be applied to evaluate Alice's work, or that it absolves Alice's work from criticism or even censure. In rejecting an extraction-based view of the researcher's relationship to the social worlds she studies, interpretive ethnography does not then create an "anything goes" alternative. Indeed, Your Honors, a work of interpretive ethnography that did not seek to centrally discuss the contours of the researcher's engagement with the social world, that did not aim to detail how the researcher generated and deployed the material that constitutes her ethnography, and that did not strive to share that material in richly specific, lushly detailed language would not just fail to persuade a readership of interpretive ethnographers, it would, literally, cease to be recognizable as a work of interpretive ethnography!

Where other modes of research and writing might prize the construction and presentation of a gleaming and flawless edifice, two key criteria for the persuasiveness of an interpretive ethnography are, first, the degree to which the ethnographer leaves up enough of the scaffolding in her finished ethnography to give the reader a thick sense of how the building was constructed, and, second, the degree to which the finished ethnography includes enough detailed specificity about the social world(s) she is interpreting. This detailed specificity allows, indeed, encourages, the reader to challenge, provoke, and interrogate the ethnographer's interpretations using the very material she has provided as an inherent part of the ethnographic narrative.[35]

JIM: To put it another way, the transparency and openness—what interpretive ethnographers often refer to as reflexivity and attention to embodiment and positionality—that DA-RT proponents see as *lacking* in deeply contextual qualitative work constitute the very hallmarks of interpretive ethnography as a mode of research, analysis, and writing. What is more, interpretive ethnography prioritizes dimensions that go beyond what is called for by DA-RT. This mode of research encourages reflexivity about positionality and an examination of the power involved in the researcher's embodied interactions with the social world. This reflexivity extends as well to the potential impacts and effects of the politically and socially legitimated "knowledge" produced through the researcher's embodied interactions with that social world.

It is by these internal relational and reflexive criteria that Alice's research should be judged, not the criteria of an extractionist view of social research alien to the research community she is working within.

ANNA: How, then, does Alice's work stand up to a set of appropriately applied criteria?

When we apply criteria consistent with the method's own self-expectations, we see immediately the conundrum that Alice and other ethnographers like her are forced into when it comes to their fieldnotes. On the one hand—and often under the legally motivated admonishments of their IRB or other ethics review protocols—ethnographers conducting research in situations like Alice's are often encouraged to anonymize, quarantine, or sometimes even destroy their fieldnotes in order to protect the identities of their research participants. On the other hand, external criteria, particularly those being applied by DA-RT and comparable movements, are institutionalizing norms that punish field researchers who fail to preserve and make public their fieldwork and other documents, attacking them as "data hoarders" and their work as unscientific if they do not do so. Although the Princeton IRB did not require Alice to destroy her fieldnotes, she later cites IRB guidelines as the reason for why she will not disclose where a scene involving her interrogation by the police takes place.[36] And so it is that both Alice's book and other ethnographic work must often navigate tensions between the anvil of a state ethics policy's requirements for anonymity and research subjects protection, and the hammer of the so-called "data transparency" movement.

Inside this space of extreme pressure, other forces also make themselves felt. Supreme among them is the sense of responsibility that the ethnographer—and certainly Alice—feels to protect her research subjects from even further surveillance, disciplining, and policing than they are already experiencing. Particularly in fieldwork on legally fraught activities, researchers may decide to sacrifice even the suggestion that any copies of their notes remain in order to stave off subpoenas and other state actions aimed at punishing their research subjects. This, we think, is what motivated Alice to destroy her notes, although the tension between the IRB and the transparency movement is the space in which those actions are being judged.

We ourselves feel that it is an extreme response—perhaps an inverted extreme to the "make-it-all-publicly-available" solution proposed by DA-RT—for ethnographers to wipe out their fieldnotes. We believe that such destruction represents an unwise course of action, not because it prevents the depositing of those notes to an online database, as the prosecutors would have it, but rather because it prevents Alice herself—or others who are trusted by her or to whom she is accountable—from going back to her fieldnotes to capture the rich, detailed descriptions and her own state of mind during both mundane and dramatic events that occurred in the course of the fieldwork. Indeed, it prevents even her research subjects from going back to her notes, should both they and Alice want them to. Here, we are in agreement with the prosecution that Alice's post hoc account of her and Mike's state of mind as they drove around town looking for Chuck's killer would have been more persuasive had she at least had access to her own, contemporaneously written fieldnotes rather than having to rely solely on her memory. In any case, Alice has already made it clear that she feels she did not go far *enough* in anonymizing her research world. She is deeply horrified at the thought that her book has led others to the 6th Street neighborhood and wishes she had done more to protect them from these types of intrusion.

We also acknowledge some weaknesses in Alice's writing. Not weaknesses of fact: she stands by every fact in the book as it is written and denies outright the first charge of "data fabrication"! But, as her defense, we do acknowledge that there may have been unintentional mistakes of chronology that create inconsistencies in the book's account, such as the one in which she reports seeing Chuck immediately before interviewing Mr. George, even though, according to her own chronology, the interview obviously could only have taken place after his death. Although scrambling chronologies was motivated by a desire to make people less identifiable, there is no reason why such scrambling had to create an internally inconsistent narrative or timeline in the book. Readers are right to approach such inconsistencies with an attitude of skepticism.

The prosecution also charges Alice with failing to conduct the kinds of "inconvenience sampling" encouraged in Mitch Duneier's aforementioned essay, analogizing her focus on a subset of the 6th Street men to Clifford Geertz's failure to look beyond the narrow slice of the village in which he was embedded. We submit that these charges are unpersuasive, for two reasons.

First, Alice's stated purpose in the book was not to represent the entirety of the 6th Street neighborhood, but rather to show the lives and social situations of men who were on the run from the police. What counts as a relevant part of an "inconvenience sample" is always first and foremost determined by the scope and focus of the study itself. Just as we would critique neither Mitch Duneier for not going to Vermont to interview the neighbors of the Christmas tree sellers who appear in his book *Sidewalk* nor Piers Vitebsky for not embedding himself in the factories that processed reindeer meat, so, too, we should not critique Alice for not examining the totality of all of the social worlds in the 6th Street neighborhood.

And second, even though Alice is interested in the lives of black men on the run from police, she does engage in a version of Mitch Duneier's extended-place method. Two entire chapters of *On The Run* explore perspectives other than those of her main ethnographic subjects. Chapter three, entitled "When the Police Knock Your Door In," provides insight on the girlfriends, mothers, and other women in these men's lives, and chapter four, entitled "Clean People," explores the lives of those men in the neighborhood who are not on the run from the law. Just as Duneier was interested in the white Christmas-tree-selling family from Vermont because of how they might further illuminate his book's main focus—the black booksellers—so too does Alice use these extensions to illuminate the lives of the people who constitute her main research interest.[37]

JIM: Having addressed the charges of "data fabrication" and "data destruction," as well as the related charges of contradictory post hoc explanations and a failure to adequately anonymize the research world, the counsel for the defense would like to continue by joining together the remaining charges that the prosecution divided between those brought by readers and those brought by research subjects. Counsel feels that it will be more intellectually productive to view the remaining charges through a lens of extreme importance to all interpretive ethnography: namely, the centrality of reflexivity about positionality and relationality in the fieldsite.

KATHERINE: Proceed.

ANNA: The remaining charges are that Alice: 1) conducted her research with prejudicial bias; 2) intended bodily, physical harm against at least one of her subjects; 3) exposed low-income communities of color to even more intensive policing and surveillance by revealing to the authorities and other outsiders their strategies and tactics of resistance; and 4) reinforced relationships of exploitation between elite universities and the low-income communities of color that often surround them. Your Honors, the common thread uniting all of these charges is that they stem directly from the positionality of the researcher in the research world, in the unavoidably embedded and embodied quality of ethnographic research.

In a classic essay entitled "Whose Side Are We On?" Howard Becker provides a prescient analysis of perceptions and accusations of bias in ethnographic work that continue to ring true to this day. In particular, and tellingly for Alice's case, Becker distinguishes between charges of bias in two different sets of power relations: those that are apolitical and those that are political. By apolitical, Becker means structures of institutionalized control where there are not overt, organized attempts to overthrow those structures. There may be discontent with the structures, and it may be profound, but no one is organizing to overthrow, overturn, or even fundamentally reform the structures. Most work environments, where there are bosses and subordinates, are apolitical in this way. These include hospitals, police, militaries, and, indeed, many of the basic institutions that reproduce the fabric of our societies.

In these situations, Becker writes, there is an implicit, and often explicit, hierarchy of credibility; a hierarchy concerning whose version of reality is to be believed and whose is not.[38] Superordinates have a near monopoly in this hierarchy, such that a university professor typically has far more power to define the relevant realities of the classroom than an undergraduate student. Indeed, if the student is to challenge the professor, it is usually within the confines of the relevant realities that the professor has already laid out. "My grade should be an A–, not a B+, because the syllabus awards three extra credit points," rather than, "Why should you make up the rules and create the syllabus and why should you be the professor and I, the student?" or even more radically, "Why should there be grades or professors or students at all?"

In politicized situations, by contrast, the power conflicts between the superordinate and the subordinate are already out in the open, in such a way that both sides are struggling to gain supremacy concerning who defines the relevant realities of a situation.

In the first situation, the apolitical one, the ethnographer is usually only accused of bias—or usually only suspects herself of bias—if she takes the subordinates' lived experiences and thoughts and uses them as the point of view from which she frames, describes, and interprets the relevant realities. This is because the superordinate has such a monopoly on the description of the given reality that anything running counter to it seems radical, subversive, or nonsensical. Most ethnographic and other social science work, argues Becker, takes the superordinate's point of view and definitions of the relevant reality as a given, but because that view is so normalized, the work is rarely accused or suspected of bias, either by readers or by the researcher herself.

In the second situation, the situation of open political conflict in which each side strives to command the definition of the relevant realities and the "facts," the ethnographer is likely to be accused of bias regardless of which perspective or point of view she takes. Her work is already politicized, from the beginning, and serves as a space of refraction for the political conflict that she studies on the ground. This is particularly true when, for whatever reason, the work becomes widely known, as is the case with Alice's book.

Becker argues that in neither the apolitical nor the political situation is it possible to conduct ethnographic or any other kind of social research that is not biased. To be biased is to have a point of view, and every piece of research contains a point of view, whether that point of view is acknowledged or not. Indeed, Your Honors, this is one of the hallmarks of interpretive ethnography: that it gives explicit attention to the power relations implied by having and representing a point of view.

Becker's analysis sheds light on the charges of bias against Alice. In some instances, we can see a naïve notion of fact-checking at play in these charges, a fact-checking which constitutes little more than not liking the experiences or point of view of the subordinate party and running back to the superordinate party for clarification of what the "real" facts are. This, in essence, is what Steven Lubet does when he phones up the Philadelphia police department to ask them if they ever check hospital logs to find people with outstanding arrest warrants. When Lubet is told no by the police, he takes that as the "real" reality; as evidence both of Alice's prejudicial bias towards her research subjects *and* of falsification of her data. Viewed through Becker's lens, the favoring of the Philadelphia police department's account of police practices over Goffman's account of how such practices are experienced by the residents of 6th Street is, in fact, a reassertion of a hierarchy of credibility. In short, on this count, Lubet is no less biased than Alice. His bias simply runs in the direction of the superordinate, while Alice's runs in the direction of the subordinate.

Second, it's interesting to note the timing of Alice's work and its subsequent publication. As she herself noted, when she first started her research:

[Pulls out and reads from a piece of paper.]

> *Public coverage of our historically high incarceration rates and the aggressive policing that has helped produce them was limited. The tough on crime position still held considerable sway in the press and in Washington.*

By the time of the book's publication, however, the police killings of unarmed black men in Ferguson, Staten Island, Baltimore, North Charleston, Brooklyn, and many other cities were capturing a great deal of media attention. Alice continues:

> *Since [the time when I conducted research] we've seen a critical shift. Politicians on both sides of the aisle are joining with activists, journalists, and practitioners to confront the fact that we are sending too many people to prison and that police conduct can be violent and dehumanizing.*[39]

In other words, Alice's work arguably straddles a fault line in which issues of policing and race moved—drawing on Becker's classification—from an apolitical context in which a hierarchy of credibility placing police at the top and poor blacks at the bottom was largely unchallenged by the broader public, to an openly politicized context in which police and organized activists struggled for control over the definition of the relevant realities. The straddling of this fault line, we argue, shapes some of the conflicting charges of bias against Alice. For some who are clinging to old hierarchies of credibility, Alice's account is biased in its anti-policeness. For others who are seeking to challenge those hierarchies, the structural features of Alice's account, including her position as a white, privileged person coming from an Ivy League institution with infinitely greater resources than the neighborhoods around it, mimicked all too closely the surveillance and police apparatus that she thought she was writing against.

We fully accept that our client conducted biased research. But our point is that *all* research is biased, in the sense that it is written from a point of view. We hold that Alice was forthcoming about the intent of her study—to produce an on-the-ground account of policed communities from the perspective of those being policed—and adequately reflexive about the larger structural issues at play. Her study was neither deceptive nor covert. Additionally, to those who take issue with Alice's privilege or the privilege of the educational institution she was a part of, or with her whiteness, her gender, her age, or her class position, we ask: under what conditions, if any, is it legitimate for people to conduct research on and represent the lives of those who are different, sometimes radically, from themselves?

These are difficult questions, and the answers are surely as messy as the realities that shape them. Still, there are two answers that we urge the court to reject in their entirety: first, that whites cannot conduct research on or with blacks or other nonwhites (or vice versa); that the rich cannot conduct research on or with the poor (or vice versa); that the European cannot conduct research on or with the indigenous (or vice versa); that the human cannot conduct research on or with the nonhuman. But, second, we equally reject a naïve approach to power; an approach reflected most often in a white privilege that seeks to deny or erase lines of difference that have been constructed through relations of oppression and domination. From this point of view, there is nothing at all problematic or difficult about researchers who cross racial, class, or other lines in order to conduct research on or with others who have been positioned radically differently by power relationships. Against both of these views, we submit that there is much to be learned by all parties involved from the strangeness that comes with being a near-total outsider to a situation, but that this strangeness must be accompanied by an abundance of reflexivity and humility.[40] Indeed, Your Honors, we suggest that this unresolvable tension between strangeness and reflexivity is one of the key traits that makes immersive ethnography so generative as an approach to the study of power.

Your Honors, we have saved for last the most difficult charge of all: that Alice fully intended bodily harm—even death—to one of her research subjects. It may sound brazen, Your Honors, but our position, which we do not hold lightly, is that this emotionally driven response on Alice's part is fully consonant with her role as an ethnographic researcher, and that, indeed, we can find echoes, traces, and reverberations of it throughout many other ethnographies involving immersion within highly fraught sites of power. Paul Rabinow recounts becoming so angry with his informant, Ali, that he kicked him out of his car and left him on the side of the road in the middle of the night. He also recounts hiking in the mountains and making love with someone who might plausibly have been defined as a research subject.[41] Timothy Pachirat writes of his struggle with the liver packers in the cooler of the slaughterhouse and his attempts to get them reprimanded by his boss.[42] Perhaps these examples—and the countless others that we do not know about because their authors have deliberately sanitized them from their final, published accounts—do not quite rise to the level of Alice's desire for lethal vengeance. But each, in its own way, demonstrates the absolute precariousness of the ethnographer in the face of real emotions that are the result of real relationships! These are formed in a space that—however much we wish to define it as a "field" or a "site" of study—is always already inextricably part of the larger world. What Alice's account provides is the valuable extreme case that illuminates a dynamic that is not only common to, but is actually required by, the basic ethnographic premise of immersion. And like all extreme cases, perhaps it is those who most recognize themselves in her who are sometimes the quickest to condemn.

THE PROSECUTOR [indignant]: I have never wished anyone dead! Behind bars, yes, but never dead!

SÉVERINE: Quiet!

ANNA: Please note, Your Honors, that we are not excusing or legitimating, in Alice or in any other, the desire for vengeance, especially vengeance to the death. But, as we know from history, from the bards, and from the daily news, the desire for vengeance is integrally part and parcel of what it means to be alive. As are, we might add, sexual lust, infatuation, anger, sadness, hope, faith, loyalty, friendship, disappointment, compassion, heartbreak, and, perhaps greatest of all, love. We are also not determining either way whether or not Alice broke the law when she drove Mike around that night to look for Chuck's killer. Did she commit a felony, as Lubet has accused her of doing? Perhaps, perhaps not. That is for a different sort of court to take up and for a different sort of jury to decide. From the perspective of adjudicating Alice's guilt or innocence according to the standards of interpretive ethnography rather than the standards of the law, the question of the *legality* of her actions is neither here nor there. Indeed, there are circumstances in ethnographic research where abiding by the law would be *unethical*, even though one would remain innocent by the standards of the state. Think, for example, of Jason De León's study of the hidden consequences of the United States' "Prevention through Deterrence" border enforcement policy that funnels migrants into deadly areas like the Sonoran Desert where they die by the thousands. To follow the law in this instance might require De León to "report" instances of "illegal" border crossings, something that would clearly be unethical from the perspective of human subjects protections.[43]

This last accusation against Alice allows us to say something very clearly: ethnographers cannot and should not strive to escape their human condition, or, less anthropocentrically, their "animality." Indeed, unlike—and perhaps in opposition to—any other method that we know of in the social or natural sciences, ethnography requires its practitioners to actively draw on their

creaturely capacities for friendship, compassion, loyalty, faith, hope, anger, sadness, lust, and, yes, even vengeance, as a precondition for the very empathic
connection that lies at the heart of the method.[44] Indeed, in this light, we
might see all other methods as attempts to harness, repress, control, or direct
such qualities through specific channels on the wager that such harnessing,
repression, and control will lead in the end to superior knowledge about the
social worlds we inhabit. Ethnography's wager is almost the exact inverse:
that it is precisely by connecting with others deeply at the level of joy, disappointment, and heartbreak that we can begin to achieve not just knowledge, but understanding...

[Anna is interrupted by rapid footsteps. Piers, Karen, and Timothy burst into
the barn, their panic palpable.]

KAREN: The wolfdog! Has anyone seen the wolfdog? Has anyone seen her?
ALICE: No! I thought she was with you!
PIERS: She was, but then...

[Piers's speech is cut off by the sound of ripping paper and shattering glass.
Momentary silence, followed by full-throated howling from the ground floor.
Alarmed, everyone rises and rushes offstage, left and right, scrambling to get
to the barn's lower level.]

## End of Act Six

## Notes

1 "I have laboured carefully, not to mock, lament, or execrate human actions, but to understand them" (Spinoza 1900 [1670]: I.4).
2 Wacquant 2005b
3 Duneier 2011
4 Duneier 2011: 2
5 Duneier 2011: 8
6 For early reviews of Goffman's book that were largely positive, see Jencks 2014, Newburn 2014, Forman Jr. 2014, Bialas 2014, Buford May 2014, Schuessler 2014, Harris 2015, Innes 2015, Sharkey 2015, Avery 2015. For highly critical reviews of Goffman's work from varying perspectives, see Sharpe 2014, Betts 2014, Lubet 2015a, 2015b, Campos 2015, Goodwin 2015, Wax 2015. For defenses of Goffman's work in light of these critiques, see Perlmutter 2014, Singal 2015, 2016, Katz 2015, Neyfakh 2015, Lewis-Krauss 2016, Manning, Jammal, and Shimola 2016, Van Maanen and de Rond 2017.
7 Lewis-Krauss 2016
8 Lubet 2015b, Manning, Jammal, and Shimola 2016
9 Lubet 2015a, 2015b, Campos 2015. For another, less critical discussion by a law professor see Forman Jr. 2014.
10 Email announcement for the conference held on October 20–21, 2017 at the Northwestern Pritzker School of Law in Chicago. See also Lubet forthcoming.
11 Campos 2015, Neyfakh 2015
12 Duneier and Back 2006
13 Campos 2015
14 Lubet 2015a
15 Lubet 2015a, 2015b, Campos 2015, Forman Jr. 2014
16 Campos 2015, Lubet 2015b
17 Lupia and Elman 2014: 26
18 Wheeler Center 2015
19 Neyfakh 2015, Lubet 2015b, Campos 2015
20 Campos 2015
21 Goffman 2014: 260
22 Lubet 2015a
23 Goffman 2015: 1
24 Campos 2015, Lubet 2015b
25 Campos 2015, Goodwin 2015, Wax 2015
26 Goffman 2014: 260
27 Wax 2015, Goodwin 2015
28 Goodwin 2015, Wax 2015
29 Campos 2015
30 Singal 2015
31 Campos 2015
32 Sharpe 2014
33 Sharpe 2014
34 There are several sophisticated treatments of this basic point. See Jackson 2016, Yanow 2014, Schwartz-Shea 2014, Wedeen 2009, Schaffer 2016, Fujii 2018.
35 See Pachirat 2009 and Yanow 2009 for further elaboration on the importance of reflexivity to interpretive ethnography.
36 "When asked by email where she was interrogated, Goffman declined to provide this information on the grounds that doing so would be 'stepping far outside the IRB guidelines for the protection of human subjects'" (Campos 2015).
37 Goffman 2014: chapters 3 and 7; Duneier and Back 2006

38  Becker 1967: 241
39  Goffman 2015
40  Alcoff 1991. My thanks to Peri Schwartz-Shea for pointing me to this piece.
41  Rabinow 2011
42  Pachirat 2011
43  De León 2015
44  "[Ethnographers] must build a complex web of relations between themselves and their subjects. Those relations are never straightforward. No matter where ethnographers might be...the emotional texture of those relationships invariably shapes the kinds of information that gets exchanged as well as the nature of the text that ethnographers eventually write. In ethnography, the personal and the professional are never separate, meaning that good ethnography is not likely to consist of bloodless prose. Put another way, doing ethnography, like living life, involves love and hate, fidelity and betrayal, and courage and fear.... Those relationships...sometimes create ethical dilemmas that no research design, no theoretical argument or set of ethical guidelines can easily resolve" (Stoller 2015; also cited in Van Maanen and de Rond 2017: 402).

# ACT SEVEN: AMONG WOLVES

The Wild still lingered in him and the wolf in him merely slept.
Jack London, *White Fang* (1911 [1906]: 305)

And here may well end the story of Buck. The years were not many when the Yeehats noted a change in the breed of timber wolves; for some were seen with splashes of brown on head and muzzle, and with a rift of white centering down the chest. But more remarkable than this, the Yeehats tell of a Ghost Dog that runs at the head of the pack. They are afraid of the Ghost Dog, for it has cunning greater than they, stealing from their camps in fierce winters, robbing their traps, slaying their dogs, and defying their bravest hunters.
Jack London, *The Call of the Wild* (2012 [1903]: 62)

## Scene

Lights come up slowly and dimly on the faces of the ten ethnographers and The Prosecutor as they stand in a semi-circle on the dirt floor of the barn.

[Lights slowly dim to complete darkness. Hold for seven seconds.]

THE PROSECUTOR: This better not be some ruse to stop the conclusion of this trial and my inevitable winning of yet another guilty verdict!

[Lights rise again, first dimly, then with full, pinpointed force on the dirt floor at the center of the semi-circle formed by the ethnographers, whose faces are now in darkness and whose bodies are only outlined in silhouette. In the middle of the circle is a pile of shredded papers. The vial once containing the Fieldwork Invisibility Potion lies empty, broken in jagged halves on the floor. After a moment, a long, chilling howl from an invisible source in the center of the ethnographers' circle fills the room. Everyone involuntarily shivers with fear, and The Prosecutor holds out his staff like a weapon.]

THE PROSECUTOR: They're real? The wolfdog and the invisibility potion are real?

[A sudden, hair-raising growl followed by a piercing scream as Piers Vitebsky throws up his left arm to shield himself against a ghostly attacker before he is thrown backwards onto the dirt.]

Growling diminishes in volume as lights fade to darkness. All goes silent.

**End of Act Seven**

# END OF PLAY

# REFERENCES

Agar, Michael. 2013. *The Lively Science: Remodeling Human Social Research*. Minneapolis, MN: Mill City Press.

Alcoff, Linda. 1991. "The Problem of Speaking for Others." *Cultural Critique* (20): 5–32.

American Anthropological Association. 2007. *American Anthropological Association's Executive Board Statement on the Human Terrain System Project*. Accessed May 20, 2014. http://s3.amazonaws.com/rdcms-aaa/files/production/public/FileDownloads/pdfs/pdf/EB_Resolution_110807.pdf

Anderson, Elijah. 1996. "Introduction to the 1996 Edition of *The Philadelphia Negro*." In *The Philadelphia Negro*. Philadelphia, PA: University of Pennsylvania Press.

Asad, Talal. 1991. "Afterword: From the History of Colonial Anthropology to the Anthropology of Western Hegemony." In *Colonial Situations: Essays on the Contextualization of Ethnographic Knowledge*, edited by George W. Stocking, Jr., 314–324. Madison, WI: University of Wisconsin Press.

Autesserre, Séverine. 2014. *Peaceland: Conflict Resolution and the Everyday Politics of International Intervention*. New York: Cambridge University Press.

Avery, Jacob. 2015. "A Philadelphia Story." *Symbolic Interaction* 38 (2): 323–325.

Bateson, Gregory. 1958. *Naven, a Survey of the Problems Suggested by a Composite Picture of the Culture of a New Guinea Tribe Drawn from Three Points of View*. 2nd edition. Stanford, CA: Stanford University Press.

Becker, Howard S. 1967. "Whose Side Are We On?" *Social Problems* 14 (3): 239–247.

Benedict, Ruth. 1980. *Races of Mankind*. Baarle-Nassau: Soma.

Bennett, James. 1981. *Oral History and Delinquency: The Rhetoric of Criminology*. Chicago, IL: University of Chicago Press.

Berlinski, Mischa. 2007. *Fieldwork: A Novel*. London: Atlantic Books.

Betts, Dwayne. 2014. "The Stoop Isn't the Jungle." *Slate*, July 10. Accessed May 18, 2015. www.slate.com/articles/news_and_politics/jurisprudence/2014/07/alice_goffman_s_on_the_run_she_is_wrong_about_black_urban_life.html

Bialas, Ulrike. 2014. Review of *On the Run: Fugitive Life in an American City*, by Alice Goffman. *International Journal of Urban and Regional Research* 39 (4): 850–852.

Blee, Kathleen M. 2003. *Inside Organized Racism: Women in the Hate Movement*. Berkeley, CA: University of California Press.

Boas, Franz. 1919. "Scientists as Spies." *The Nation* 109 (20 December): 797.

Boo, Katherine. 2012a. *Behind the Beautiful Forevers*. New York: Random House.

————. 2012b. *Acceptance Speech. 2012 National Book Award for Nonfiction.* Accessed June 17, 2015. www.nationalbook.org/nba2012_nf_boo.html#.WRZNqVPytE4

Booth, Charles. 1892. *Life and Labour of the People of London*. London: MacMillan.

Bourdieu, Pierre. 1977. *Outline of a Theory of Practice*. New York: Cambridge University Press.

Brannigan, Augustine, Ian Nicholson, and Frances Cherry. 2015. "Introduction to the Special Issue: Unplugging the Milgram Machine." *Theory & Psychology* 25 (5): 551–563.

Buford May, Reuben A. 2014. "*On the Run: Fugitive Life in an American City*, by Alice Goffman." *City and Community* 13 (4): 412–413.

Bulmer, Martin. 1986. *The Chicago School of Sociology: Institutionalization, Diversity, and the Rise of Sociological Research*. Chicago, IL: University of Chicago Press.

Burawoy, Michael. 1998. "The Extended Case Method." Sociological Theory 16 (1): 4–33.

Campos, Paul. 2015. "Alice Goffman's Implausible Ethnography." *The Chronicle of Higher Education*, August 21. Accessed January 23, 2017. http://www.chronicle.com/article/Alice-Goffmans-Implausible-/232491

Canadian Institutes of Health Research, Natural Sciences and Engineering Research Council of Canada, and Social Sciences and Humanities Research Council of Canada. 2010. *Tri-Council Policy Statement: Ethical Conduct for Research Involving Humans*. Ottawa, ON: Interagency Secretariat on Research Ethics.

Chanlat, Jean-François. 2014. "The Forgotten Contribution of the French Schools of Anthropology to the Foundations of Anthropological Perspectives in the Anglophone Universe: A Comment on Morey and Luthans." *Journal of Organizational Ethnography* 3 (1). Accessed September 13, 2016. doi: 10.1108/JOE-02-2014-0004

Clifford, James. 1990. "Notes on (Field)notes." In *Fieldnotes: The Makings of Anthropology*, edited by Roger Sanjek, 47–70. Ithaca, NY: Cornell University Press.

Clifford, James and George Marcus, eds. 1986. *Writing Culture: The Poetics and Politics of Ethnography*. Berkeley, CA: University of California Press.

Conrad, Joseph. 1973. *Heart of Darkness*. London: Penguin.

Coon, Carleton S. 1980. *A North Africa Story: The Anthropologist as OSS Agent 1941–1943*. Ipswich, MA: Gambit.

Cruikshank, Barbara. 2016. *Machiavellian Optimism: Cultivating and Sustaining the Spirit for Political Life as an Endless Struggle*. Unpublished manuscript, June 1 version. Microsoft Word file.

De Atkine, Norvell B. 2004. "The Arab Mind Revisited." *Middle East Quarterly* 11 (3): 47–55.

De León, Jason. 2015. *The Land of Open Graves: Living and Dying on the Migrant Trail*. Oakland, CA: University of California Press.

Douglass, Frederick. 2017 [1845]. *Narrative of the Life of Frederick Douglass, an American Slave*. New York: Quarto.

Du Bois, William E. B. 1899. *The Philadelphia Negro: A Social Study*. Philadelphia, PA: University of Pennsylvania Press.

————. 1903. *The Souls of Black Folk*. Chicago, IL: A. C. McClurg & Co.

————. 1940. *Dusk of Dawn: An Essay Toward an Autobiography of a Race Concept*. New York: Schocken.

————. 1968. *The Autobiography of W.E.B. Du Bois: A Soliloquy on Viewing My Life from the Last Decade of Its First Century*. New York: International Publishers.

Duneier, Mitchell. 1994. *Slim's Table: Race, Respectability, and Masculinity*. Chicago, IL: The University of Chicago Press.

————. 1999. *Sidewalk*. New York: Farrar, Straus and Giroux.

————. 2002. "What Kind of Combat Sport is Sociology?" *American Journal of Sociology* 107 (6): 1551–1576.

————. 2006. "Garder sa tête sur le ring? Sur la négligence théorique et autres écueils de l'ethnographie." ["Keep his head in the ring? On theoretical neglect and other pitfalls of ethnography."] *Revue française de sociologie* 47 (1): 143–157.

————. 2011. "How Not to Lie with Ethnography." *Sociological Methodology* 41 (1): 1–11.

————. 2017. *Ghetto: The Invention of a Place, the History of an Idea.* New York: Farrar, Straus and Giroux.

Duneier, Mitchell and Les Back. 2006. "Voices from the Sidewalk: Ethnography and Writing Race." *Ethnic and Racial Studies* 29 (3): 543–565.

Duneier, Mitchell, Barry Alexander Brown, Ovie Carter, Cornel West, Kim Hopper, and Jane Jacobs. 2010. *Sidewalk: A Film by Mitchell Duneier and Barry Alexander Brown.* Princeton, NJ: Princeton University.

Duneier, Mitchell, Philip Kasinitz, and Alexandra Murphy, eds. 2014. *The Urban Ethnography Reader.* New York: Oxford University Press.

Ehrenreich, Barbara. 2001. *Nickled and Dimed.* New York: Henry Holt.

Ellison, Ralph. 1952. *Invisible Man.* New York: Random House.

Elman, Colin and Diana Kapiszewski. 2014. "Data Access and Research Transparency in the Qualitative Tradition." *PS: Political Science & Politics* 47 (1): 43–47.

Emerson, Robert M., Rachel I. Fretz, and Linda L. Shaw. 2014. *Writing Ethnographic Fieldnotes.* 2nd edition. Chicago, IL: The University of Chicago Press.

Engels, Friedrich. 1984 [1845]. *The Condition of the Working Class in England from Personal Observation and Authentic Sources.* Moscow: Progress Publishers.

Feldman, Martha, Jeannine Bell, and Michele Tracy Berger. 2003. *Gaining Access: A Practical and Theoretical Guide for Qualitative Researchers.* Walnut Creek, CA: AltaMira.

Fitzgerald, Maureen H. 2005. "Punctuated Equilibrium, Moral Panics and the Ethics Review Process." *Journal of Academic Ethics* 2 (4): 315–338.

Flyvbjerg, Bent. 2001. *Making Social Science Matter: Why Social Inquiry Fails and How It Can Succeed Again.* Oxford: Cambridge University Press.

Forman Jr., James. 2014. "The Society of Fugitives." *The Atlantic*, October 2014. Accessed October 29, 2015. www.theatlantic.com/magazine/archive/2014/10/the-society-of-fugitives/379328/

Fox, Richard G. 1972. "Rationale and Romance in Urban Anthropology." *Urban Anthropology* 1 (2): 205–233.

Fujii, Lee Ann. 2018. *Interviewing in Social Science Research: A Relational Approach.* New York: Routledge.

Gans, Herbert. 1962. *Urban Villagers.* New York: Free Press.

Geertz, Clifford. 1973a. "Thick Description: Toward an Interpretive Theory of Culture." In *The Interpretation of Cultures,* 3–30. New York: Basic Books.

————. 1973b. "Deep Play: Notes on the Balinese Cockfight." In *The Interpretation of Cultures,* 412–453. New York: Basic Books.

Gezari, Vanessa. 2013. *The Tender Soldier.* New York: Simon & Schuster.

Glaser, Barney and Anselm Strauss. 1967. *The Discovery of Grounded Theory: Strategies for Qualitative Research.* New Brunswick, NJ: Aldine Transaction.

Go, Julian. 2016. "The Case for Scholarly Reparations." *Berkeley Journal of Sociology*, January 11. Accessed September 2, 2016. http://berkeleyjournal.org/2016/01/the-case-for-scholarly-reparations/

Goffman, Alice. 2014. *On the Run: Fugitive Life in an American City.* Chicago, IL: University of Chicago Press.

————. 2015. "A Reply to Professor Lubet's Critique." Accessed October 27, 2016. www.ssc.wisc.edu/soc/faculty/docs/goffman/A%20Reply%20to%20Professor%20Lubet.pdf (4 pp.).

González, Roberto J. 2007. "Towards Mercenary Anthropology? The New US Army Counterinsurgency Manual FM 3-24 and the Military-Anthropology Complex." *Anthropology Today* 23 (3): 14–19.

————. 2009. *American Counterinsurgency: Human Science and the Human Terrain.* Chicago, IL: Prickly Paradigm Press.

————. 2015. "The Rise and Fall of the Human Terrain System." *Counterpunch*, June 29. Accessed November 7, 2015. www.counterpunch.org/2015/06/29/the-rise-and-fall-of-the-human-terrain-system/

Goodman, Nelson. 1972. *Problems and Projects*. Indianapolis, IN: Bobbs-Merrill.

Goodwin, Michele. 2015. "Invisible Women: Mass Incarceration's Forgotten Casualties." *Texas Law Review* 94: 353–386.

Gough, Kathleen. 1967. "New Proposals for Anthropologists." *Economic and Political Weekly* 36 (2): 1653–1655, 1657–1658.

————. 1968. "Anthropology and Imperialism." *Monthly Review* 19 (11). Accessed November 12, 2015. https://archive.monthlyreview.org/index.php/mr/article/view/MR-019-11-1968-04_2

————. 1993. "'Anthropology and Imperialism' Revisited." *Anthropologica* 35 (2): 279–289.

Graeber, David. 2006. *Fragments of an Anarchist Anthropology*. Chicago, IL: Prickly Paradigm Press.

Gray, Bradford H. 1981. *Human Subjects in Medical Experimentation: A Sociological Study of the Conduct and Regulation of Clinical Research*. Huntington, NY: R. E. Krieger Pub. Co.

Hamper, Ben. 1986. *Rivethead: Tales from the Assembly Line*. New York: Warner Books.

Haraway, Donna. 1988. "Situated Knowledges: The Science Question in Feminism and the Privilege of Partial Perspective." *Feminist Studies* 14 (3): 575–599.

Harris, A. 2015. Book Review: *On the Run: Fugitive Life in an American City*. *Theoretical Criminology* 19 (1): 131–143.

Harris, Charles H. and Louis R. Sadler. 2003. *The Archaeologist was a Spy: Sylvanus G. Morley and the Office of Naval Intelligence*. Albuquerque, NM: University of New Mexico Press.

Hasan, Hakim. 1999. "Afterword." In *Sidewalk* by Mitchell Duneier, 319–330. New York: Farrar, Straus and Giroux.

Hayward, Clarissa Rile. 2000. *De-Facing Power*. Cambridge: Cambridge University Press.

Ho, Karen Zouwen. 2009. *Liquidated: An Ethnography of Wall Street*. Durham: Duke University Press.

Hull House. 2010. *Hull House Maps and Papers: A Presentation of Nationalities and Wages in a Congested District of Chicago*. Charleston, SC: Nabu Press.

Humphreys, Laud. 2009. *Tearoom Trade: Impersonal Sex in Public Places*. Chicago, IL: Aldine Transaction.

Innes, M. 2015. Book Review: *On the Run: Fugitive Life in an American City*. *The British Journal of Sociology* 66 (2): 392–394.

Jackson, Patrick Thaddeus. 2016. *The Conduct of Inquiry in International Relations: Philosophy of Science and its Implications for the Study of World Politics*. 2nd edition. London: Routledge.

Jackson, Zakiyyah Iman. 2013. "Animal: New Directions in the Theorization of Race and Posthumanism." *Feminist Studies* 39 (3): 669–685.

Jencks, Christopher. 2014. On America's Front Lines. *The New York Review of Books*, October 9. Accessed August 22, 2016. www.nybooks.com/articles/2014/10/09/americas-front-lines/

Jerolmack, Colin and Shamus Khan. 2014. "Talk is Cheap Ethnography and the Attitudinal Fallacy." *Sociological Methods & Research* 43 (2): 178–209.

Jonsson, Hjorleifur. 2005. *Mien Relations: Mountain People and State Control in Thailand*. Ithaca, NY: Cornell University Press.

Kaku, Michio. 2008. *Physics of the Impossible: A Scientific Exploration into the World of Phasers, Force Fields, Teleportation, and Time Travel*. New York: Doubleday.

————. 2016a. "*Science Fantastic Live* with Dr. Michio Kaku." Accessed February 2, 2017. http://mkaku.org/home/radio/

————. 2016b. "The Future of the Mind." Accessed February 10, 2017. www.youtube.com/watch?v=YKpzo47iyhE

Katz, Jack. 2015. "Email Communication with Eugene Volokh." In Eugene Volokh, "Prof. Alice Goffman, 'On the Run,' and driving a gang member around, looking for a mutual friend's killer." *The Washington Post*, June 2. Accessed December 5, 2016. www .washingtonpost.com/news/volokh-conspiracy/wp/2015/06/02/prof-alice -goffman-on-the-run-and-driving-a-gang-member-around-looking-for-a-mutual- friends-killer/?utm_term=.3421eaace719

Keesing, Roger M., Malcolm Crick, Barbara Frankel, Jonathan Friedman, Elvin Hatch, J. G. Oosten, Rik Pinxten, Jerome Rousseau, and Marilyn Strathern. 1987. "Anthropology as Interpretive Quest [and Comments and Reply]." *Current Anthropology* 28 (2): 161–176.

Khan, Shamus Rahman. 2013. *Privilege: The Making of an Adolescent Elite at St. Paul's School.* Princeton, NJ: Princeton University Press.

King, Gary, Robert O. Keohane, and Sidney Verba. 1994. *Designing Social Inquiry: Scientific Inference in Qualitative Research.* Princeton, NJ: Princeton University Press.

Laitin, David D. 1999. "Seeing Like a State: How Certain Schemes to Improve the Human Condition Have Failed (Review)." *Journal of Interdisciplinary History* 30 (1): 177–179.

———. 2003. "The Perestroikan Challenge to Social Science." *Politics & Society* 31 (1): 163–184.

Leach, Edmund Ronald. 1954. *Political Systems of Highland Burma: A Study of Kachin Social Structure.* London: London School of Economics and Political Science.

Leibow, Elliot. 1967. *Tally's Corner: A Study of Negro Streetcorner Men.* New York: Routledge and Kegan Paul.

Lewis, David L. 2000. *W.E.B. Du Bois.* New York: H. Holt.

Lewis-Krauss, Gideon. 2016. "The Trials of Alice Goffman." *The New York Times Magazine*, January 12. Accessed November 27, 2016. www.nytimes.com/2016/01/17/magazine/ the-trials-of-alice-goffman.html

London, Jack. 1911 [1906]. *White Fang.* London: Macmillan & Co.

———. 2012 [1903]. *The Call of the Wild.* New York: Dover Publications, Inc.

Lubet, Steven. 2015a. "Did This Acclaimed Sociologist Drive the Getaway Car in a Murder Plot?" *New Republic*, May 27. Accessed January 4, 2017. https://newrepublic.com /article/121909/did-sociologist-alice-goffman-drive-getaway-car-murder-plot

———. 2015b. "Ethnography on Trial." *New Republic*, July 15. Accessed December 31, 2016. https://newrepublic.com/article/122303/ethnography-trial

———. Forthcoming. *Interrogating Ethnography: Why Evidence Matters.* New York: Oxford University Press.

Lundblad, Michael. 2015. *The Birth of a Jungle: Animality in Progressive-Era US Literature and Culture.* New York: Oxford University Press.

Lupia, Arthur and Colin Elman. 2014. "Openness in Political Science: Data Access and Research Transparency." *PS: Political Science & Politics* 47 (1): 19–42.

Malinowski, Bronislaw. 1922. *Argonauts of the Western Pacific: An Account of Native Enterprise and Adventure in the Archipelagoes of Melanesian New Guinea.* Long Grove, IL: Waveland Press.

———. 1929. "Practical Anthropology." *Africa: Journal of the International African Institute* 2 (1): 22–38.

Manning, Philip, Sarah Jammal, and Blake Shimola. 2016. "Ethnography on Trial." *Society* 53 (4): 444–452.

Marcus, George E. 1995. "Ethnography in/of the World System: The Emergence of Multi-Sited Ethnography." *Annual Review of Anthropology* 24 (1): 95–117.

———. 1998. *Ethnography Through Thick and Thin.* Princeton, NJ: Princeton University Press.

Marlowe, Christopher. 1994. *Dr. Faustus.* Mineola, NY: Dover.

Marvin, Garry. 2012. *Wolf.* London: Reaktion Books.

Mathers, Samuel Liddell MacGregor. 1932. *The Book of the Sacred Magic of Abramelin the Mage.* Chicago, IL: De Laurence.

McCoy, Alfred W. 2006. *A Question of Torture: CIA Interrogation, from the Cold War to the War on Terror.* New York: Metropolitan Books/Henry Holt and Co.

McFate, Montgomery. 2005a. "The Military Utility of Understanding Adversary Culture." *Joint Forces Quarterly* 38: 42–48.

———. 2005b. "Anthropology and Counterinsurgency: The Strange Story of their Curious Relationship." *Military Review* 85 (2): 24–38.

McFate, Montgomery and Janice Laurence. 2015. "Introduction: Unveiling the Human Terrain." In *Social Science Goes to War: The Human Terrain System in Iraq and Afghanistan*, edited by Montgomery McFate and Janice Laurence, 1–44. New York: Oxford University Press.

Mears, Ashley. 2011. *Pricing Beauty: The Making of a Fashion Model.* Berkeley, CA: University of California Press.

Milgram, Stanley. 2010. *Obedience to Authority.* New York: Pinter & Martin.

Mills, C. Wright. 2001. *Sociological Imagination.* Oxford: Oxford University Press.

Morris, Aldon. 2015. *The Scholar Denied: W.E.B. Du Bois and the Birth of Modern Sociology.* Oakland, CA: University of California Press.

Munck, Gerardo L. and Richard Snyder. 2008. *Passion, Craft, and Method in Comparative Politics.* Baltimore, MD: Johns Hopkins Press.

Nader, Laura. 1972. "Up the Anthropologist: Perspectives Gained from Studying Up." In *Reinventing Anthropology*, edited by Dell H. Hymes, 284–311. New York: Vintage Books.

Newburn, Tim. 2014. Book Review. On the Run: Fugitive Life in an American City. *LSE Review of Books*, July 10. Accessed April 14, 2015. http://blogs.lse.ac.uk/lsereviewofbooks/2014/07/10/book-review-on-the-run-fugitive-life-in-an-american-city-by-alice-goffman/

Neyfakh, Leon. 2015. "The Ethics of Ethnography." *Slate*, June 18. Accessed June 18, 2016. www.slate.com/articles/news_and_politics/crime/2015/06/alice_goffman_s_on_the_run_is_the_sociologist_to_blame_for_the_inconsistencies.html

Nicolini, Davide, Silvia Gherardi, and Dvora Yanow. 2003. *Knowing in Organizations: A Practice-Based Approach.* Armonk, NY: ME Sharpe.

Pachirat, Timothy. 2009. "The Political in Political Ethnography: Dispatches from the Kill Floor." In *Political Ethnography: What Immersion Contributes to the Study of Power*, edited by Ed Schatz, 143–162. Chicago, IL: University Press Chicago.

———. 2011. *Every Twelve Seconds: Industrialized Slaughter and the Politics of Sight.* New Haven, CT: Yale University Press.

Pader, Ellen. 2006. "Seeing with an Ethnographic Sensibility." In *Interpretation and Method: Empirical Research Methods and the Interpretive Turn*, edited by Dvora Yanow and Peregrine Schwartz-Shea, 161–174. Armonk, NY: ME Sharpe.

Park, Robert Ezra, Jitsuichi Masuoka, and Preston Valien. 1975. *Race Relations: Problems and Theory: Essays in Honor of Robert E. Park.* Freeport, NY: Books for Libraries Press.

Patai, Raphael. 1973. *The Arab Mind.* New York: Scribner.

Perkins, John. 2004. *Confessions of an Economic Hit Man.* San Francisco, CA: Berrett-Koehler.

Perlmutter, David. 2014. "In Defense of Ethnography." *The Chronicle of Higher Education*, June 26. Accessed July 7, 2016. www.chronicle.com/article/In-Defense-of-Ethnography/231191

Peterson, Roger Tory. 2001. *A Field Guide to Western Birds: A Completely New Guide to Field Marks of all Species Found in North America West of the 100th Meridian and North of Mexico.* Vol. 2. Boston, MA: Houghton Mifflin Harcourt.

Petraeus, David. 2015. "Forward." In *Social Science Goes to War: The Human Terrain System in Iraq and Afghanistan*, edited by Montgomery McFate and Janice Laurence, vii–xi. New York: Oxford University Press.

Polanyi, Michael. 1966. *The Tacit Dimension.* Garden City, NY: Doubleday.

Price, David. 2000. "Anthropologists as Spies." *The Nation*, November 2. Accessed August 11, 2016. www.thenation.com/article/anthropologists-spies/

————. 2005. "America the Ambivalent: Quietly Selling Anthropology to the CIA." *Anthropology Today* 21 (6): 1–2.

Rabinow, Paul. 2011. *Reflections on Fieldwork in Morocco*. Berkeley, CA: University of California Press.

Reverby, Susan M. 2013. *Examining Tuskegee: The Infamous Syphilis Study and its Legacy*. Chapel Hill, NC: University of North Carolina Press.

Ricoeur, Paul. 1970. *Freud and Philosophy: An Essay on Interpretation*. New Haven, CT: Yale University Press.

Rock, Paul. 2001. "Symbolic Interactionism and Ethnography." In *Handbook of Ethnography*, edited by Paul Atkinson, Amanda Coffey, Sara Delamont, John Lofland, and Lyn Lofland, 26–38. London: SAGE Publications.

Roulet, Thomas J., Michael J. Gill, Sebastian Stenger, and David James Gill. 2017. "Reconsidering the Value of Covert Research." *Organizational Research Methods* 20 (3): 487–517.

Said, Edward. 2006. "Representing the Colonized: Anthropology's Interlocutors." In *Jean-François Lyotard: Critical Evaluations in Cultural Theory, Volume II*, edited by Victor E. Taylor and Gregg Lambert, 366–385. London and New York: Routledge.

Salemink, Oscar. 2003. *The Ethnography of Vietnam's Central Highlanders: A Historical Contextualization, 1850–1990*. Honolulu: University of Hawai'i Press.

Sanjek, Roger, ed. 1990. *Fieldnotes: The Makings of Anthropology*. Ithaca, NY: Cornell University Press.

Sanjek, Roger. 1991. "The Ethnographic Present." *Man*, New Series, 26 (4): 609–628.

Sanjek, Roger and Susan W. Tratner, eds. 2015. *eFieldnotes: The Makings of Anthropology in the Digital World*. Philadelphia, PA: University of Pennsylvania Press.

Schaffer, Frederic Charles. 2014. "Thin Descriptions: The Limits of Survey Research on the Meaning of Democracy." *Polity* 46 (3): 303–330.

————. 2016. *Elucidating Social Science Concepts: An Interpretivist Guide*. New York: Routledge.

Schrag, Zachary M. 2010. *Ethical Imperialism: Institutional Review Boards and the Social Sciences, 1965–2009*. Baltimore, MD: Johns Hopkins University Press.

Schuessler, Jennifer. 2014. "Fieldwork of Total Immersion." *The New York Times*, October 23. Accessed October 31, 2016. http://nyti.ms/1mVAGsr

Schwartz-Shea, Peregrine. 2014. "Judging Quality: Evaluative Criteria and Epistemic Communities." In *Interpretation and Method: Empirical Research Methods and the Interpretive Turn*, 2nd edition, edited by Dvora Yanow and Peregrine Schwartz-Shea, 120–146. Armonk, NY: ME Sharpe.

Schwartz-Shea, Peregrine and Dvora Yanow. 2009. "Reading and Writing as Method: In Search of Trustworthy Texts." In *Organizational Ethnography: Studying the Complexities of Everyday Life*, edited by Sierk Ybema, Dvora Yanow, Harry Wels, and Frans Kamsteeg, 56–82. London: SAGE Publications.

————. 2012. *Interpretive Approaches to Research Design: Concepts and Processes*. New York: Routledge.

Scott, James C. 1985. *Weapons of the Weak: Everyday Forms of Peasant Resistance*. New Haven, CT: Yale University Press.

————. 1998. *Seeing Like a State: How Certain Schemes to Improve the Human Condition Have Failed*. New Haven, CT: Yale University Press.

————. 2009. *The Art of Not Being Governed: An Anarchist History of Upland Southeast Asia*. New Haven, CT: Yale University Press.

Sharkey, Patrick. 2015. Reviewed Work: *On the Run: Fugitive Life in an American City* by Alice Goffman. *Social Service Review* 89 (2): 407–412.

Sharpe, Christina. 2014. "Black Life, Annotated." *The New Inquiry*, August 8. Accessed March 30, 2015. https://thenewinquiry.com/black-life-annotated/

Singal, Jesse. 2015. "The Internet Accused Alice Goffman of Faking Details in Her Study of a Black Neighborhood. I Went to Philadelphia to Check." *New York Magazine*, June

18. Accessed June 21, 2016. http://nymag.com/scienceofus/2015/06/i-fact-checked-alice-goffman-with-her-subjects.html

———. 2016. "Three Lingering Questions from the Alice Goffman Controversy." *New York Magazine*, January 15. Accessed July 4, 2016. http://nymag.com/scienceofus/2016/01/3-lingering-questions-about-alice-goffman.html

Spinoza, Benedict. 1900 [1670]. *The Chief Works of Benedict De Spinoza, Volume 1: Introduction, Tractatus Theologico-Politicus, Tractatus Politicus*. London: George Bell and Sons.

Stack, Carol. 1974. *All Our Kin: Strategies for Survival in a Black Community*. New York: Harper Torch Books.

Stark, Laura. 2014. *Behind Closed Doors: IRBs and the Making of Ethical Research*. Chicago, IL: University of Chicago Press.

Stoller, Paul. 2015. "Alice Goffman and the Future of Ethnography." *Huffington Post*, June 15. Accessed July 13, 2016. www.huffingtonpost.com/paul-stoller/alice-goffman-and-the-future-of-ethnography-_b_7585614.html

Thomas, William Isaac and Florian Znaniecki. 1918. *The Polish Peasant in Europe and America: Monograph of an Immigrant Group. Volume One*. Boston, MA: Richard G. Badger, The Gorham Press.

Thomson, Jennifer. 2009. "Pregnancy, Power and Commodity: An Ethnographic Glance at Pregnant Experience." Unpublished manuscript, May 1 version. Microsoft Word file.

Tolkien, John R. R. 1966 [1937]. *The Hobbit; or, There and Back Again*. Boston, MA: Houghton Mifflin.

Tolstoy, Leo. 1920 [1869]. *War and Peace*. London: Walter Scott Pub. Co.

Tsing, Anna Lowenhaupt. 1993. *In the Realm of the Diamond Queen: Marginality in an Out-of-the-Way Place*. Princeton, NJ: Princeton University Press.

———. 2015. *The Mushroom at the End of the World: On the Possibility of Life in Capitalist Ruins*. Princeton, NJ: Princeton University Press.

Valeriano, Napoleon and Charles Bohannan. 2008. *Counter-Guerrilla Operations: The Philippine Experience*. New Delhi: Pentagon Press.

van den Hoonaard, Will C. 2011. *The Seduction of Ethics: Transforming the Social Sciences*. Toronto, ON: University of Toronto Press.

Van Maanen, John. 1991. "Playing Back the Tape: Early Days in the Field." In *Experiencing Fieldwork: An Inside View of Qualitative Fieldwork*, edited by William B. Shaffir and Robert A. Stebbins, 31–42. Thousand Oaks, CA: SAGE Publications.

Van Maanen, John and Mark de Rond. 2017. "The Making of a Classic Ethnography: Notes on Alice Goffman's on the Run." *Academy of Management Review* 42 (2): 396–406.

Vaughan, Diane. 2004. "Theorizing Disaster." *Ethnography* 5 (3): 315–347.

Venkatesh, Sudhir Alladi. 2009. *Gang Leader for a Day: A Rogue Sociologist Crosses the Line*. London: Penguin Books.

Vitebsky, Piers. 2005. *The Reindeer People: Living with Animals and Spirits in Siberia*. Boston, MA: Houghton Mifflin.

Wacquant, Loïc. 2002. "Scrutinizing the Street: Poverty, Morality, and the Pitfalls of Urban Ethnography 1." *American Journal of Sociology* 107 (6): 1468–1532.

———. 2004a. *Body & Soul: Notebooks of an Apprentice Boxer*. Oxford: Oxford University Press.

———. 2004b. "Following Pierre Bourdieu into the Field." *Ethnography* 5 (4): 387–414.

———. 2005a. "Carnal Connections: On Embodiment, Apprenticeship, and Membership." *Qualitative Sociology* 28 (4): 445–474.

———. 2005b. "Nothing Beyond its Reach." *The Chronicle of Higher Education* 51 (49): B14.

———. 2010. *Urban Outcasts: A Comparative Sociology of Advanced Marginality*. Cambridge: Polity Press.

———. 2011. "Habitus as Topic and Tool: Reflections on Becoming a Prizefighter." *Qualitative Research in Psychology* 8 (1): 81–92.

———. 2015. "For a Sociology of Flesh and Blood." *Qualitative Sociology* 38 (1): 1–11.

———. 2016. *Body & Soul: Notebooks of an Apprentice Boxer.* Revised and expanded edition. New York: Oxford University Press.

Wax, Amy L. 2015. "Negatively Sixth Street." *Commentary* 139 (6): 37–40.

Wedeen, Lisa. 2002. "Conceptualizing Culture: Possibilities for Political Science." *American Political Science Review* 96 (4): 713–728.

———. 2009. "Ethnography as Interpretive Enterprise." In *Political Ethnography: What Immersion Contributes to the Study of Power,* edited by Ed Schatz, 75–94. Chicago, IL: University of Chicago Press.

———. 2010. "Reflections on Ethnographic Work in Political Science." *Annual Review of Political Science* 13: 255–272.

Wheeler Center. 2015. "Conversation Between Jo Case and Katherine Boo." Accessed July 16, 2016. https://www.youtube.com/watch?v=eMqglnW5M_w

Wilkinson, Cai. 2014. "On Not Just Finding What You (Thought You) Were Looking For: Reflections on Fieldwork Data and Theory." In *Interpretation and Method: Empirical Research Methods and the Interpretive Turn,* 2nd edition, edited by Dvora Yanow and Peregrine Scwartz-Shea, 387–405. Armonk, NY: ME Sharpe.

Yanow, Dvora. 2009. "Dear Author, Dear Reader: The Third Hermeneutic in Writing and Reviewing Ethnography." In *Political Ethnography: What Immersion Contributes to the Study of Power,* edited by Ed Schatz, 275–302. Chicago, IL: University of Chicago Press.

———. 2014. "Thinking Interpretively: Philosophical Presuppositions and the Human Sciences." In *Interpretation and Method: Empirical Research Methods and the Interpretive Turn,* 2nd edition, 5–26: Armonk, NY: ME Sharpe.

Yanow, Dvora and Haridimos Tsoukas. 2009. "What is Reflection-in-Action? A Phenomenological Account." *Journal of Management Studies* 46 (8): 1339–1364.

Yanow, Dvora and Peregrine Schwartz-Shea. 2015. "Framing 'Deception' and 'Covertness' in Research: The Legacy of Milgram, Humphreys, and Zimbardo for Regulating Social Science Research Ethics." American Political Science Association Annual Meeting.

———. 2016. "Encountering Your IRB 2.0: What Political Scientists Need to Know." *PS: Political Science & Politics* 49 (2): 277–286.

Zimbardo, Philip G., Craig Haney, W. Curtis Banks, and David Jaffe. 1972. *Stanford Prison Experiment: A Simulation Study of the Psychology of Imprisonment.* Philip G. Zimbardo, Incorporated.

# INDEX

literature 32, 52, 73n88, 81, 83–4, 114
locations 27, 30, 31, 65; *see also* fieldsites
Lubet, Steve 139, 143–4, 146, 154, 156

Malinowski, Bronislaw 28, 50–1, 54
mapping 44
maps 86
maximum variation 92–3
McFate, Montgomery 48
Mead, Margaret 51
memory 144, 151
Milgram, Stanley 97, 98–100, 112
military 10–11, 48, 50–3, 67, 102
mnemonics 115–16
modelling, formal 46
morals 32, 98, 101, 136
mourning 143
*Mushroom at the End of the World: On the Possibility of Life in Capitalist Ruins, The* 8; mushrooms, matsutake 5, 25, 28–9, 42–3, 82

Nader, Laura 60, 62
narrations *see* fieldnotes
neutrality 19, 102, 106, 131n44

*Obedience to Authority* 97–8
objections 135
objectivity 10, 19, 56, 79, 114
observations 15, 31, 113
omens 46–7
*On the Run: Fugitive Life in an American City* 8, 60, 133–5, 138–40, 143–4, 146–7, 152; hospital logs 141, 154

Park, Robert E. 55–6
participants 58–9, 98, 108, 122, 142, 145–7, 150
peacekeeping (peacekeepers) 27, 29, 52–3
*Peaceland: Conflict Resolution and the Everyday Politics of International Intervention* 8, 28
plantations 41–2
poetry 117
points of view 119–21, 153; researcher's 144–5
police departments 6, 81, 99, 111–12, 141, 151–2, 154; *see also* Lubet, Steve
policing 86, 100, 146, 150, 152, 154
*Polish Peasant in Europe and America: Monograph of an Immigrant group Volume One* 54–5, 82
political agendas 31
political changes 89

political science 39–40, 76
politicians 15
populations 10, 91, 96, 142, 146–7
positionality 19, 62–3, 65–7, 80, 115, 137, 149; researchers' 39, 76, 100, 151–2
positivism 15, 80, 113, 138, 147
power 33–4, 56, 63, 75, 137–8, 149, 153; authority 44–5; autobiographical 78; dynamics 48–9, 58, 65–7, 100–1; researchers 97, 155; stories (storytelling) 40; structures of 88
prediction 18
Project Camelot 52
propaganda 51–2
protection 101, 146, 151
public interest 134–5, 138–9
publicity 107

questions 31, 83, 138, 139, 141; *see also* research, questions

Rabinow, Paul 103–6, 108, 155
racism 55–7, 59, 76, 97, 111, 147, 154
rapport 20, 59, 105–8
readers 137, 140, 144
recognition (professional awards) 33, 95
recollections 144, 151
reflexivity 39, 101, 118–19, 123, 149–50, 152, 155
regression 33, 46
*Reindeer people: Living with Animals and Spirits in Siberia* 8, 24, 77, 79, 119, 126
relationality 42, 104, 108, 148, 150, 152
relationships 51, 58, 60, 65, 75, 101, 115; building 103–8; transitions 127; viewpoints 137
relationships, interspecies 39
reliability 138, 141
research 19–20, 29, 32–3, 35–6, 40, 75; covert 98–101; questions 32, 34, 80–5, 111–12
researchers 10, 20, 31–2, 57, 66–7, 76–7, 118; methods 94; as narrator 121; qualities required 112, 117
Research Ethics Committee 96
research questions 32, 34, 80–5, 111–12
research subjects *see* participants
resistance 31, 93
respect 59, 105–6
responsibility 127, 141
rights 137, 140, 146–7
rigor 10, 16, 32, 40, 50, 79
risk-taking 83
rituals 144

antiplantation-